The Best of Jim Coleman

The Best of Jim Coleman

Fifty Years of Canadian Sport from the Man Who Saw It All

Compiled by Jim Taylor

HARBOUR PUBLISHING

Harbour Publishing Co. Ltd.
P.O. Box 219
Madeira Park, BC
V0N 2H0
www.harbourpublishing.com

Edited by Alicia Miller
Interior Design by Mary White
Cover design by Peter Read
Cover and Coleman author photo by Gerry Kahrmann / *Province*
Printed and bound in Canada

Harbour Publishing acknowledges financial support from the Government of Canada through the Book Publishing Industry Development Program and the Canada Council for the Arts, and from the Province of British Columbia through the British Columbia Arts Council and the Book Publisher's Tax Credit through the Ministry of Provincial Revenue.

Library and Archives Canada Cataloguing in Publication

Coleman, Jim
The best of Jim Coleman : fifty years of Canadian sport from the man who saw it all / compiled by Jim Taylor.

ISBN 1-55017-359-6 / 978-1-55017-359-8

1. Sports—Canada—History—20th century. I. Taylor, Jim, 1937- II. Title.

GV585.C64 2005 796'.0971'09045
C2005-903201-4

For Maggie, who let me play with the time machine

Acknowledgement

For D'Alt, for Jim, and for the matchless memories.

THE ODDS AGAINST this book ever being published were so long that not even Johnny Needle-Nose would have risked a $2 show ticket on it.

Toronto's Woodbine Race Track, where Jim Coleman is remembered with affection, backed the project early on, but it would have gone no further without the generous support of two great Coleman fans, Vancouver businessmen Gerry Strongman and Peter Kains.

Strongman's lifelong friend from high school and college days was the late D'Alt Coleman, Jim's son. Strongman's business partner, Peter Kains, also had a Coleman connection: his father and Jim had been friends and fellow tenants in Mrs. Minion's rooming house in Brandon, MB, where the young Coleman was launching his career as correspondent for the Winnipeg *Tribune*. Years later, as Coleman moved west, Strongman and Kains would lunch with him, enthralled by the man as much as by the sporting tales he spun.

When they read a story by reporter Jim Morris about my dream of bringing the works of the great Canadian sports legend back into print, they called friend and retired Vancouver *Sun* columnist Trevor Lautens, who knew about such things. Lautens got us all together with a willing publisher and we were off.

Sometimes, the longshots do come in.

—JIM TAYLOR

Contents

Foreword

THIS BOOK WAS BORN in fourteen cardboard flower boxes—the long, narrow kind florists use to transport long-stemmed roses—found in the bottom drawer of a paint-chipped and dented old filing cabinet in a basement storage locker. Given that the top two drawers contained a half-century's worth of paper-trail minutiae—cheque stubs, receipts, bank statements, expense accounts ("Some of my most creative work," Jim Coleman used to say)—now destined for a shredder or garbage bag, it was an unlikely place to mine gold.

There had always been rumours of a Jim Coleman filing cabinet, and what might be in it if indeed it existed. What does a columnist-cum-legend collect along the way? The guy wrote sports forever. What if he kept a diary? What unpublished tidbits might his notes contain?

Frankly, I'd forgotten the filing cabinet rumour. All I knew was that my friend had been dead for better than a year—slipping away quietly of heart failure in 2001 after an apparent full recovery from a broken hip suffered at age eighty-nine as he climbed into a taxi headed for the Vancouver *Province* to treat his readers to another crop of memories. Now his widow Maggie was changing apartments, and we were sorting through Jim's things to decide what to keep and what should go elsewhere.

The books were packed; the tributes and trophies and accolades stored; the top hat and morning coat he'd worn to so many runnings of the Queen's Plate hung in a garment bag on the edge of the closet door. We were done.

"Mind you," she said, "there is the storage locker in the basement . . ."

We had to take the locker door off by unscrewing the hinges. Jim was big on keys but not on key tags. A locksmith was called to open the filing cabinet. And there they were—fourteen boxes, the corners torn or the lids ripped on some, but each carefully tagged with a faded orange sticker on one end: "Vancouver *Daily Province* 1939–42," "Toronto *Telegram* 1943–44," "The *Globe and Mail* 1945–46," all the way to 1986. And in them, clipped from the parent papers—or later in the Southam days when he was Canada's first syndicated sports columnist, from any paper that carried them wherever in Canada he happened to be—the near complete collection of the most famous, best-loved sports columnist this country has ever produced.

"Migawd, Maggie," I whispered. "We've found a time machine."

If you were studying the development of sport in this country and in North America, how would you feel if you found interviews with hockey players of the 1930s at the time they were playing? How about a conversation with a young Montreal Royals baseball player named Jackie Robinson, the year before Branch Rickey dared to bring him up to the Brooklyn Dodgers as the first Negro player to break the major league colour barrier? Or a 1943 interview with former world heavyweight boxing champion Jack Johnson at age sixty-five, sitting in a circus tent as the main attraction of a ten-cents-a-ticket carnival freak show, recalling the day in 1908 when he first won the title he held for eight years and, along with it, hatred from the white world because he had beaten their best and refused to accept that a black man was supposed to know his place?

What would it be worth to you, to read the recollections of a man who was there when Warren Stephens threw the first touchdown pass in a Grey Cup game in 1932, but who could gently remind you that the first passes in a cup game had actually been thrown in 1929 by a left-handed centre named Jersey Campbell who'd snap the ball, drop into the backfield for a lateral, and heave the ball downfield to an open teammate while the opposing players stood there wondering what the hell just happened?

What would be their archival value, these on-the-spot slices of sporting history plus first-person reportage on hockey through the decades, from the day the Victoria Cougars won the 1925 Stanley Cup with a wide-eyed young Coleman in the stands, to that magical night in Moscow in 1972 when Paul Henderson scored the Summit Series winner for Team Canada to end the eight-game showdown with Russia that forever reshaped our national game?

How important would such a reference library be, particularly when all these events and hundreds more were chronicled by one man who, as fan or reporter, was there for all of them?

There will never be another Jim Coleman. The times and technology will never allow it. Never again will a man file a blow-by-blow boxing story to his paper by dictating it to a telegrapher—"brass-pounders" they called them—who tapped out the words in Morse code. There'll be no more typing out a story, grabbing a cab to the telegraph office and pounding on the back door to rouse an operator so he can file it NPR (Night Press Rates) Collect.

Typewriters have given way to laptop computers, though never for Coleman, who refused to learn the new technology, sticking to typewriter and paper to the end. "A few more years," he lamented, "and no one in this business will know the meaning of 'carriage return.'" Jet flights, interminably extended seasons and deadlines shortened by the death of the afternoon newspaper mean no more of those long between-game train trips when reporters and athletes could and would share booze and stories that would find their way into print an edition or so down the road.

Coleman loved trains. His father, D'Alton Corry Coleman, was a railroad man who began as an engineer's clerk with Canadian Pacific in 1889 and rose through the ranks to become president of the line from 1942 until his retirement in 1947. His position allowed him to share with his sons his lifelong love of sports and open doors to adventures beyond the dreams of small boys.

Train tickets would arrive at University School in Victoria and the little boy and his younger brother, Rowan, would ride across the country in the care of conductor or baggage man, to be met by his father—often in a limousine—and taken to the big horse race, or to an Allan Cup hockey game, or to a Cubs game at Wrigley Field, or to the New York

Yankees' Florida training camp to watch Babe Ruth and Lou Gehrig, or to a heavyweight title fight in which Jack Dempsey kayoed Jack Sharkey. Out of those trips, those games, those years and the writing ones that followed came a couple of memoirs—the incomparable *A Hoofprint on My Heart* and the sequel *Long Ride on a Hobby-Horse*—and fourteen flower boxes containing the words of a man whose work won him membership in five Canadian Halls of Fame (news, sports, racing, hockey and football) and the Order of Canada.

The characters he made famous are here—Johnny Needle-Nose, the Blow-Back Kid, Knifey, Sir Sidney Mole, Deacon Allen, the Good Kid, Sir Benjamin Stockley and the rest—along with dogs, bears, wrestlers, Hall of Famers and ham-and-eggers who tried and sometimes even succeeded, at least a little bit. Coleman's people.

There is lots of hockey. And Canadian football. Horse racing, of course, including the tales from the shedrows that only he could tell. Dogsled racing, the Curse of the Muldoon, Duke Ellington's phantom trombonist, the toughest cat in Toronto, and the Indian who conned the cavalry and rode off into the sunset.

Other eyes, other friends, might have chosen differently. These choices are mine, based on memories and retellings in those matchless lunchtime bull sessions I miss so much it hurts.

Some of the words may jar. But they are Coleman's words, and they fit within the context of the times in which they were written. "Black" had not yet replaced "Negro" when Coleman met Jackie Robinson. During the war years, Japan and Germany were the enemy, and derogatory terms like "Jap" and "Nip" or "Kraut" and "Hun" were burned into the North American vocabulary. Coleman wrote them as a chronicler of his time. In the forty-odd peacetime years I knew him, he'd have bristled at their use in speech or print.

In his mid-eighties, Jim Coleman held daily court in the cafeteria of Pacific Press, home of the Vancouver *Sun* and *Province*. He never meant to; it just kept happening. He'd go upstairs for lunch and within minutes the table would be jammed with reporters, pressmen, ad salesmen, circulation managers—all gathering to discuss the previous night's results, the teams that were and the teams that had been, with a man who'd seen them all. On his birthday, much to his disgust and despite heated warnings that it had best not happen again this year or by the Lord Harry there'd be hell to pay, they brought him cakes and insisted he make a wish and blow out the candles. They loved him. He knew it, was humbled by it and basked in the friendships. Finding the Coleman table was no trick. You just headed for the laughter.

And the stories rolled on.

The Toronto Blue Jays, having a little problem with the recalcitrant George Bell, were they? What about it, Jim?

"George Bell?" Coleman said thoughtfully. "I knew him when his name was Jorge, and nobody gave a damn."

Vancouver Canucks, making a run for the Stanley Cup in 1994?

"Pretty good," he admitted. "Of course, the Vancouver Millionaires *won* the thing in '15. And Lester Patrick and his brothers had a better league out here than the NHL but couldn't challenge for the cup. A bigger arena, too, the one on Denman Street right here in Vancouver. Bigger than any in the East until it burned down. Then all the better players were sold and shipped east and that did it for western hockey until the Canucks got their franchise in 1970 . . ."

To some of the younger reporters on the *Province* staff, the Coleman gatherings were a bit of a mystery. His heyday had come and gone before they were born. There were new hotshots on the sports pages now, an endless and interchangeable array of talking heads on the tube. History was yesterday; ancient history the day before. Okay, he wrote a little nostalgia column two or three times a week, but big deal. Almost everybody in it was dead.

"How come you spend so much time with that old guy?" one of them asked me.

"In the first place, his name is Mr. Coleman," I said. "Second, he is my friend. And third, I'm going to school."

I went to Coleman's school for almost thirty years. Mostly he never knew it was in session. Tangle-footed and grass-green to the column-writing dodge, I stapled myself to his coattails at every opportunity, from the 1972 Winter Olympics in Sapporo to the Canada–Russia hockey series seven months later, to Canadian Football League games and playoffs and Grey Cups too numerous to count. He didn't teach writing. In all those years I never saw him go over someone else's copy. With word and deed, he taught professionalism.

Terry Jones, the Edmonton *Sun* sports columnist, remembers the Hamilton Grey Cup game in 1996 when he and Coleman decided they'd write their columns at the *Sun* chain's paper, the Hamilton *Spectator.*

"I shook hands with everybody in the office I knew," he says. "Jim went around and introduced himself to everyone he *didn't* know."

Everyone in our business has a Jim Coleman story. All of them are like that, tales of kindness and helpfulness and a shared understanding of the joy that came when you got the words just right.

He knew he was a little bit famous. He just never understood why.

One lunchtime in the cafeteria, the talk somehow got around to epitaphs and what each of us would like carved on our tombstones. "That's easy," Jim Coleman said. "Just put 'He was a sportswriter.' That's enough."

Sure. And Michelangelo was a guy who did ceilings.

—JIM TAYLOR

1

1939–42

Foster the Microphone Mahout

Vancouver *Daily Province*
April 12, 1939

FEARLESS FOSTER HEWITT, that titan of the tonsil twisters, was at it again last night.

Hockey fans in thousands of Vancouver homes battled one another for vantage points around the radio as Fearless Foster, his voice shrilling above the cacophony in Maple Leaf Gardens, chanted his familiar war cry, "He shoots! He scores!"

Thousands of dinners grew cold on neglected platters as the much-maligned mahout of the microphone lured citizens from the refectory table to listen to his description of the grim goings-on involving the Boston Bruins and Toronto Maple Leafs.

Much criticism has been heaped on Hewitt's curly noggin. He has been pilloried conversationally more than any other member of the Canadian syntax-slaughtering industry, which of course includes the entire roster of sportswriters and radio announcers.

The basis of the beef against him is that he is a "homer." He is accused of favouring the Maple Leafs in his weekly broadcasts. There are those of his critics who are unkind enough to suggest that he is blind in one eye and can concentrate on only one team. That team, the critics continue, is arrayed in the livery of Mr. Conny Smythe's Toronto club.

Taken in its broader aspects, the charge against Mr. Hewitt is grossly unfair though it cannot be denied that his voice rises three or four octaves and a note of triumph creeps into it when he announces that the Leafs have scored another goal.

There is none who can deny that the little guy does an extremely efficient job of describing the Saturday night festivities at Maple Leaf Gardens and brings pleasure into the homes of millions of Canadians who are unable to witness the hurly-burly of National Hockey League warfare from $2.20 box seats.

What does it matter if he *is* a homer, chums? If you don't like him you can twirl the dials of your static-stunned wireless and listen to *Amos 'n Andy*. Fearless Foster has been broadcasting the Toronto games for nearly ten years and it is only natural that he should develop a very real affection for the Maple Leafs during an association of such duration. The same thing happens to sportswriters who, like radio announcers, are sentimentalists in addition to being mildly punch-drunk.

The sportswriters fortunately don't have to write their stories at the scene of battle. They can go back to their hotel rooms and pen dispassionate reports after a period of suitable meditation, stimulated perhaps by a beaker of hops and the mellowing conversation of convivial companions.

For instance, this correspondent was once a camp follower of the Winnipeg Blue Bombers rugby club. I loved them dearly. On some of those rare occasions when they have been beaten I have rushed to the typewriter and, seething with indignation, written something along the following lines:

> CALGARY, October 10—The Winnipeg Blue Bombers were robbed here this afternoon by three blind men who were posing as officials. If those guys are officials, I'm the Queen of Siam. They should be hanged. Our club was twenty points better than the Calgary Bronks and yet we were beaten 20–5. We wuz robbed.

This correspondent has never telegraphed such a dispatch.

Some celebrant invariably has knocked on our door and the sheet of copy has nestled forgotten in the typewriter for many hours. Then, in the grim dawn of the next day this reporter has clambered out of bed, tiptoed to his typewriter through the broken glass on the bedroom floor, placed a fresh sheet of paper in the machine and, in the measured prose of the *Daily Province* editorial page, has written something along this line:

> CALGARY, October 11—Calgary Bronks defeated Winnipeg Blue Bombers 20–5 here yesterday afternoon in a game that was featured by excellent officiating. The Bombers were outplayed at every turn . . .

Elsie Shows Her Knees

Vancouver *Daily Province*
November 10, 1939

THE MOST HAPPY NEWS OF THE WEEK emanates from Reno, a garish desert oasis of twenty thousand people that has received more than its share of inquisitive international attention since the town became the acknowledged centre of the great American divorce industry.

The news dispatch that is causing such widespread cheer states that the University of Nevada authorities have agreed that Miss Elsie Crabtree "will be allowed to show her knees."

As it is entirely possible that some of you aren't aware of the details of the case, it should be explained that Miss Elsie Crabtree is the University of Nevada's drum majorette. Furthermore, Elsie is a drum majorette of surpassing comeliness and, up until recently, she led the cheering at the University of Nevada football games clad in a costume that was somewhat abbreviated.

Needless to say news of this pulchritudinous performance was noised abroad and attendance at the football games soared to unprecedented levels. The college's football team, which glories in the name of the Wolf Pack, has never been a particularly puissant force on the American gridiron, but this year Elsie has inspired them to the extent that they have been bopping more highly favoured rivals.

All went well until last week when the university authorities decreed that Elsie must henceforth wear a skirt extending nigh unto her ankles. Immediately there were shrill cries of indignation that echoed throughout the republic from the rock-ribbed coast of Maine to California's silver strand. The fans demanded a refund on their season's tickets and the football team refused flatly to win a game until Elsie's dimpled knees were in view once more.

The authorities have capitulated. Miss Crabtree's underpinnings may again be admired at the regular admission prices. All is well in Reno.

This reporter believes that he has discovered a method of inspiring the Nevada Wolf Pack to win the national football championship and a bid to the Rose Bowl:

She is a tasty enchilada;
Her dimpled knees and twinkling toes
Have sparked the boys of old Nevada
To defeat their conference foes.
Though this may sound like arrant whimsy,
The Wolves perhaps could sweep the land
If Mrs. Crabtree's daughter Elsie
Were replaced by Sally Rand.

The Clancys of Ottawa

Vancouver *Daily Province*
January 3, 1940

IF YOU ARE A CONSTANT READER of the daily blats you will have observed that Frank "King" Clancy, the shillelagh-swinging Celt from Ottawa, is still slugging sundry citizens across the chops. King Clancy is acting in this bellicose fashion despite the fact that he has retired from active participation in the sanguinary sport of puck-chasing and has donned the uniform and attendant dignity of a National Hockey League referee.

Early in the current NHL campaign M. Clancy was officiating in Montreal one night when some of the loyal Montreal customers questioned his judgment. As a matter of fact, four or five of these customers questioned his judgment so seriously that they clambered over the boards and slithered across the ice to remonstrate with M. Clancy personally.

The gendarmes rushed to the rescue, but instead of saving the referee—as is customary in such situations—the gallant constabulary was forced to succour the spectators who had invaded the ice surface. Clancy was laying about him with such violence and evident pleasure that his attackers were in sore need of police intervention.

Clancy was refereeing in Montreal again last week when four players who had been showing trifling animosity all evening suddenly began to bop one another with their cudgels. Clancy plunged into the fray to separate the combatants, but his peacemaking tactics were so vigorous that the players stopped bopping one another with their cudgels and all began to bop Clancy. When the King disposed of them, he gave major penalties to only two, ruling that the two others hadn't hit him hard enough to draw blood.

M. Clancy's singularly violent behaviour comes as no surprise to those who remember him in his playing days. He wasn't much bigger than a well-fed Saskatchewan jackrabbit, but he could tear 'em down. When those big forwards roared in on the Ottawa defence, King Clancy would hit them and they would collapse as if they had been shot through the knees.

Conny Smythe paid fifty thousand dollars for Clancy and Hurricane Hector Kilrea and Ferocious Francis Finnegan. Clancy represented thirty-five thousand dollars of this outlay and it was the shrewdest investment that Constantine ever made because Clancy's flaming spirit drove the Toronto Maple Leafs to championship heights.

And Clancy came by his fighting spirit honestly as those people who knew his illustrious sire, King Clancy the elder, will tell you.

Up until today I had thought that my doctor had lived a blameless life, but it now appears that my doctor was born in Ottawa. He told me that he was at Ottawa College in 1904 when King Clancy the elder was in attendance at that institution.

My doctor says that Mr. Clancy was playing rugby for the Ottawa Rough Riders and was receiving a few bob for his athletic endeavours but, in order to keep things on the up-and-up, the Ottawa management gave Mr. Clancy and several other stars an education at Ottawa College. Now this was a very strict institution and when Mr. Clancy and his colleagues won the Canadian rugby championship and wished to celebrate, they were deeply shocked to find that the priests wouldn't allow them to ferry any firewater onto the premises.

Mr. Clancy the elder was quartered on the third floor of the building and he evolved the splendid scheme of rigging a vast system of ropes and pulleys and lowering the smallest boy in the college to the ground. The smallest boy was commissioned to run to the nearest grocery store and purchase twelve quarts of Mr. Labatt's best malt beverages. When he returned with the suds, he was to yank the rope twice and Mr. Clancy would haul him back into the dormitory.

Unfortunately this scheme was overheard by Father Duffy, a young and portly priest from Boston. Father Duffy watched as the boy was lowered to the ground and, after a reasonable interval, yanked the rope twice himself.

Mr. Clancy and some assistants hauled on the ropes manfully.

"My, my," Mr. Clancy observed, "it seems that our young friend is bringing back one of the brewery horses as well as the beer."

Just then Father Duffy's noggin hove into view at the window and Mr. Clancy gave a startled yelp but didn't lose his presence of mind. He lowered Father Duffy rapidly but cinched the ropes, leaving the young priest suspended between the first and second storeys of the college building.

There is only one thing about this story that worries me. The doctor left without telling me what happened to Father Duffy. I wonder how he reached the ground? Perhaps he is still hanging there between the first and second storeys, though chances are that the vultures and jays have picked his bones clean because that was back in 1904.

Best in the West

Vancouver *Daily Province*
January 6, 1940

I'm sorry to bring it to your attention, chums, but our athletic competitions of today are anemic and shoddy exhibitions when one compares them with the imbroglios of recent yesteryear.

This sad fact was brought to my notice one day this week when this alley of aches was visited by H.H.C. "Torchy" Anderson. Mr. Anderson's journalistic endeavours in the past few years have carried him into the world of paunchy and verbose politicians and tycoons, but there was a time when he enjoyed the carefree and unfettered existence of a sports reporter. He was in a reminiscent mood on the occasion of his visit to this corridor of convalescents and consequently I was privileged to hear of Sam Whiting, one of the gaudiest characters in the gaudy history of the gaudy West.

Samuel first broke into the limelight when the Canadian Pacific Railway decided to build a large dam in Bassano, Alberta. Mr. Whiting immediately conceived the idea of selling the available real estate in the Bassano district. He plunged into this task and invented the spectacular and historic slogan: "Bassano—Best in the West by a Dam Site!"

Now hockey was the outstanding game of the pre-war period and, like all good promoters, Sam Whiting realized that his town must have a good hockey team. In his opinion the talent in the surrounding area was of inferior quality, so he unlimbered his cheque book and descended on the old Kootenay League, purchasing an entire team including such stars as famed goalie Chuck Clark and the Bishop brothers.

The rivalry between the Calgarys and the Bassanos was very intense, and the citizens of these places would wager great gobs of "Spanish" on their respective teams. Mr. Anderson remembers one game he saw when the Calgarys invaded Bassano. Mr. Whiting and his associates had wagered so mightily with their Calgary rivals that the resultant payoff, regardless of the outcome of the game, would be one of the major financial transactions of the generation.

The Calgary side included such luminaries as the celebrated Cook brothers of Taber and Scotty Davidson, who was killed in the Great War. These were the days, mind you, when the country roads were white with the bleaching bones of hockey referees whose decisions had offended the sensibilities of the hometown fans. This particular game was contested bitterly and when the score was tied at the end of regulation time, both teams agreed to play twenty minutes of overtime.

Play had scarcely resumed before Bassano scored a goal. At this juncture, one of the Bassano gamblers produced a skilfully concealed pair of scissors and proceeded to cut the belt that operated the light plant.

The rink was plunged into darkness and the jubilant Bassanos claimed victory because the game couldn't be completed. But the Calgarys took an extremely narrow-minded view and insisted that they would stay on the ice until the light plant was repaired. The plant was repaired after a long delay and—horror of horrors—the Calgarys subsequently scored two goals that won the game for them.

Well gentlemen, that was the signal for some very bitter exchanges of words and blows among the spectators. The referee disappeared in the scuffling and when he was next seen, a grim-looking posse of Bassano citizens was escorting him into the Bassano Hotel. To the vast amazement of the assembled Calgary celebrants the referee climbed onto a table and, in a quavering voice, announced that all bets were off due to the fact that the game hadn't been completed within the prescribed time limit.

Those were the days, of course, when the referee of an athletic contest could cancel the wagering on a technicality. The indignant Calgarians claimed afterwards that one of the Bassano posse was carrying a noosed rope that he was waving significantly before the eyes of the frightened referee.

In light of this occurrence it is only fair that Calgary should have grown to be quite a city while Bassano, the brainchild of Sam Whiting, is still only a whistle stop on the CPR mainline.

The Great Reformation

Vancouver *Daily Province*
March 5, 1940

M. JEAN PUSIE, the gallant Gallic screwball who is known professionally as "the Chamblis Chameleon," visited me one night last week. M. Pusie was accompanied by Guy Worthington Patrick, the patient puck entrepreneur.

"From now on I will do just as Guy says," said M. Pusie. "If he tells me that I am to stay back on the defence I will stay on the defence. Of course, I will still rush once or twice a period to please the customers. But from now on I will do just as Guy says."

To emphasize his sincerity, M. Pusie struck himself on the breast with his right hand. The blow echoed thunderously, reminding his audience of the impressive basso profundo music that floods the theatre when the name of a Metro-Goldwyn-Mayer production is flashed on the screen.

Mr. Patrick beamed affectionately. "Jean is a good boy," he said. "It is true that in the past he has been a bit headstrong and impetuous but he has decided to reform and for the rest of the season he will do just as I say."

Those of us who were fortunate enough to journey to the Vancouver Forum last night were privileged to witness an example of this splendid new relationship between M. Pusie and his manager. During the hectic third period, Bobby Rowe, the Portland manager, engaged in an acrimonious discussion with referee Cameron Proudlock and, finally reaching the limits of his patience, leaned over the railing and sloshed Proudlock on the chops.

M. Pusie was playing on the Vancouver defence when Rowe roughed the ref.

"Sacré bleu! In fact, zut alors!" M. Pusie muttered in amazement. "This is highly irregular. Rowe cannot strike the referee because Rowe is not in uniform! I remember well that when I was playing for the St. Rose du Lac Habitants in the Quebec Dimanche Matin League there was a strict rule that nobody but players in uniform could attack the referee!

"Hmmm," mused M. Pusie, stroking his lantern jaw. "Rowe is clearly attempting to infringe on the rights of the players! Pusie will feex!"

And with no further adieu M. Pusie skated over to the Portland bench, swung his ham-like right fist and creased Bobby Rowe athwart the schnozzle, thereby avenging referee Proudlock and repelling an abortive attack on the constitutional rights of all hockey players.

Well gentlemen, at this juncture the roof fell in and after several minutes of highly vigorous pushing and shoving, we saw Mr. Patrick exert his amazing new influence over his most colourful hireling.

While M. Pusie was raging about the ice, his fellow players and that eminent insurance agent, linesman Siggurdur Frank Frederickson, were attempting to soothe him. Mr. Patrick gazed out over the swirling players and beckoned to Pusie with supreme confidence.

"Come Jean, my little cabbage," said Mr. Patrick. "Come to the players bench like a good boy."

M. Pusie hesitated only momentarily when he heard Mr. Patrick's gentle voice. Then turning toward his manager he screamed, "To hell wit' you, too!" He tore himself loose from his captors, broke his hockey stick into two pieces and hurled the fragments at Mr. Patrick's startled noggin. Mr. Patrick realized that something was amiss. Shedding a silent tear he removed his spectacles, handed them to a bystander and awaited developments.

This morning, word that Pusie and Rowe have been fined one hundred dollars each for their part in last night's fracas has seeped through to my country estate in the trackless jungles of Little Mountain. This is a gross and startling miscarriage of justice!

I believe that the Mr. Rowe involved in this case is the same Mr. Rowe who has howled consistently about the officiating in the league. I believe further that this is the same Mr. Rowe who, in a fit of petulance, pulled his team out of the playoffs a couple of years ago when a league ruling failed to meet his approval. This is the same Mr. Rowe who urges his players to "cut 'em down" when Vancouver teams visit the glorified bowling alley that serves as a rink in Portland. In view of these circumstances I feel that the league should give Pusie a one-hundred-dollar honorarium instead of fining him.

It has come to my attention that some of the local customers are losing patience with M. Pusie and accusing him of dirty tactics. I would merely point out to them that no one was injured when Pusie went berserk last night. As a matter of fact when Pusie gets into a fight he customarily is the only person who is injured when the bodies are carried away.

Fish Story

Vancouver *Daily Province*
December 1, 1942

THIS PROBABLY IS A BIT OUT OF SEASON, but this department had a visitor last night who reminded us that the Modern Art of Telling Lies is dominated completely by that hardy sect known as the Piscatory Prevaricators.

The Piscatory Prevaricators' pre-eminence is due to the fact that they are more imaginative than most of their competitors. No fisherman ever returns from an excursion into the wilds without insisting that he hooked at least one fish that made Jonah's whale look like a suckling bass.

Last night's visitor was Vic May, a scribe from the Saskatoon *Star-Phoenix,* who recalled a trip that Gar Wood, the celebrated speedboat merchant, made into Saskatchewan in search of finny delicacies.

It seems that Gar Wood, who once was accused of excessive guile when he descended to petit larceny to snatch the Harmsworth Trophy from Kaye Don of Great Britain, deserves to be ranked in the upper brackets of Piscatory Prevaricators.

Mr. Wood, several fellow fishermen and their guide were sitting around the campfire one evening during their Saskatchewan safari. Their imaginations had been stimulated a trifle by several libations of rum and maple syrup, a medicinal concoction that has been known to discourage the most robust bacteria.

The guide, who must have been sitting rather close to the fire, announced suddenly that only two weeks previous he had caught a rainbow trout weighing seventeen pounds. Now everyone well knows that a rainbow trout weighing more than five pounds would be claimed immediately by the Smithsonian Institution.

"Hmmm," said Mr. Wood solemnly, "undoubtedly a very large fish. That reminds me of a day when my father and I were fishing on Lake Ontario. A terrific storm came up, so we started to row for shore. Just then my father's line nearly was yanked out of his hand. We thought he had hooked a rock, but with our combined efforts, we managed to reel in the line. On the end of it was a boat's lantern.

"The lantern was covered with mud and slime, but we managed to clean it off. My father looked at it closely. I hardly expect you to believe it, but this lantern had been dropped overboard by my father and grandfather when they were fishing in the same spot nearly forty years earlier."

Mr. Wood stared into the campfire for a second and then continued.

"The incredible part of the story is that, after we got the muck and slime cleaned off, we discovered that the lantern still was alight despite the fact that it had been underwater for forty years."

The guide took another sip of his medicine.

"I can believe most of that story, Mr. Wood," he said. "Undoubtedly you are an honest man. I believe it is possible that you hooked the same lantern that had been lost forty years earlier. But you'll pardon me if I'm a bit puzzled by the fact that the lantern still was alight."

"Well," said Mr. Wood craftily, "if you take twelve pounds off your rainbow trout, I'll blow out my lantern."

Elmer the Bear

Vancouver *Daily Province*
December 4, 1942

THE SPORTSWRITERS FOR THE EVENING JOURNALS have dealt at some length with the height, brawn and vigorous athletic behaviour of the Winnipeg Blue Bombers. In view of the excellent manner in which the scribes have described the physical attributes of the Winnippeggers, it appears that this department has no choice but to deal solely with the intellectual qualifications of the invaders.

There is a widespread belief that football players—and the gentlemen associated with them in an executive capacity—are, as a rule, strong in the back and weak in the noggin. This, we suggest, is a misconception.

For instance, there is the famous example of how the Winnipeg Football Club dealt with a great crisis. The Winnipeg Football Club, as far as we can ascertain, is the only football club that has been presented with a full-grown, ravenous bear as a mascot.

The Winnipeg Football Club invariably has been guided by an executive that represents every stratum of the province's economic and social structure, from the premier of Manitoba to the bootblack at Winnipeg's Royal Alexandra Hotel.

During the season in question the Winnipegs had two brothers named McBean in minor executive capacities. Now one of the brothers happened to be the Winnipeg district manager for an American airline. The president of the airline sent a telegram to McBean saying that he would like to procure "a bear rug."

McBean, who was of a somewhat whimsical turn of mind, sent a few coureurs de bois into the northern woods with instructions that they were to get him "a bear *cub*."

In due course, an extremely startled railway express clerk telephoned McBean to tell him that his specimen of northern fauna had reached Winnipeg and would he kindly "come down and take the blankety-blank thing out of here."

The McBean brothers made a leisurely journey to the railway station where, to their infinite delight, they were greeted by a huge, three-hundred-pound bear bearing the label "Call Me Elmer."

While spectators cowered at a respectable distance, the uninhibited McBeans led Elmer from his cage and hailed a hack piloted by one Butch Dobrians. Butch had faced the gunfire and mud of Passchendaele with equanimity, but he has described the ensuing ride as the most terrifying experience of his life. The McBeans shoved Elmer into the back seat of the hack and lolled on each side of him with their arms draped affectionately around his neck. Mr. Dobrians's customary aplomb was shattered when the bear, slavering slightly at the jowls, insisted on licking his ears.

The boys realized that Elmer was a trifle too large to make a suitable gift for the president of the airline, so they reasoned that Shea's Brewery would be an excellent spot to which to repair while they discussed the beast's future. Accordingly, they led him into the gloomy confines of this gargantuan suds foundry.

Elmer was left to his own devices while the McBean brothers toyed with a few noggins of hops and discussed his well-being. After two hours of earnest debate with similarly disposed well-wishers, they decided it would be an excellent idea to present Elmer to the Winnipeg Blue Bombers, who were playing a league game in the immediately adjacent Osborne Stadium.

But when they started to look for Elmer, it was evident that, in some inexplicable manner, he had found his way into the beer vats. He had developed a definite list to starboard; he was licking his chops gleefully; his eyes were more than a trifle bloodshot; and obviously, Elmer was in the advanced stages of intoxication.

It was with extreme difficulty that the McBeans and six willing assistants persuaded Elmer to don a Winnipeg sweater once worn by Bob Fritz. And then they led him from the premises and, with due ceremony, presented him to the Winnipeg Football Club at the game's halftime interval.

We would like to conclude the Saga of Elmer on a happy note, but this is impossible. After the game, the president of the club—either Frank Hannibal or Les Isard, both of whom have accompanied the Blue Bombers on their current safari—was commissioned to take Elmer to the Royal Alexandra Hotel in a taxi.

But Elmer, regretful to say, was beginning to feel the results of his debauchery. He was sullen and uncooperative. To be brutally frank, Elmer was suffering from one of the worst copper-bottomed hangovers ever seen in western Canada.

He was definitely sulky when Mr. Isard (or Mr. Hannibal) coaxed him into a taxi. And when Mr. Isard (or Mr. Hannibal) attempted to cajole him with flippant comments on the game, Elmer turned, lifted a stout paw and dealt Mr. Isard (or Mr. Hannibal) a whack upon the chops.

But this is where the executive brilliance of the Winnipeg Football Club came into full prominence.

Mr. Isard (or Mr. Hannibal) did not strike back at Elmer. Very craftily, Mr. Isard (or Mr. Hannibal) wiped the blood from his chin and decided sagaciously that the members of the Winnipeg Football Club would eat Elmer at their annual banquet, which was scheduled for the following Saturday.

Which they did.

The Toronto Hurricanes may outplay the Winnipeg Bombers on Saturday, but it's obvious that the local Hurricanes will never outsmart 'em.

MIA

Vancouver *Daily Province*
June 10, 1942

RED DUTTON'S OLDEST BOY JOE has been reported missing after aerial operations against the enemy.

Joe Dutton was twenty-one when he went overseas and he was just like your son, or just like those kid brothers of yours and mine, and just like the rest of the youngsters from down the block who tossed aside their books and hockey sticks and answered the call so willingly.

Young Joe was a bomber pilot. His number came up a few nights ago. There's still a chance that he may have come down safely, but no one can tell for certain about these things.

Hundreds of our finest young men have paid with their lives for our freedom already, and their passing has been marked only by a brief line in the casualty lists. And so when we pay this brief, awkward tribute to Joe Dutton, we pay homage to your sons and your kid brothers.

It just happens that we didn't know your boys—and that was our loss—but we knew young Joe when he was a tiny kid. We know his old man, too; his friendship is something of which we're proud.

Red is just like a lot of the rest of us. He loves his kids with a fierce pride. When Joe and Joe's eighteen-year-old brother Alex joined the air force, the old man ranted and swore and told them that they were too young.

But they had him there.

They reminded him that he was only seventeen when he went overseas with the Princess Patricia's Canadian Light Infantry in the last war. He gave up the argument.

These youngsters, who are face to face with death, achieve a mature wisdom and insight that is denied to the rest of us on the sidelines.

On Good Friday a letter was published in this paper. It was a letter written by another Canadian youngster just before he went on a bombing raid. He never came back, and the letter was delivered to his parents after his death.

Perhaps it has no place on the sports page, but then—on second thought—it should have been printed on every page in the paper. It should have been printed in large black type. It was a message full of unassuming gallantry.

It is reprinted here in the hope that it may bring a measure of comfort and hope to those of you, like the Duttons, who are parents. It said in part:

> I am the lucky one, as I have gone to the land where there is no time. It will be only a momentary lapse in the infinite before you

are all with me—and so, courage! To you who are left behind is a task—a huge task. A new world order must be created where men can live in peace and plenty without fear or prejudice. It is up to you to see our job finally completed.

It looks as if they have passed the ball to us. Don't muff it.

The Boxing Bellhops

Vancouver *Daily Province*
January 26, 1942

DEACON ALLEN, the scholarly sage of Bashed Beak Boulevard, is bleeding internally these days because he has learned that he missed an opportunity to promote one of the epic bouts of the current century. Although the bout took place some weeks ago, the Deacon's sense of personal loss still is extremely acute and, even today when he is watching a couple of his own hirelings go through their grimaces in the gymnasium, there are times when a soulful sob is wrenched from between his lips. These sobs cause some consternation among the onlookers who do not realize that the lachrymose sounds come from the innermost recesses of a tortured spirit.

The Deacon's sorrow is caused principally by the fact that the bout was strictly a "one-way" proposition in which he couldn't have failed to make himself a couple of yards of long green.

The circumstances were these: An extremely wealthy gentleman who is given to moments of whimsy took up quarters in a hotel. For the purpose of the story, we will not identify the hostelry and will refer to the whimsical gent only as Mr. X.

Well, Mr. X was a high-spirited gent and there were times when he adopted rather novel methods of dissipating his wealth. He purchased fur coats for chorus girls and distributed one-hundred-dollar bills in hospitals and generally had one heck of a time.

Mr. X had one favourite bellhop who performed many important functions for him, such as meeting the taxis when they arrived with shipments of cough syrup and making trips to the downstairs drugstore to purchase supplies of soda bicarbonate for Mr. X.

Well one day Mr. X asked him, "Who's the toughest bellhop in the hotel?"

"That is a moot point," answered the bellhop, who was an expert in double-talk, particularly when conversing with guests who stay awake after two o'clock in the morning.

"Here's seven hundred dollars," said Mr. X, peeling off a roll of bills. "I want you to stage an elimination tournament on the condition that I see the bout between the two finalists."

The bellhop pocketed the seven hundred dollars, gave two hundred dollars to the bell captain and decided to forget about this latest manifestation of Mr. X's peculiar form of fun. However, several weeks later, Mr. X returned to the hotel, summoned the bellhop and demanded to know the names of the two finalists in his boxing tournament.

"Well," said the bellhop, thinking quickly, "it has dwindled down to me and the bell captain."

"Capital," roared Mr. X. "We will stage the finals in my suite tonight!"

At the appointed hour the bell captain and the bellhop entered Mr. X's suite and discovered, to their horror, that a miniature boxing ring had been erected in the sitting room. Not only that, but about twenty or thirty of Mr. X's uninhibited friends had assembled as spectators.

"But we have no boxing outfits," protested the bellhop.

"I have them right here," boomed Mr. X jovially, producing gloves, trunks, shoes and even aluminum protective devices.

So the long and short of it was that the two bellboys clambered into the ring and slugged the bejabbers out of each other while the guests applauded enthusiastically. Finally, when they lay gasping in pools of their own blood, Mr. X tossed another $250 in $10 bills over the prostrate bodies.

The whole affair still grieves Deacon Allen. He figures that he would have been willing to promote the Battle of the Bellhops for twenty-five percent of the gross, and there wouldn't have been any rental or advertising charges!

Mr. Saperstein's Road Show

Vancouver *Daily Province*
August 20, 1942

ABE SAPERSTEIN is visiting our town. Mr. Saperstein is the globular little character who is making a strong bid to assume the mantle of the late Phineas T. Barnum, the world's greatest entrepreneur of freaks and colourful zanies.

As an illustration of how far Mr. Saperstein rides in advance of his rivals, we would point out that Mr. Saperstein is the only sports promoter who has been able to discover a baseball catcher who can play nine innings while seated in a rocking chair behind home plate.

In case genial Abe's name is unfamiliar to any of you, we should explain that he's the man who manages the affairs of Satchel Paige and the Kansas City Monarchs. As a matter of fact, the Monarchs constitute only one of eighteen Negro baseball teams whose affairs he supervises. And we would do him an injustice if we ignored the fact that he is the proprietor of the Harlem Globetrotters, the world's greatest basketball team.

Mr. Saperstein has two occupations apart from going to the bank to cash the large dividend cheques from his athletic agencies. He spends one-half his time scanning the flora and fauna of North and South America in search of rare and eccentric athletic specimens. The other half of his time he spends searching for hillsides and mountain peaks on which there is sufficient space to write the adjectives with which he is pleased to describe his sportive attractions.

Abe, an enormously likable little citizen, is addicted to adjectives, the mildest of which is "colossal." He describes most of his events as "smashing!"

Perhaps you might be interested in hearing how he happened to assume the "Black Man's Burden." Well, about sixteen years ago he was a professional basketball player out of Chicago, and a Negro ballroom proprietor needed someone to manage the basketball team that he owned. He picked Abe.

Abe put the Negro casaba-tossers on their feet and, when the Chicago Giants of the Negro American League lost fifty thousand dollars in one season, they persuaded Abe to manage them. Ever since that time, he has made a more-than-comfortable living handling the affairs of Negro sports organizations.

His major fame has been gained from the activities of the Harlem Globetrotters. The Globetrotters have visited more towns than a Fuller Brush salesman. Incidentally, Ted Strong, who played in the outfield for the Kansas City Monarchs last night, is the key man on the Globetrotters and is regarded as the greatest basketball player in the world. As proof of Strong's versatility, he also leads the Negro American League in hitting.

But Mr. Saperstein's current pride and joy is a baseball team known as the Cincinnati Ethiopian Clowns. The Clowns have been outdrawing the Cincinnati Reds in their own bailiwick and they gross more per season than any other Negro club with the exception of Paige and the Monarchs.

Abe discovered the Clowns in Miami. Employing his flair for the theatrical, he persuaded all the players to change their names to Ethiopian cognomens. For instance, Ed Davis, the celebrated pitcher, promptly became "Peanuts Nyasses."

Nyasses is much funnier than Al Schacht. And he can pitch better than Schacht. Nyasses holds two decisions over Paige this summer.

The Clowns also feature Pepper Bassett, the gentleman who catches while seated in a rocking chair.

"He can catch like a fiend but he can't hit a lick," says Saperstein, whose frankness is one of his most engaging qualities. Mr. Saperstein wouldn't attempt to fool anyone about Paige. "Satch is ten years past his prime," he says, "but he's still one of the best in baseball."

"Do you see that Frank Duncan out there," he said, pointing to the field. "He's the manager of and sub-catcher for this Kansas City club. He must be fifty years old. He's the only man in the world who caught for both Paige and Dizzy Dean when they were in their prime. He did it in 1934 when Dizzy took a big-league team on a barnstorming trip. Duncan has visited more countries than any other man in baseball. He's made two trips around the world. Wottaman!

"Say, did I tell you about my new basketball player for the Globetrotters? His name is George Atkins, he's only twenty-one and he's seven feet one inch tall. He'll be smashing when he grows up."

We'd like to tell you more about Saperstein but he left abruptly to select a few mountain peaks on which to write his adjectives if ever he should decide to bring the Ethiopian Clowns to town.

2

1943–44

The Mighty Cleghorn

Toronto *Telegram*
January 18, 1943

Frank "King" Clancy, whose scars are legion, was reminiscing Saturday on the time-honoured subject "Hockey Axemen Whom I Have Known." This is a subject on which Mr. Clancy is well-qualified to speak because every axeman of any importance in the past twenty years has taken a few clouts at Mr. Clancy in the line of duty.

Mr. Clancy hails from Ottawa and civic pride naturally prompted him to put in a few votes for fellow Ottawans. He spoke affectionately of Harold Starr, the brutal beer baron who once at Maple Leaf Gardens felled Clancy in exactly fourteen seconds with a reverse hammerlock and a flying-mare. "A powerful fellow, that Starr," said Clancy judiciously, "but a trifle crude."

The King also marked a few ballots for Aubrey Siebert and George Boucher and Clinton Benedict, the genial goalie. Mr. Clancy recalled, with a nostalgic sigh, the Stanley Cup game in Vancouver when Mr. Benedict lifted his stick over his head and fractured Alf Skinner's ankle with a single well-aimed blow.

As Benedict ambled cheerfully to the penalty box, he handed his goalie stick to Clancy, adjuring him, "Look after this until I get back."

The effervescent Thomas Patrick Gorman, who was handling the Ottawa club at the time, immediately flashed dispatches to Ottawa telling of Clancy's heroic work as stand-in goalie.

Wrote Mr. Gorman, inflamed with enthusiasm: "Clancy, pirouetting like a ballet dancer, caught the flying pucks with the super nonchalance of a great baseball catcher. He stopped a dozen shots that were ticketed for goals."

Clancy regards Gorman's dispatch as one of the century's finest examples of sportive prose, but he says that there was only one minor inaccuracy. In the interests of truth, he revealed that he didn't stop a single shot while Benedict was off the ice. As a matter of fact, his Ottawa mates checked the Vancouvers so resolutely that they didn't get past centre ice.

But Mr. Clancy finally yielded the information that the greatest axeman of all time was Sprague Cleghorn. In fact, Clancy also said that, in his opinion, Cleghorn was the greatest of defencemen.

Clancy fingered a particularly prominent scar on his nose and said, "Personally, I only once had trouble with Cleghorn, and that was enough. Cleghorn took great delight in murdering all members of the Ottawa team but, when I broke in as a kid, he never touched me."

One night when Les Canadiens were playing in Ottawa, Sprague broke away from the play and had only one man to beat. Clancy pursued the mighty Cleghorn down one wing and, as they reached the lone defenceman, the King called for a pass.

The mighty Cleghorn made one of the few mistakes of his career and passed to Clancy.

Clancy expected Cleghorn to decapitate him for perpetrating such a felony, but Cleghorn said nothing.

At the end of the period, the two teams left the ice through the same gate. As Clancy was about to enter the Ottawa dressing room he heard a soft voice behind him say, "Oh, King!"

Thinking that some feminine admirer must be seeking his autograph, Clancy turned and—BOOM! When he regained consciousness, Clancy was being carried into the dressing room and, seeing Father Fallon in the background, he assumed naturally that the priest had been summoned to administer the last rites of the church.

"Yes," said Clancy on Saturday, rubbing his nose thoughtfully, "Cleghorn was a wonderful hockey player, but a bit short-tempered."

Toronto the Tough

Toronto *Telegram*
March 5, 1943

FOUND: A HOCKEY PLAYER who says that Toronto was "the toughest town on visiting players" that he visited in his twenty-five years of connection with the game.

But before the chamber of commerce gets indignant, it should be pointed out that the player in question is Si Griffis, who retired from active hockey competition twenty years ago. And the tough treatment of which the celebrated Mr. Griffis complained was handed out during the 1918 Stanley Cup series between the Toronto Arenas and the Vancouver Millionaires.

You should drop around this year, Mr. Griffis! Our current professional team is both hospitable and deferential toward its opponents. For the past two weeks our team hasn't even bothered to defeat a visiting team!

There was a day, though, when Toronto was a tough town, when defeat weighed heavily on the citizenry, and the city fathers, constabulary and local players combined threats and blandishments to thwart hockey invaders.

Mr. Griffis, who was one of the greatest defencemen of all time, was talking to Johnny Park of the Vancouver *Daily Province* recently and told him of the Millionaires ill-starred invasion of the Queen City, to which some uncouth outlanders still refer as "Hogtown."

Before the first game of the series, the Vancouver players were huddled in their dressing room at the Mutual Street Arena when a large gentleman strode through the door. The large gentleman had a large mustache and large feet that were extremely flat. He glared at the assembled Vancouverites and told them that he was a police official. "If any of you," he roared, "so much as swings a stick or a fist at our innocent Toronto players, I will put you under arrest immediately."

Mr. Griffis, who was depositing his bridgework in a glass of water at the time, arose and answered thunderously, "Go back and tell that Toronto gang that if they try any of their butchery, I personally will hack them to pieces with this piece of hickory."

After this pleasant exchange of amenities, the 1918 Stanley Cup series got under way.

Ten minutes after the start of the game, the late Mickey MacKay, who was playing centre for Vancouver, complained to Mr. Griffis that Toronto's Harry Mummery had been slashing at his ankles. Mr. Mummery was only slightly smaller than the Centre Island Ferry, but on the next three rushes Griffis laid him low, and from that point forward Mummery desisted from carving his initials on MacKay's thighs.

It was a bitter series, but Toronto won the final game by a single goal.

Charlie Querrie, who managed the victorious Arenas, remembers the winning goal vividly. Corbett Denneny stole the puck at centre ice, sizzled through the Vancouver defence and beat Hughie Lehman with a perfect shot. Our Corbett was so excited that he burst out bawling until the mascara ran all over the front of his nice jersey.

The Toronto team in that historic series was managed by Querrie and coached by Dick Carroll. Happy Holmes was in goal and the defence was composed of Mummery, Ken Randall and Harry Cameron. The forwards were Rusty Crawford, Harry Meeking, Denneny, Reg Noble, Alf Skinner and Jack Adams, who now manages the Detroit Red Wings.

The Vancouver team had Lehman in goal; Griffis, Art Duncan and Lloyd Cook on defence. The forwards included MacKay, Cyclone Taylor, Barney Stanley and Ran McDonald.

In the present emergency, it seems expedient that city council should do something to help the Leafs. Mayor Conboy should send a posse of policemen to the Montreal train on Saturday morning and inform the disembarking Canadiens that they will be lodged in the Toronto sneezer if they do not accept defeat willingly on Saturday night.

Mr. Griffis's references to Harry Mummery caused this department to recall the last time we saw Mummery in action. It was an exhibition game in Brandon, and Mummery weighed exactly 335 pounds. His uniform was tailored specially by the Brandon Tent and Awning Company. His defence mate in this exhibition game was another old pro, Bobby Benson, who weighed 142 pounds with a demijohn of rum in his hip pocket.

At last reports, Harry was a locomotive engineer for the Canadian Pacific but the railway was considering retiring him on pension because too many of its locomotives were becoming lopsided from carrying Mummery on his errands of commerce.

Students of hockey doubtless will be interested to know that Griffis considered Tommy Phillips to be the greatest of all hockey players. It is all the more interesting when you recall that for many years Griffis was a teammate of the famous Cyclone Taylor.

Phillips, when he was snowbound in his house, would take a stick and puck into the attic and practise shooting at a bull's eye. At a distance of twenty feet he could shoot a puck into a tomato can on two out of three attempts.

One night Phillips scored two goals in Kenora but the puck went through the posts so fast that the goal umpire, who was wearing a mask to protect his face, didn't see either of the shots. It was in the days before there were nets on the goals.

"I'll bet you that bird raises his hand the next time I shoot one," muttered Phillips.

Phillips swept down the ice again. The puck went through the goal and struck the goal umpire square on the jaw. The unfortunate gentleman raised his right hand high in the air and toppled over, unconscious.

When Hattie and Daisy Donned the Mitts

Toronto *Telegram*
March 20, 1943

In recent years psychologists have been pondering the serious implications of the physical ascendancy of the Female of the Species. The Battle of the Sexes has been going badly for our side, and only a few weeks ago Miss Roberta Rosenfeld, uttering shrill cries of triumph, broadcast the news that Women have divested themselves of the last shred of fragile femininity and invaded the field of professional pugilism.

Chortling happily, Miss Rosenfeld produced a press dispatch that said that two female gladiators had slugged the bejabbers out of each other in a Victoria Arena, and six hundred customers had gathered to watch this horrendous display.

Saddened by the news, the operator of this bureau sought solace in the muscle salon of Sir Benjamin Stockley and beseeched the scholarly sock-savant to build us up physically to the stage where we would have a reasonable chance to withstand the robust assaults of our five-year-old daughter.

"Tush!" quoth Sir Benjamin, when he heard the news. "Women boxed professionally in England forty-five years ago." With which, Sir Benjamin strode into his trophy room to produce the evidence. He lifted a crate containing two dozen mousetraps that he had purchased in one of his carefree moments, cast aside a suit of medieval armour, threw three snaffle bits and six billiard cues onto the floor and finally snagged two faded photographs out of the litter.

The pictures were of two ladies named Daisy Dudley and Hattie Stewart. They were arrayed in tights and wore small boxing gloves, and they had assumed attitudes of beady-eyed truculence with their fists extended.

Dashing Daisy tipped the beam at 150 pounds and Herculean Hattie weighed a neat 170, minus her lipstick and mascara. From an examination of the faded photographs, it was a little difficult to ascertain that they were ladies, but Sir Benjamin assured us such was the case.

"Could 'it like 'ell, too," said Sir Benjamin, cuffing the head of a stray dog, which apparently had been bivouacking in a packing case for the past couple of months and had emerged, blinking, from his sanctuary.

Daisy and Hattie used to tour the country fairs in England forty-five years ago, challenging all comers. No females were sufficiently misguided to accept the challenge, but invariably several country bumpkins, who were mildly foxed with the grape, would essay to take a few clouts at the bellicose damsels. And invariably, Daisy and Hattie would knock the chappies on their piazzas.

Occasionally, of course, the unsuspecting males would attempt to grab the ladies in affectionate embraces while in the ring. But the ladies were prepared for this. They wore stout brogans, equipped with steel toes, and they would kick the unfortunate gentlemen in the ankles or any other portion of the anatomy that presented a sporting target.

The saga of Dashing Daisy and Herculean Hattie must be encouraging news for the Mere Male. The little story shows that, after all, the Female hasn't progressed inordinately in the past forty-five years.

Bye-bye, Bojangles

Toronto *Telegram*
April 27, 1943

WE SEE BY THE PUBLIC PRINTS that Bill "Bojangles" Robinson, the famed Negro backward-sprinter, finally has been defeated. Of course, Bill Robinson is probably better known to you as the world's best dancer. (And that includes Fred Astaire, Ray Bolger, Dave Castilloux and Bill Ritchie of Brown's Sports & Cycle Company!)

For the past thirty years, Bill Robinson has imbued the modern art of terpsichore with an air of vivacity and humour. He has been the star of innumerable Broadway shows; he has toured the world; he is the unofficial mayor of Harlem; and—along with Paul Robeson, Marian Anderson and Joe Louis—he has received more international attention than any other member of his race.

And for the past thirty years, Bojangles has been running backwards faster than most men can run forward. Whenever he visited a city, Bojangles would challenge the area's best sprinter, asking only for a 25-yard handicap in a 100-yard race. We recall seeing him on one occasion racing Cyril Coaffee, who at that time held the world record for the 100 yards. Robinson had crossed the finish line and was tapping out the first four bars of "Runnin' Wild" when Coaffee finally reached home plate.

Well Bojangles must be over sixty now and it wasn't until last week that he was beaten. A lad named Jim Keating of San Francisco State College defeated him in a race that was staged to boost the sale of war bonds. Incidentally, Keating ran the 100 yards in 9.5 seconds. Robinson still must be a pretty spry old boy.

There have been several other characters who have travelled backwards to enter the Hall of Fame. For instance, Carl Fischer, who toiled for the Maple Leafs baseball team in 1941, received international attention simply because he lost more games consecutively than any other pitcher in organized baseball.

We recall, too, a character named Ptomaine Joe who occupied a starring role in the stories that H.C. Witwer wrote about a fictional pugilist named Kid Roberts. Ptomaine Joe had a rugged constitution, but he couldn't lick his lips. Consequently, he determined to win himself the title of "World's Gamest Loser." He lost every fight on a technical knockout but invariably he was still on his feet at the finish, albeit cut and bleeding.

And now Jack "Deacon" Allen, the fight promoter, is employing the same technique. He walked in here last night and announced proudly, "The opener on Tuesday's fight card will be the worst bout in history. I guarantee this positively, and anyone who doesn't agree with me can get a refund at the box office."

More than likely, he'll pack the joint!

How Do You Like Your Trout?

Toronto *Telegram*
May 1, 1943

TODAY MARKS THE OPENING of the fishing season for speckled trout.

Today, millions of speckled trout who have been minding their own business and living exemplary lives are about to have their bucolic mode of existence rudely dislocated. They are about to be assaulted and chivvied by rapacious human beings. We hate to think of it, chums, but it's a sure-pop that a large percentage of the speckled trout in the rivers and lakes of Ontario are destined, in the near future, to finish their careers on a large platter, nestling among such outlandish neighbours as boiled potatoes and hothouse tomatoes.

This situation seems grossly unfair. The speckled trout is part of a civilization that is older than that of the human being. The speckled trout annoys no one, but lives in peace with every man. The speckled trout does not destroy the fruit in the orchards. The speckled trout does not prey upon the stalks of wheat or flax. The speckled trout, unlike the mosquito, does not bite the human being, raising unsightly lumps. The speckled trout does not vote illegally at elections.

The only point that can be raised to the speckled trout's detriment is the fact that occasionally he exhibits cannibalistic tendencies and eats smaller fish without bothering to cook them. But we feel that this is the speckled trout's own business—and to hell with it!

The speckled trout does not owe any money. The speckled trout merely spends all his time lying quietly in a shady pool, occasionally yawning and emitting a stream of bubbles that pop to the surface like that stuff they put in champagne. Occasionally, too, the speckled trout lays eggs, which seems a pretty damn silly occupation for anything other than a hen; but the point is that the speckled trout seems happy.

Now, let us look at the other side of the picture.

The human being who hunts the speckled trout is called an angler. Under ordinary circumstances, he is an eminently sensible character who lives a regular life and never beats his stenographer.

But what happens to him when he goes fishing? He gets up at some unearthly hour before dawn. He spends the day standing up to his hips in cold water or perched precariously on some rock. He permits himself to be devoured, without protest, by large, angry black flies. He patiently unravels knotted fishing lines and he doesn't lose his temper even when his hook gets caught in the branch of an overhanging tree. He sits up half the night ruining his eyes while he plays cards by the light of an oil lamp and ruining his digestive tract by filling it with corrosive fluid.

But does he complain? No, a thousand times no. He thinks that he's having a wonderful time.

This angler, of course, is the same man who, when he is home, suddenly develops fallen arches when his wife asks him to carry the ashes out into the lane. This angler, who lives such a spartan life in the wilds, is the same fellow who screams for justice when the heat in his apartment falls below seventy degrees Fahrenheit. This angler, who exhibits such remarkable patience when pursuing the speckled trout, is the same fellow who threatens to sue the Toronto Transit Company when the streetcar service is thirty seconds late.

It's all very confusing. Small wonder that the human being has gotten the world into such a hell of a mess. It's high time that we turned the whole works over to the speckled trout.

An angler, patient he is when he fishes,
But just ask him, chum, to wash those dishes!

The Legend of Charlie Conkle

Toronto *Telegram*
July 22, 1943

A FEW WEEKS AGO we made fleeting reference to Charlie Conkle, "the midget Hercules of Hamilton." Conkle, who is operating a service station now in Hamilton, will be seventy years old on August 5, but in his heyday he was reputed to be the toughest rough-and-tumble fighter in the history of North America.

Undoubtedly the passage of years has embellished the Conkle legend, but as one veteran sports scribe once told us, "Any story you hear about the feats of Charlie Conkle, no matter how fantastic it sounds, is almost certain to be true."

Conkle never weighed more than 142 pounds, but he wrestled Frank Gotch when Gotch was world champion and weighed 238. He beat the bejabbers out of boxers who outweighed him by twenty pounds, and one Hamilton constable is reputed to have said that the only way to win a decision over Conkle "is to shoot him with a pistol before he gets within punching distance."

They say that Conkle has made a financial success of the service-station business because he didn't find it necessary to make the capital outlay for equipment, such as jacks, to hold cars off the ground while tires are being removed. They say that Conkle simply holds the car in the air with one hand and changes the tire with his free maulie.

A gentleman who publishes a local scratch sheet has brought our attention to the occasion on which Conkle returned to the ring at the age of thirty-nine and kayoed a Boston toughie who weighed 167 pounds.

At the time Conkle was managing a fighter in Hamilton. The fighter was matched with a man-eater from Boston, and Conkle, knowing that his own boxer was on the verge of being punch-drunk, tried to get out of the bout when he took his first look at the Boston battler. The Bostonian was a simian-looking citizen of enormous strength, and it was obvious that he could slaughter Conkle's fighter.

In the course of the parley over the cancellation of the bout, the Bostonian sneered at Conkle, "Both you and your so-and-so fighter are yellow."

Mr. Conkle blew clear through the roof and landed running.

"Why you blankety-blank such-and-such," he howled, "I'll fight you myself."

Conkle realized immediately that he had made a tactical error. His opponent was only twenty-seven years old and reputed to be the toughest man in his division. Conkle was twelve years older and hopelessly out of condition, but he insisted on going through with the bout.

However, he had the foresight to stage a pre-fight conference with the referee who, quite naturally, was sympathetic to the Conkle cause.

"The first time we clinch," Conkle told him, "break us up and walk between us slowly. But the second time you break us up, walk between us—but *quickly*!"

The referee was a most co-operative citizen, and after a few seconds of ineffectual milling, the fighters fell into a clinch. The referee broke them up slowly. The second time they clinched he walked quickly between them. The referee reported afterwards that he heard a sound that gave him the impression that someone had dynamited the peak off Hamilton Mountain. He turned around quickly and saw Conkle leaning over the ropes, talking to a blonde in the front row. Conkle's opponent was lying on the canvas, slumbering blissfully, and it was many hours before he was able to sit up and take nourishment.

They'll tell you, too, about the time that Conkle wrestled Frank Gotch in Hamilton. Gotch outweighed the pride of Hamilton by ninety-six pounds, but it took the world champion twenty-eight minutes to pin his doughty little foeman.

Our favourite story about Conkle concerns the occasion on which he wrestled the champion of Japan in Charleston, South Carolina. Japanese wrestling is a modified form of mayhem, but the champ met his match in Conkle, who had served his apprenticeship in one of the continent's finest schools of street fighting.

They fought for five hours and thirty-eight minutes—and it was the Jap who finally quit.

Conkle still was on his feet at the finish, though he had suffered seven broken fingers, one broken thumb and a fractured bone in one leg. Wottaman! They tell us that he's anxious to join the army in order to lead the eventual assault on Tokyo.

Li'l Arthur

Toronto *Telegram*
August 20, 1943

"JUST A DIME—TEN CENTS!" bellowed the banjo-eyed blonde as she waved the microphone a few inches in front of her tonsils. "Just a dime to see the world's greatest collection of freaks. See the amazing wool-covered men—the wool grows on their bodies just like on the back of a sheep!"

The crowd edged toward the huge circus tent. The atmosphere was permeated by the odours of sizzling hot dogs, pink lemonade and a dozen noxious candy confections.

"This way to the big show," barked the banjo-eyed blonde. "See the two-faced man; see the amazing sword swallower. Only a dime—ten cents!"

We shoved through the mob. We walked past the sword swallower and the lady snake charmer. We sidled through the crowd that surrounded the sheep-faced men. We pushed our way down to the far end of the tent, and there in a darkened corner, sat Li'l Arthur!

The great frame was draped over a kitchen chair. He wore a neat blue suit and his feet were encased in brogans of obviously fine quality. He wore a beret. He adopted a beret in the days when—along with Sparrow Robertson and Sheriff McGeehan and Jeff Dickson and a score more expatriates—he was one of the ornaments of Harry's New York Bar in Paris.

Li'l Arthur was paring his nails with a large knife. He looked up slowly and his famous gold teeth were visible for a flickering instant as he smiled a half-hearted greeting. Li'l Arthur was morose and lonely in his own small corner. That in itself wasn't unusual. Li'l Arthur has been lonely for more years than he can remember.

You see, Li'l Arthur committed the unpardonable sin of winning the heavyweight championship. Li'l Arthur was a Black Man, and in 1908, when he won the championship, a Black Man was supposed to know his place.

Li'l Arthur beat Tommy Burns in Australia to win the title. He had kayoed old Bob Fitzsimmons and Fireman Jim Flynn, and he had beaten the great Sam Langford. And then, when he came back to the United

States, he kayoed the mighty Jim Jeffries in fifteen rounds. That was a bad thing to do—Li'l Arthur was a Black Man, and Jeffries was the athletic hero of the white races.

Then Li'l Arthur got into some trouble. It was bad trouble, but the thing that made it worse was the fact that he was a Black Man. The police were after Li'l Arthur, and he was forced to go into hiding. He became an outcast, a man who wandered from country to country, and eventually he settled down in Paris where people permitted him to live his own life without interference.

Li'l Arthur yielded his championship to the white races in Havana in 1915. He lay quietly on his back, with his hands raised, covering his head to protect his eyes from the sun, while the referee counted "ten" over him, and Jess Willard was declared world champion.

Probably Li'l Arthur still considers Paris to be his home. He lived in Spain for several years, but invariably he returned to Paris. They understood him in Paris, and there were sympathetic friends like Sparrow Robertson, the ageless little man who was the sports editor of that famous paper called the Paris *Herald*. The Sparrow is dead now, and the rest of those friends fled Paris when the war clouds gathered. There was nothing left for Li'l Arthur, so he returned to America.

The years haven't marked him greatly. His sixty-five summers rest lightly on his massive body. His skin is fresh and young-looking, and there is a spark that lies deep in his sleepy eyes.

As he sat in the hot tent, one hand flicked out through the air in an incredibly swift and graceful gesture. A tiny fly was clutched between two huge fingers. The insect hadn't been harmed. Arthur regarded it thoughtfully for a second and set it free.

When he speaks there is just a trace of bitterness in his deep but gentle voice.

"Years ago I was in Vancouver," he said. "Victor McLaglen was there, and he was broke and hungry. He wanted a chance to fight me. I broke a contract to let him have the bout. I beat him, but he got a stake out of it. A couple of years ago, McLaglen had a chance to get me a job in the movies. I needed that job badly. McLaglen didn't do it for me."

Li'l Arthur looked into space for a second, then resumed his manicure.

As we left the tent, the banjo-eyed blonde still was barking into the microphone. The men and women and small children crowded around her curiously.

"See the amazing sheep-faced men!'" she counselled. "See the original Popeye! See Jack Johnson, the former heavyweight champion of the world and the greatest boxer of all time. Just a dime—ten cents!"

Just a dime—ten cents!

The Lady, the Lord and the Hermit

Toronto *Telegram*
September 24, 1943

TAKE YOUR NOSE OUT OF YON BOWL OF BORSCHT, Terence, and list ye to a tale of a sporting gentleman who was crossed in love.

This is a true story, Terence, and it's all about a couple of belted earls and the Epsom Derby and a beautiful tomato named Florence. If you wish for any corroboration of this tale, you need only consult any history of the derby.

Well it was like this, see.

It was the year 1867, and a gent named Mr. Chaplin was engaged to this delectable tomato named Lady Florence Paget. Mr. Chaplin was subsequently named Viscount Chaplin, but at the time of our story he was struggling along with a name no more important than that of Joe Blow, the Oxbow amateur golfer.

This Mr. Chaplin was a sportsman, however, and he owned a noble steed called Hermit that had been nominated for the derby. But Hermit was strictly a longshot. No one believed seriously that he would win the derby unless his jockey gave him the hot seat with a large battery.

So one day Mr. Chaplin and this gorgeous tomato, Lady Florence Paget, went to London's Regent Street to shop for her trousseau. When they reached the lingerie department, Mr. Chaplin, who was a gentleman and a scholar, withdrew from the shop and sat in his carriage, puffing on a Burma cheroot. This was in 1867, of course, long before the Mere Male mustered sufficient nerve to venture unescorted into a lingerie department to purchase a brassiere for his ever-loving wife.

So Mr. Chaplin sat there for an hour or so, gnawing on a succession of cheroots, until finally evening descended, and the lady who operated the lingerie shop started to close up for the night. Mr. Chaplin approached her courteously and asked what had become of Lady Paget.

We regret to report that Lady Florence had ratted on Mr. Chaplin. While he was sitting there, blissfully contemplating his forthcoming marriage, she had taken it on the Jesse Owens and dashed through the back door of the lingerie shop. There, in a back alley, she had met the young Marquis of Hastings, and he had carried her off and had her churched before Mr. Chaplin had finished his first cheroot.

To make it worse, even the most charitable critics of the period agreed that Lord Hastings was "a wild rakehell," which, Terence, is just another way of saying that he was a lush.

Mr. Chaplin, of course, felt considerably upset by this turn of events, and he felt no cheerier when, two days before the derby, his gallant steed Hermit bled badly after a gallop. It looked as if Hermit wouldn't get to the post unless he was carried there by several representatives of the St. John Ambulance Corps.

Lord Hastings, for his part, wasn't satisfied with his triumph over his rival. He mortgaged his home and wagered five hundred thousand dollars that Hermit *wouldn't* win the derby. As a matter of fact, he went into hock more than considerably to make this wager, and it was rumoured that Lady Florence was forced to post some of that Regent Street lingerie as security.

The Epsom Derby of 1867 was one of the most amazing in history. A violent storm raged over Epsom Downs and the course was swept by rain and snow. In an excess of gloom, Mr. Chaplin betook himself to the big tree at Tottenham Corner and prepared to watch his rival's final triumph.

But Chaplin reckoned without Hermit. The horse, giving an almost incredible display of gameness, fought his way through the storm and won by a neck from Marksman.

Lord Hastings was ruined, and they say that ultimately he shot himself through the pimple.

Mr. Chaplin's fortune was made. Hermit was sent to the stud and for many years his stud fees brought Mr. Chaplin forty-five thousand dollars annually—which ain't hay, Terence!

All of which goes to show that even a gorgeous tomato with a title is only a selling plater around the racetrack.

And, Terence, while we're on the subject of steeds, we should explain to you that perfidious conduct in the nineteenth century wasn't confined to tomatoes.

We were reading the other day about a gentleman named Honest John Day, who trained horses for Lord George Bentinck. Honest John was much revered in his day, though merely because he had an unfortunate habit of keeping copies of his correspondence, his reputation suffered quite a severe knock after he'd passed to his final reward.

Someone was rummaging among his papers and discovered two letters written by him, both on the same day. One was written to Lord Bentinck and the other to a prominent bookmaker.

The letter to Bentinck read: "My Lord—The colt is quite fit and has done a rattling gallop. I fancy he is bound to win. Pray, back him for all you can on Monday next if only you can get a fair price."

But the letter to the bookmaker read: "Dear Joe—The long-legged lord will be at Tattersall's on Monday. Lay him all you can. The horse is a dead one!"

The knave!

Knifey's Christmas

Toronto *Telegram*
December 13, 1943

DURING THIS SEASON OF THE YEAR most citizens are slugging themselves lustily across the nut with a rubber hammer as they attempt to devise schemes for digging up a small bundle of scratch in order that they may tuck a couple of gewgaws into the toe of the Old Doll's nylons on Christmas morning. Most of us are chock full of the ruddy old Yule spirit but, unfortunately, suffering from financial anemia. Simply to restore the Mere Male's faith in human nature, we intend to tell you the little story of "How Knifey Got His Christmas Stake" or "Lester's Luck Ain't Always Lousy."

The hero of our little tale is Mr. L.R. Knifong, a maverick from Austin, Texas, who is one of the authentic characters of the turf. Knifey is a drawling, shuffling, dead-pan gentleman with a warm heart and a gentle sense of humour. Mr. Knifong was christened Lester Knifong, but this is something that is mentioned seldom in public, and if someone is sufficiently ill-advised to ask Knifey what his initials stand for, Mr. Knifong merely fixes him with a hard look.

Knifey has been in the hoss business for many, many years, and from it he has done no more than eke out a fair living. Mr. Knifong has an excellent system for concealing the fiscal facts in connection with himself. When Mr. Knifong meets one of his many friends, he will borrow a cigar, thus dissuading any but the most insensitive friends from asking any questions concerning his financial resources.

Well, Knifey was down here this autumn with a couple of sterling beasts named Hoops My Dear and Frilly. Mr. Knifong's luck was neither good nor bad, but he made a small score and shipped to Bay Meadows.

Mr. Knifong, being a gentleman of Celtic origin, is in the habit of speaking quietly to his horses, and there are many horsemen who vow that the horses speak back to Mr. Knifong. In any event, things were far from good at Bay Meadows, and in the early mornings Mr. Knifong could be seen walking around the track followed by Frilly and Hoops My Dear. Mr. Knifong, observed from a distance, could be seen to be gesticulating angrily and the horses to be hanging their heads and looking very ashamed.

It was noticeable, too, that there were very few oats around the Knifong barn, and when Knifey went into the stalls to feed the horses, the other residents of the shedrow could hear snarls coming from the stalls. It was rumoured that Knifey and Frilly and Hoops My Dear were dividing the oats and arguing about it. Knifey could be heard muttering, "You so-and-sos had better win pretty soon or there ain't going to be any Christmas tree!"

When it became obvious that Mr. Knifong's frail constitution wasn't benefiting from this diet of oats, Judge George Schilling, the well-known racing official, telegraphed Jim Speers in Winnipeg and reported: "Knifey soon will be down to riding weight."

But two days later, Judge Schilling wired again and reported: "All is well."

So this is what had occurred in the interim.

Knifey entered Frilly and Hoops My Dear in two separate races on the one program. Then Mr. Knifong reached into the heel of his shoe and produced a five-dollar note. He walked over to the parimutuel machines and wagered the five-dollar note on Frilly. It was a tight fit, but Frilly got up in time to win by a lip and pay $124 for $2. Mr. Knifong was somewhat irked when Frilly came back. "What do you mean by scaring me half to death?" he muttered and chased her into her stall.

Then Knifey took his fresh roll of $310 and bet it on Hoops My Dear. Good old Hoops bounced home and paid $30 for $2. Mr. Knifong's original five-dollar investment yielded him a total of $4,650. In addition, the two purses brought him another $1,400, which made a total of $6,050 for a single afternoon's work.

Mr. Knifong locked his two equine friends in their stalls and shuffled off to buy a Christmas tree. On his way out of the track he met Judge Schilling and borrowed *two* cigars.

The story of Mr. Knifong's latest adventures somehow has filled us with happiness. Who ever said that there's no Santa Claus?

Shaggy Horse Story

Toronto *Telegram*
January 3, 1944

WHILE YOU'RE STANDING IN LINE waiting for your blood transfusion, you might as well hear the story of "The Horse that Played Baseball." Stand well back, boys, and don't let any of this stuff get squirted over your jabot.

Well, it was this way, see! This horse was reading the sports page one day when he noticed that the manager of a professional baseball club had inserted an advertisement seeking a pitcher. So the horse says, "Well I'm not working, so I might as well go down and snare that job."

So the horse goes to the manager of the baseball club and tells him that he is prepared to pitch. The manager of the ball club takes another gander at the horse and wipes his hand over his eyes. Then he says to himself, "Oh, wotthehell—I might as well take a chance on it. We're in last place, anyhow, and it might help the attendance if the horse really can pitch."

The next day the club is playing the Throttlebottom Rovers, so the manager sends the horse out to the mound. The horse looked pretty good while he was warming up. His curve was breaking nicely and his fastball had a real hop on it.

The first batter goes up to the plate and—zzzzip—the horse throws a strike right past him. The horse takes the ball again and—zzzzip—strike TWO! So the horse just keeps on throwing that high hard one and—zzzzip, zzzzip, zzzzip—he fans the first three men on nine pitched balls.

Naturally, the customers are cheering like mad when the horse tosses aside his glove and strolls back to the dugout. The manager pats the horse on the back and says, "Boy, if you can hit like you can pitch, we'll use you in the clean-up spot."

The first batter goes up to the plate and fans. Then the next man walks and the third hitter manages to get a scratch single. So the horse goes up to the plate, carrying the bat, and he sees that his teammates are perched on first and third bases.

Well, the horse has a nice, easy swing and the opposing pitcher sizes him up carefully. Then the pitcher throws one down there and—WHANGO!—the horse hits the ball clear over the left-field fence. The two baserunners start to run, but the umpire yells, "Foul ball!"

The pitcher throws again and—WHANGO!—the horse hits the ball over the left-field fence again. Everybody starts to run, but it's another foul. Incredible though it may sound, the horse hit the first five pitches over the left-field wall and all of them were fouls.

The pitcher tried a change of pace then, but he missed the corner of the plate, and the count went to two strikes and one ball. The pitcher threw another curve that missed the corner, and the count moved to two strikes and two balls. Then the pitcher threw one down the crack and—WHANGO!—the ball went over the right-field fence. Well, so help me, Hannah, it was another foul. As a matter of fact, the horse then proceeded to belt three successive foul balls over the *right*-field fence.

Well, the pitcher was pretty nearly worn out, and his next pitch was one that floated up there, looking as big as a cantaloupe. So—WHANGO!—the horse kissed it on the nose and the ball soared clear over the centre-field fence, 415 feet away.

The customers went daffy and the two baserunners started to leg it for home. The man from third scored and the man from first came scampering home, and then—all of a sudden—everyone noticed that the horse hadn't moved away from the plate.

The manager dashed out of the dugout and bellowed, "Run, you dummy!"

But the horse just stood there. The customers all shouted, "Run, run, run!" but the horse just stood there.

So the manager, who was frantic with exasperation, rushed up to the horse and screamed, "Can't you run, you sap?"

"Hell," says the horse, "if I could run I wouldn't be here—I'd be at Tropical Park."

The Deacon's Alberta Assassin

Toronto *Telegram*
January 15, 1944

UNLIKE OTHER PRIZEFIGHT PROMOTERS and managers, Deacon Allen is one citizen to whom the word "heavyweight" is an anathema. The Deacon's adventures with heavyweights have been somewhat unfortunate. Last year he had a heavyweight in the person of Howard Chard, but just when fame and fortune appeared likely to beckon the pugilistic duo, Chard was persuaded to take a prolonged vacation at the expense of the government.

Some years earlier the Deacon managed a heavyweight gent who rejoiced in the name of Yale Okun. When, under Mr. Allen's guidance, Okun made his New York debut in Madison Square Garden, the results were disastrous. The celebrated Damon Runyon, who was writing sports at the time, tottered into print the next morning with the sage observation that, undoubtedly, Mr. Okun had been the inspiration for that famous war cry, "Hold 'em, Yale!"

However, viewed in retrospect, Mr. Allen is of the opinion that his most unfortunate experience with heavyweights occurred in Vancouver about eight years ago. Maximilian Baer, the butcher boy from Livermore, California, was the current world heavyweight champ, and the Deacon imported him to Vancouver for a bout.

There was only one trifling obstacle: every one of the heavyweights within two hundred miles of Vancouver took to the high hills when they heard that Baer was coming to town. Effusively, they declined to box Baer, even if he promised to fight with one hand tied behind his back.

This setback left Allen in a weakened condition, and when his resistance was at its lowest ebb he was approached by a persuasive young Athenian named David Cavadas. Catching Allen with his guard down, Cavadas persuaded him that he should match Baer with one James J. Walsh, "the Alberta Assassin."

"I might have known that this egg would lay an egg," says Mr. Allen now, as he looks back upon the event without rancour.

However, the Deacon was desperate, and he clutched at the flimsy straw. At considerable expense the Alberta Assassin was freighted in from the cattle ranges of Alberta. Mr. Allen and Mr. Cavadas were there to greet him. Allen confesses today that he shuddered in horror when he saw James J. Walsh clamber off the brake beams of the freight car.

With the utmost alacrity, the Alberta Assassin was rushed to a gymnasium where, behind carefully barred doors, he boxed a few rounds with a waiter from a nearby suds foundry.

The Deacon swooned, victim of an attack of vertigo, when he saw the Alberta Assassin essay to throw a punch. As a matter of fact, if the walls of the gymnasium hadn't been constructed of particularly stout material, the Deacon would have fallen into the street below and would have been trampled to death by the five o'clock crowd.

When he recovered consciousness, Allen, with a great effort, calmed his snapping nerve ganglia and grabbed Cavadas. "Take your fighter home to bed," he snarled bitterly, "and have him down here for a workout at six o'clock tomorrow morning."

"Why at six o'clock?" gasped the injured Mr. Cavadas. "None of the fight writers or prospective customers will be up to watch us then."

"That's what I mean," answered the Deacon wearily. "That way, neither of us will get murdered."

The next night a goodly crowd had gathered in the Vancouver Arena, capacity eleven thousand, to watch Baer trade punches with the Alberta Assassin.

Baer entered the ring to a thunderous accompaniment of cheers and boos. The Alberta Assassin entered the ring, and there was a hushed silence. When James J. Walsh removed his bathrobe, there were shouts of outright disapproval. When the Alberta Assassin threw his first punch the customers started to clap their hands and stamp their feet.

Then Baer waved his fist and struck Walsh in the stomach.

The breeze sent the Alberta Assassin flat on his kisser. With the screams of the outraged citizens dinning in his ears, the Deacon fled into the night.

Some five hours later the Deacon emerged from a sanctuary where he had been taking internal applications of healing medicines. He had taken sufficient anesthetics, according to the doctor in charge at the establishment, so that he would be unable to feel any knife wounds. The Deacon looked to the west and saw that the skies were red with flames. He looked again and saw that the arena had burned to the ground.

Of course, the fire was only a coincidence but, to this day, the Deacon isn't convinced that one of his indignant clients didn't light a match to the arena after the show was over.

The Shue Moy Solution

Toronto *Telegram*
May 5, 1944

In surveying the sporting accomplishments of the United Nations, the majority of experts overlook the Chinese. The Chinese are accustomed to being ignored—they had been fighting the Japanese for nearly ten years before anyone offered them assistance.

The Chinese are extremely interested in sporting pastimes, particularly those with gambling aspects. The Chinese are dab hands at fan-tan and mah-jong; they bet the races vigorously; and at least one Chinese friend of ours, Luey Gow of Calgary, has a flourishing stable of thoroughbreds.

In Vancouver for some years there was the Chinese Students soccer team. The Students made quite a shambles of the league and precipitated several interesting donnybrooks. On one such occasion their opponents were the City Police, and when the ambulances arrived the field was littered with the bodies of stalwart constables.

Under ordinary circumstances, though, the Chinese were Vancouver's best citizens. They minded their own business, and they would become irked only when the authorities attempted to interfere with their gambling. We recall that during the Depression not a single Chinese family was on relief. The wealthier members of the large Chinese community provided all necessary food, clothing and lodgings for their countrymen who were unemployed.

The Depression wasn't just an *ordinary* depression. In Vancouver, most of us were about four feet underground.

Well the cops were ordered to knock over the Chinese lottery, an institution that was operated by an elderly, scholarly and generous gentleman named Shue Moy. The lottery had operated for many years without bothering anyone, and Mr. Shue was hurt and bewildered when the gendarmes began paying frequent visits. However, he weighed the situation calmly and within a few weeks he had routed the forces of the law.

When the police raided the lottery headquarters they would find several hundred Chinese there. The police would issue summonses to all of them. The next morning two hundred Chinese would arrive in court and plead guilty to being inmates of a gaming house. They were fined ten dollars, with the option of ten days in jail instead. All of them would take the ten days in jail.

Thus the city was compelled to feed the two hundred Chinese for ten days. This meant that the city was forced to provide six thousand meals.

The police commission soon realized what Mr. Shue was doing. When he heard of an impending raid he would fill his lottery headquarters with jobless Chinese whose relief was being provided by the wealthier members of the Chinese community.

The police never again bothered the Chinese lottery.

Damned clever, these Chinese!

This department regrets to report that probably we have been responsible for a serious breach in Chinese-Canadian relations.

For some time now we have been dealing with a laundry operated by the Lam Brothers, On-The Lam and Leg-Of Lam. Leg-Of was a merry-faced fellow with a keen interest in the gentle art of improving the breed. In order to curry his favour we gave him feed-box information on the turf turtles. These gallant steeds met with indifferent success, but one morning last autumn we whispered in his ear, "Bet Western Prince and Broom Time. They can't miss today."

Just as we were leaving with our clean shirts we heard Leg-Of ripping the cash register off its base, and seconds later he was disappearing down the street with the cash register under his coat.

"Oh happy fellow," we whispered, staring after him in friendly fashion. "Tonight he will be a millionaire."

We would like to draw a veil over the rest of this unhappy story, but in some completely inexplicable fashion Western Prince and Broom Time both ran in the can that afternoon.

It was a week before we recovered sufficiently to visit the laundry to collect our shirts. Leg-Of wasn't in evidence. On-The was standing behind the counter and somehow he didn't greet us in true Rotary Club fashion.

"Where's our old pal, Leg-Of?" we asked, forcing a timid smile.

"Eighty-five cent for shirts," answered On-The.

"Yeah, but where's Leg-Of?" we persisted.

"Eighty-five cent," said On-The, inexorably. Somehow, we didn't want to make an issue of it. We haven't seen Leg-Of since then.

Lately, On-The has been giving us other people's shirts. None of those shirts fits us.

Somehow, we don't want to make an issue of that, either. Obviously, On-The is a hard man!

A Little Dry-Cell Humour

Toronto *Telegram*
July 7, 1944

THAT SUBTLE FELLOW, Mr. Appas Tappas, was referring humorously today to the fact that a swarm of bees invaded the paddock at Fort Erie yesterday afternoon. With a nostalgic sigh, he suggested that there might have been some astounding upsets if the bees had accompanied a few of the horses to the post. Said Mr. Appas Tappas, chuckling happily into the ribbon of his typewriter: "In the old days riders often made a noise like bees buzzing in the ears of their horses. Some of them, who had been beaten regularly in the past, got home winners."

Mr. Appas Tappas was referring obliquely to one of the most important contributions to horse racing, viz. the invention of the dry-cell battery. The dry-cell battery accomplished the same thing for horses that Gartersnake's Little Liver Pills accomplished for human beings. It was excellent for horses with that "tired, rundown feeling."

In such cases, it was necessary only to touch a small dry-cell battery to the horse's flank. Immediately the horse's eyes would brighten; his chest would swell; he would leap in the air and shout loudly that he was Man o' War. Of course, occasionally one of these noble beasts would jump right into the upper gallery of the judges' stand and create considerable confusion therein. The dry-cell battery was banned generally after several such incidents because it destroys the dignity of the judges if a horse chases them around their cupola.

This handy little dry-cell battery, which improved a horse's health so rapidly, was known generally as "the old persuader," or "the joint," or merely "the thing."

We recall once meeting a groom friend of ours who grasped us by the lapels and whispered hoarsely, "Bet on Mr. Beefsteak."

"That hide," we replied bitterly, "has been last every time he has started this year."

"Bet on him," persisted the groom.

"But why?" we asked.

"Well," said the groom, looking over his shoulder, "if they stick a light globe in his mouth this afternoon, he'll be all lit up like a Greek church!"

And there is an expatriated western groom with whom we were chatting the other day.

"Do you remember so-and-so?" we asked, mentioning a horse that ran with remarkable inconsistency some years ago.

"Do I remember so-and-so?" screamed the groom, practically knocking himself out with laughter. "We called him the Presto-Lite Kid!"

The handy dry-cell battery still is in existence, though it is a bold jockey who will venture to use one on a decently policed racetrack.

There was one owner in Montreal who employed the handy dry-cell battery to awaken his sleeping grooms by touching the instrument to their bare feet. Invariably, they jumped out of bed and dashed twice around the track before he could get them pulled up. Then it was necessary to put halters over their heads and cool them out in the walking ring for forty minutes before they could sit down to breakfast.

The Thrush on the Flying Trapeze

Toronto *Telegram*
July 19, 1944

It was recorded on these pages yesterday that Jack Doyle, known facetiously in biff-and-boff circles as "the Irish Thrush," has abandoned boxing in favour of a career as a singer. This is a move that will be hailed with ecstatic approval by all those who have been misguided sufficiently to pay good money to witness M. Doyle's strange antics in the ring.

There is indisputable evidence that Doyle wasn't the best heavyweight, but there is no evidence to show that he wasn't the worst heavyweight of his time. In examining his record, you will discover that his most impressive victory was scored in London, England, over that amiable eccentric, Kingfish Levinsky. Levinsky's greatest asset was his sister-manager, Leaping Lena Levinsky, whose conduct was so uninhibited that eventually she wound up in a quiet room in a carefully guarded rest home. As far as the Kingfish's fistic record is concerned, there is no reputable testimony that he was able to lick his lips.

There have been other prominent athletes who were noted as singers. Earl Sande, the top jockey of his day, trained to be an opera star, but he wasn't equipped with a sufficiently large stomach to vie with the ranking bassos in those Wagnerian roles. Imagine Sande wooing one of those Wagnerian contraltos. It would have looked like a mouse trying to crawl up an elephant's trunk.

Frank Swoonatra essayed to be a boxer but discovered that it was more profitable to have his sports jacket ripped from his shoulders by impressionable autograph-seekers. Pepper Martin and Dizzy Dean were noted musicians when they performed for the St. Louis Cardinals in the era of the Gas House Gang, but inevitably, it was necessary to get rid of them. The trainer of the club insisted that, after one of their songfests, it took two days to clear the air in the dressing room.

The most effective singer-athlete of whom we have heard was a reformed racetrack tout who, after being run out of the country for touting a Pinkerton into betting five hundred dollars on a losing ten-to-one shot, decided to seek another vocation. His name was Willie Nittlewit, and in the days of his extreme youth he had trained to be a circus acrobat. As a matter of fact, he had trained as a trapeze artist but was forced to quit because his hands were shaped so peculiarly that he couldn't grab one of those guys flying through the air. His hands had twisted into a permanently contorted position through his proclivity for clinging to those two-ounce glasses in the old saloon days.

Well, Willie was a sharp guy and he realized that there was no important dough, anyhow, in being one of those regular trapeze artists. The customers only get cricks in their necks watching the regular trapeze artists and they are liable to lose interest every time that the man passes selling hot dogs or Eskimo pies.

Consequently Willie decided to be a trapeze artist with a novel dodge. He took singing lessons from a broken-down operatic baritone and, after practising in his bathtub eight hours a day for two years, he mastered all the trills, tremolos and gusty sighs from the famed aria from *Boris Godunov* (the opera of the same name, chums).

Not only does he master this aria but he sings it while hanging from his feet on a flying trapeze.

Well, right from the start, Willie's act killed them. He played fourteen consecutive weeks in the Palace Theatre in New York. Few of the patrons there had heard the aria from *Boris Godunov*, let alone a guy singing the aria from *Boris Godunov* while hanging from his heels.

Willie was booked for a triumphal European tour and he knocked them dizzy in London, Paris, Amsterdam, Vienna and waypoints.

Then came the day when Willie was so famous that he was told that he was to appear in a command performance before the King of Sweden.

The joint was packed that night and there was more precious metal on display in the audience than you'd find on the lists of all the stockbrokers in Toronto. So Willie gets up there and hangs by his heels and starts to give with the vocal pipes. He is giving in good voice and the audience is entranced—but then it happens.

Willie's voice cracks on a top note. The audience gasps in astonishment. Willie tries to go on, but his voice sounds like someone calling a herd of Arkansas hogs. Desperately, the manager of the opera house rings down the curtain. Willie is ruined. He departs on the first cattle boat for America. After hearing his voice, they toss him into a pen with some of the steers.

The mystery was solved late. Willie was a case of arrested development. His voice never had broken till that night in the Swedish opera house when he had reached the age of thirty-seven. Even today, he sounds like the foghorn at the Eastern Gap.

We saw him today. He was trying to tout a Pinkerton at Fort Erie.

But, to get back to our theme, we are glad to see that Jack Doyle finally has taken up singing as a means of living. We will make one suggestion: after viewing M. Doyle's record, we would suggest that he would feel more at home if he did all his singing while lying flat on his back.

Those Days When the Fix Was In

Toronto *Telegram*
October 11, 1944

Walter Richey, the quiet, business-like fellow who has enjoyed an excellent season in his first year as official starter on Ontario racetracks, was a jockey in his younger days. Richey doesn't insist that he was the best jockey on the North American continent, but many of his admiring friends insist that he was the fastest broken-field runner ever to toss a pair of riding boots through irons.

About thirty years ago Walter was performing in the gay, carefree atmosphere of Montreal's Delorimier Park, a racing plant that was frequented by uninhibited wagerers who liked above all to wager on "sure things." In order that there should be several of these "sure things" in each day's program, these gamblers would approach the jockeys and speak to them very, very seriously. In some cases, it was necessary to give a jockey a slight boff across the ears to emphasize the seriousness of the conversation.

So one afternoon, Richey was riding a gallant steed named Commerata for Russell Padgett. There was no parimutuel betting at dear old Delorimier in those days, and the bookmakers took a very dim view of things when heavily backed favourites bounced home in front. Accordingly, they made a practice of discouraging such favourites from winning.

Well, for reasons of their own, the members of the fraternity decided that it wouldn't be wise for Commerata to win this particular race, so a delegation of the Amalgamated Gambling and Bookmaking Trades waited on Richey. They spoke to him very seriously and told him that it would be a very bad thing if Commerata won. It wasn't necessary for them to boff him across the ears—Mr. Richey awoke early in the morning.

But just as the horse was being saddled for the race, Mr. Padgett, the owner, grabbed Richey by the shoulder and rasped into his ear. "Mr. Richey," he said, "I understand that there is some business being done in this race. If Commerata doesn't win, I will kill you in small pieces."

Mr. Padgett was a large, burly man and he had been known to rip a Manhattan phone directory in twain with his bare hands. Richey knew what to do, and Commerata won the race by many lengths.

Later that evening Richey—with Willie Morrissey and two other companions—was out strolling and reached the corner of St. Catherine and St. Lawrence Main. That is a very tough corner and it was extremely tough that night.

Too late, Richey and his companions realized that they had picked the wrong place for a stroll. As they reached the corner they were approached by a large band of gentlemen who wore the sorrowful look common to bookmakers and gamblers.

It was then that Richey gave his remarkable performance of broken-field running. Employing M. Morrissey as a blocker for the first five yards, he broke clear through the centre of the mob of gamblers without a hand being laid on him, reversed his field and sprinted down St. Catherine Street with no one between him and the goal line.

An alert cabbie—there were horse-drawn cabs then and very few automobiles—saw his plight and whipped his horse into a gallop. As Richey came abreast of the cab, he scrambled aboard and thumbed his nose at his pursuers.

"That cab-driver's horse was faster than Commerata," he says thankfully today.

There was another time when a friend prevailed upon Richey to act as racing secretary and clerk of the scales at a Carolina track. Richey was owner-trainer of a horse at the time, but the friend told him to bring the horse along and run it in someone else's name.

So one day, Richey was performing his duties at the Carolina track when a claim was placed in the box. The claim was for Richey's horse.

Richey went to the presiding steward and said, "This claim is out of order."

"Why?" asked the presiding steward, indignantly.

"Well, judge," said Richey, "I happen to be the fellow who owns the horse."

"Well, that's tough on you, Richey," said the presiding steward, "because I happen to be the fellow who's *claiming* the horse."

Ah, those carefree days!

Getaway Day

Toronto *Telegram*
October 23, 1944

GETAWAY DAY! The last short lap in a ninety-eight-day race to get into the county alms house. Fifteen thousand human beings gambling desperately in a hopeless attempt to break even. Fifty thousand parimutuel tickets lying in the dust. The sun sinking slowly behind the backstretch. The shadows lengthening but the fifteen thousand humans, oblivious of the swift coming of evening, rooting stridently for a long shot. Fifteen thousand suppers waiting at home. The chill wind whispering a warning that winter is riding north on the wings of an Atlantic gale.

Getaway Day! Topcoats and furs. Faces white and drawn with strain. There isn't much laughter in this crowd—just the harsh, rueful kind that accompanies that peculiar twist of the fingers when useless tickets are ripped and tossed underfoot. This crowd has no time to admire the horses, to notice the way in which they bow their necks and tug steadily against the rider's hold. This crowd is in a hurry to get to the parimutuel wickets.

This, too, is Getaway Day for Big Fish and Spring Moon and Izaak Walton. This is the end of the road for them, the last stop. They're too old now to run anymore, and the racing officials have exiled them to a life of ease in lush pastures where they may snatch a few morsels of vicarious glory by telling lies to younger generations.

This is Getaway Day, too, for old Cuba and many of his generation. Cuba is the aged Negro valet who lies desperately ill in hospital and whose health is such that never again will he be able to return to his racetrack chores.

There are other old men who, buttoning their coats tighter against the evening wind, remember those other winters in the South when there were yearlings to break and the sun shone brightly in December; when Black Gold ran at Fair Grounds; and when, every morning after the work had been done, there was a crap game in the shade of some shedrow and even when you went broke, always there was someone to give you "shipping money." Now the passage of time has dimmed their eyes and they have only memories of the thrill that comes from that incomparable sight—the early morning sun splashing the sleek coat of a yearling as he sprints down the stretch, his shadow racing ahead of him against the white rails of the inner fence. This is winter again, and the clock will tick slowly for them from now until April.

Stand at the bottom of the home stretch after the last race has been run on Getaway Day and you can smell loneliness in the air.

The lights glimmer fitfully in the parimutuel sheds. You can hear the shuffling of human feet as the bettors move in long lines toward the payoff wickets. The infield is littered with refuse: half-eaten frankfurter buns, bottles, tickets, and more tickets.

The human beings, shuffling disgustedly into the night, are unaware of the air of urgency that still permeates the stable area. Grooms—muttering maledictions against the equine race, the weather and the astounding frailty of beasts and humans—reach for blankets to toss over the steaming backs of horses that have just returned from the unsaddling post. Anxiously, they scan the skies and walk their equine charges purposefully in circles to cool them out.

The last lights flicker out in the parimutuel sheds. The wind moans as it sweeps down the stretch, petulantly whisking newspapers out of its path.

A stallion lifts his head as he is led into his stall. He sniffs the air wisely. He knows that winter is coming and his labours are over for another year.

Somewhere a horse whinnies and kicks the back of his stall resoundingly. He whinnies again. He sounds like a young horse, perhaps a yearling colt, impatient to meet his destiny.

That's Getaway Day!

Sancho's Last Hand

Toronto *Telegram*
December 29, 1944

Mr. David Ambersley—who is known as "Irish Davy" in convivial debating circles and whose underlying faith in the essential integrity of human nature is such that invariably he is shocked and stunned by police reports that lawless persons are abroad in the land—was ruminating yesterday on the peril of financial investments.

Normally, Mr. Ambersley is a resident of Van Wagner's Beach, outside Hamilton, but he is in residence at the King Edward in Toronto over the holiday season. His precipitous flight from Van Wagner's Beach was occasioned by the fact that the winter winds drove the gulls inland and they perched overnight on Ambersley's roof. When they awoke in the early dawn these gulls were given to emitting raucous and vulgar vocal renderings of their kind, a circumstance that drove Ambersley to distraction. He said feelingly, "There is nothing in the world that sounds as bad as a gull unless it is a North of Irelander trying to sing 'The Wearin' o' the Green.'"

So in the course of conversation, Irish Davy got around to a character named Sancho O'Dwyer, who flourished in the fabulous city of New York in the early days of the current century. Sancho ran a table-stakes poker game in New York, and he was known as a broad-minded and generous fellow who would shove out your eye, stick a grape in the empty eye socket and tell you that it looked twice as good as the original orb. In addition, Sancho, who didn't believe in taking unnecessary chances, had a couple of guys playing for him in the poker game, merely to protect his investment of course.

When inoffensive Canadian gamblers visited New York it was their custom to stick their schnozzles into Sancho O'Dwyer's poker game, and he mulcted and persecuted them in a manner that was little short of scandalous.

Sancho's headquarters were on the fifth floor of a neighbourhood hotel, and he locked his doors at noon sharp. No one could get into that room after that hour and no one left unless he had tapped-out and needed a small blood transfusion. But the main point was that no one was permitted to enter the hotel suite after noon.

Now Sancho O'Dwyer was a highly avaricious fellow, and he wasn't content merely with clipping his customers in the poker game. In addition, he would take wagers on horses from his customers, though such was considered a very lawless practice.

Well, one day a set of Hamiltonians went down to New York and in the course of their adventures they happened to pop into Sancho O'Dwyer's little joint on the fifth floor of the neighbourhood hotel. They arrived very shortly before noon sharp, and just as soon as they had taken off their coats and loosened the laces in their store-bought shoes Sancho O'Dwyer locked the door—on the inside of course.

The game got under way, and within two hours a gent whom we will call Hamilton Harry was in the crease for five C's. It was very quiet in the room—so quiet, in fact, that the players could hear one of those organ grinders playing in the street. The organ grinder was playing a fine old ditty entitled "When Irish Eyes Are Smiling."

Sighing sadly, Hamilton Harry called for a scratch sheet and exclaimed, "I'm hooked for five C's, so I might as well bet on a steed named Cup Cake in the first at Belmont." To cut it short, Cup Cake won and paid six-to-one, and Hamilton Harry was in there with a fifty-dollar wager.

Shortly afterwards Hamilton Harry still was doing badly at the tables, and it was so silent that down in the street they could hear the organ grinder playing "The Sidewalks of New York." Hamilton Harry dipped into his right shoe, pulled out a century note and bet on Millie's Mother in the second at Belmont.

Sancho O'Dwyer was watching the tables closely, but he managed to tear himself away long enough to telephone to a fellow who should know, and he discovered to his horror that Millie's Mother had won and had paid off at three-to-one.

Mr. Ambersley did not wish to bore his listeners with a recount of the afternoon's complete transactions, but suffice to say, the Canadians were three-thousand-dollar losers to the poker game by five o'clock the same evening. But at the same time Sancho O'Dwyer was hooked for thirty thousand dollars on the horses and he was a gone pigeon. To be exact, he was cleaned out of cash and credit, and it was necessary for him to close the joint and sell the furniture at fire-sale prices in an attempt to avoid the bailiffs.

To you and you and you, it is obvious of course what had happened. The Canadians had become a bit weary of losing their dough to Sancho O'Dwyer.

On their arrival in New York they had hired the organ grinder who had a repertoire of twenty musical numbers. They had a confederate stationed in a corner cigar store where he was getting flashes of the race results from the track. When the organ grinder played "When Irish Eyes Are Smiling" it meant that the number-two horse had won the first race at Belmont. Number two was Cup Cake. When he played "The Sidewalks of New York" it meant that number eighteen had won. Number eighteen was Millie's Mother in the second heat.

Mr. Ambersley, chuckling evilly, revealed that the Canadians never went back to Sancho O'Dwyer's after that famous afternoon. To be truthful, they *couldn't* go back to Sancho O'Dwyer's because Sancho O'Dwyer was out of the table-stakes poker and bookmaking business.

When last they heard of him, Sancho O'Dwyer was first mate aboard a barge on the Gowanus Canal in Brooklyn, which was just what he deserved, the mealy-mouthed little snitch.

As far as is known, Sancho O'Dwyer will go down in history as the only guy who ever went broke betting on musical programs.

3

1945–46

Alas, Poor Mervin

Toronto *Globe and Mail*
May 5, 1945

WITH VICTORY IN EUROPE JUST AROUND THE CORNER it's difficult to concentrate on unimportant things, but Johnny Needle-Nose happened to mention another of those talking-dog stories yesterday.

It seems that Wilbur Jones of rural Ohio was sent to Harvard by his parents. He had a dog named Mervin to which he was deeply devoted. His farmer parents decided that Mervin should accompany him to college. Soon after he arrived at Harvard he learned about the dice games in nearby Boston. He dipped his beak into the dice games, and the first thing you know he was hooked for five hundred bananas.

He had no money, but he was an ingenious chappie. He knew that his parents believed Mervin was the smartest dog in the world, so he sent them the following telegram: "Dr. Brawn of psychology department believes Mervin so smart that he wants to teach him to speak English. Please send $500."

The parents were elated and promptly mortgaged their farm to raise the five hundred dollars, which they sent to Wilbur.

But Wilbur made the horrible mistake of visiting the dice games in an attempt to retrieve his five hundred bananas. The first thing he knew he was hooked for another five hundred seeds.

Promptly he wired his parents: "Mervin now knows how to speak English, and Dr. Brawn thinks he can teach him to READ. Please send another $500 for this course."

The gleeful parents, seeing visions of a vaudeville career for their dog, took a second mortgage on the farm and wired Wilbur another five hundred dollars.

Eventually it came time for him to go home on his summer holidays. He disposed of Mervin quietly, boarded the train and finally greeted his father at the depot in rural Ohio.

"What," asked the father as he watched Wilbur disembark alone, "became of Mervin?"

"Well, it was this way," said Wilbur, taking his father by the arm solemnly and leading him to a quiet corner. "The dog learned how to read English, and he became awfully smart. As we were getting near home this morning I was shaving in the washroom and the dog was sitting there reading the newspaper. He turned to the sports page and happened to notice the race results.

"Suddenly he turned to me and said, 'I wonder if your mother knows about the time that your Old Man lost that farm near Warrensville because he mortgaged it to bet one thousand dollars on Bimelech, the year that Gallahadion won the Kentucky Derby?'

"Well," said Wilbur, "I was pretty sure that you'd never told Mother about losing that thousand bucks, so I took out that straight-edged razor that you gave me before I left for college and I cut Mervin's throat from ear to ear!"

The couple stood there, tears streaming down their faces.

"Son," the father said brokenly, "are you sure that Mervin is dead?"

VE Day

Toronto *Globe and Mail*
May 9, 1945

THE WAR ISN'T OVER. The war isn't over for the maimed, the blind and the bereaved. The war isn't over for the weak and the hungry. The war isn't over for our own dead. The war isn't over until we have learned to recognize another Ethiopia, another Spain when we see it. The war isn't over until Gentile can live with Jew, and intolerance and bigotry have been banished. The war isn't over until Negroes can play baseball on the same field with whites.

The war isn't over until China, which for a decade has stood against aggression, has been freed.

This war was fought for a simple principle that has been established, time and time again, on the streets of our own Canadian cities. It's the principle that, reduced to simple terms, reads: no bully is going to shove the little fellows around.

When Hardy Walked the Falls

Toronto *Globe and Mail*
July 2, 1945

THAT IMPETUOUS FELLOW, Red Hill, is going to write another chapter in the strange history of Niagara Falls next Sunday when he makes the trip through the Niagara River Rapids and the famed Whirlpool in a steel barrel.

He will use the same barrel in which his celebrated sire—the *original* Red Hill—made three trips through the same obstacle course. Incidentally, it is the same barrel, too, in which George Stathakis tried it in 1930. Stathakis somehow got wedged behind the Falls and it was fourteen hours before they could extricate the barrel. He had sufficient air only for three hours and he was dead when the rescue squad finally reached him.

Anyhow, there should be a good "house" on hand for the event next Sunday, and it is to be trusted that the gents with the tin cans get around and collect enough money to buy sufficient liniment to heal Red's aching joints.

Now comes a correspondent, N.E. Hardy of Brantford, to point out that most historians who have dealt with the daffy doings at Niagara have overlooked the feats of a native Torontonian, James E. Hardy, who died six years ago at the age of sixty-four.

The correspondent can point to these feats with justifiable pride because, after all, James Hardy was his father.

The historians have devoted most of their space to the feats of Blondin (Jean-François Gravelet) who walked across Niagara Gorge on a tightrope, carried a man on his back, made the trip on stilts and, once, cooked an omelet while on the tightrope.

However, Hardy gave sixteen performances at the Falls in 1896 on a cable 265 feet above the Rapids and more than one thousand feet long. Hardy gave these performances, not on a thick ship's hawser such as Blondin used, but on a slender three-quarter-inch wire cable. The American and Canadian press of the time agreed that Hardy had out-Blondined Blondin.

His son writes:

> In 1897, even before people had recovered from their surprise, Hardy again caused a profound sensation by crossing the Genesee Gorge at Rochester, New York, on a cable 1,400 feet long and 245 feet above the Genesee River, a feat he accomplished no less than twenty-one times.
>
> In 1903, America again rang with his name and his fame when he performed over the great Montmorency Falls in Quebec, giving seventy-one performances and causing thousands to again shudder at his daring achievements. Montmorency Falls are the highest on the American continent, and Hardy's cable was suspended over the brink of the falling water, 350 feet high and 460 feet long.
>
> Hardy went on to gain more laurels and to become known throughout the amusement world as the "Greatest Exponent of Aerial Art." He devoted his entire life to the profession and appeared during his career at the principle places of amusement, both in Europe and America, where only the premier artists of the day were engaged. The following are only a few of the many places at which he appeared during his long career: Alexander Palace, London, England, for the entire season of 1898 and a return engagement for the following season of 1899; Crystal Palace, London, England, for the entire season of 1900 and a return engagement for the following seasons of 1901 and 1902 including a command performance for His Majesty King Edward VII; Eastman Gardens, Liverpool, England, for a

> ten-week engagement; Tower Gardens, Liverpool, England, for an engagement of eighteen consecutive weeks; New York Hippodrome, New York City, for an engagement of fifteen weeks; Luna Park, Coney Island, New York, for many seasons; the Canadian National Exhibition on numerous occasions.
>
> Mr. Hardy adds:
>
> I would also like to make it clear that Hardy was the only man in the aerial business that performed extraordinary feats with an ordinary Cleveland street bicycle on a high wire without the aid of any fake or counterbalance whatever, and that no man ever rode a bicycle across Niagara Falls—this being an absolute impossibility due to the difficulties experienced in guying the cable and also on account of the wind current in the Gorge.
>
> Hardy died in Toronto on May 11, 1939, at the age of sixty-four, after more than forty years in the profession, in which time he did more to advertise Toronto in all parts of the world than any one person, perhaps with the exception of old Ned Hanlan.

He encloses numerous clippings concerning his father's exploits. As an example, the Detroit *Free Press* wrote: "The most skilful artist the world has yet produced."

The New York *World* was even more succinct, writing: "Hardy's feat over Niagara was simply marvelous."

We trust that Red Hill will receive similar good press next Sunday.

The Sad, Sad Saga of Sam South

Toronto *Globe and Mail*
September 6, 1945

JOHNNY NEEDLE-NOSE, who is so careful that he drinks his coffee with an interlocking grip, was sitting in a canvas deck-chair in a patch of sunlight at the end of the shedrow. A gentle breeze rustled the giant elms overhead, and in the nearest stall a horse kicked the wall fretfully.

"Quiet please, Man o' War," muttered Johnny Needle-Nose without opening his eyes. Naturally, the horse wasn't Man o' War because, to be truthful, Johnny Needle-Nose never owned a horse that was worth more than $3.85 in cash. On the majority of tracks the stewards always examined Johnny's horses carefully to be sure that they carried the standard equipment of four legs.

A fly settled on Johnny's nose. It was a large fly and an angry-looking fly. It lifted up its hind feet and kicked Johnny's nose bitterly. Johnny opened his eyes, then crossed them as he peered thoughtfully at the fly. "Must be a B-29," drawled Johnny, and he closed his eyes again.

The Blow-Back Kid was sitting against the wall, rolling a pair of dice with Professor Mole. Suddenly Blow-Back asked, "Did you know Pittsburgh Phil, Johnny?"

"Like a brother," said Needle-Nose flatly, without opening his eyes. The fly kicked him in the nose again, but he ignored the fly. The fly sulked and flew into the first stall to annoy Johnny's horse.

"Did you know Bet-a-Million Gates?" asked Blow-Back.

"Like a brother," replied Needle-Nose flatly.

"Were they good or just lucky?" asked Professor Mole.

"Lucky," said Needle-Nose, "but not as lucky as a guy named Sam South who blew into Juarez one winter, sleeping in a freight car with Knifey's horses. In those days a guy had to be awfully tired to sleep with Knifey's horses because they were so thin their ribs clanked together whenever the wind blew, and they rattled like canes in an umbrella rack.

"He didn't start off by being lucky, but he got lucky all of a rush," continued Johnny Needle-Nose. "First of all, he was bonked by a cross-eyed cop in Chicago who mistook him for Dion O'Banion. He had a fractured noggin and they chucked him in a public ward. He was unconscious for twenty-seven days and he contracted athlete's foot and trench mouth.

"He got out of there and finally arrived in Omaha, Nebraska, on the rods. It seems he was a dead ringer for a heist guy named Little Solomon and the Omaha cops lugged him in for a bank job. This Sam South was identified as Little Solomon by the bank watchman, and they sentenced him to ten years for a job he hadn't done. He was making little ones out of big ones for seven years until Little Solomon was converted by Billy Sunday, got religion and confessed that he had done the job.

"By the time that Sam South got out, he had lost forty pounds and his face was the colour of wallpaper in Leo Belanger's cookhouse at Stamford Park. You can understand that by this time a guy would be about ready to sleep with Knifey's horses, even on a windy night."

Johnny Needle-Nose stared into space for a moment and then reached under his canvas chair for a small jug of Dr. Oswald Dunsmore's Household Remedy. He took a gulp out of the bottle. The fly, which was sitting on his nose again after having stopped annoying the horse, promptly fell to the ground, as stiff as a new boot.

"So he blew into Juarez," continued Needle-Nose, "and it was a wet winter day. He was so thin that you could have threaded him through the eye of a needle, and he didn't have a bean because Knifey and his horses had arrived strictly COD.

"But he walked into the betting ring just before the first race. He was walking with his head down, and he noticed something shining in the mud. He leaned down and found it was a Mexican silver dollar. So he took it to Tom Shaw, and Shaw said that he would give him a fifty-cent marker for it, so Sam South bet the fifty cents on a steed that was thirty-to-one.

"Well, the steed bounced home on top, and there was Sam South with a score of fifteen dollars. He walked over to the cookhouse and had a big plate of ham and eggs and three cups of coffee. Then he went right back to that betting ring and plunked his remaining fourteen skins on another steed that won and paid three-to-one. So by the end of the second race Sam South had parlayed a stray Mexican buck into forty-two dollars.

"The payoff was that Sam South picked all seven winners that wet afternoon. He never backed away, and he kept parlaying that dough. By the end of the day he was more than twenty thousand dollars richer, and Tom Shaw paid him off in crisp new banknotes, all in bundles with thick rubber bands around them. There was Sam South, who had been plugged by a cross-eyed cop and sent to college unjustly, walking out of Juarez racetrack with more than twenty thousand dollars."

"Geez," said the Blow-Back Kid respectfully, "did he get himself a new car and a new suit?"

"Geez," said Professor Mole, "did he take a good, warm bath?"

"No," said Johnny Needle-Nose slowly. "Sam South went over to El

Paso and rented a hotel room. He sat down on the bed and started to count those bundles of money. He cut his finger on the sharp edge of a one-hundred-dollar bill and got blood poisoning."

Johnny Needle-Nose reached under the canvas chair and took another short dull thud of Dr. Oswald Dunsmore's Household Remedy.

"Sam South was dead in three hours," said Johnny, his voice lowering slightly.

The Blow-Back Kid and Professor Mole stood up, removed their hats and stood with heads bowed for a full minute. The Blow-Back Kid looked into the sunny morning; his gaze drifted down the backstretch and rested on a bluebird sitting on the whitewashed inner rail.

"That was a very tough break for Sam South," he said.

"No," said Johnny Needle-Nose very indignantly. "No, Sam South just couldn't stand prosperity."

Johnny Needle-Nose closed his eyes again. The Blow-Back Kid and Professor Mole picked up their dice and tiptoed away. The horse inched his head over the stall door and sniffed the sweet clover in the air. The sun caressed the long shedrow and probed the shadows under the trees with long, slender fingers of light. It was a beautiful morning.

Thereby Hangs a Tail

Toronto *Globe and Mail*
October 5, 1945

THE REGULAR PATRONS of Vasilisius Venezelos Metaxas's Soda Bicarbonate Grill are all agog concerning the story of the remarkable manner in which the gin-rummy championship of South Toronto Street was settled on Wednesday night. The participants in the final round were two local sportsmen known whimsically as the Beast and Doc. The scene of the battle was a well-known club, the members of which are extremely interested in various manifestations of the investment business.

As the two contestants started on the final game the atmosphere was tense. The other members were clustered around the small table and the lights glared down hotly. It was a battle of such titanic proportions that even the Senior Blimp and the Junior Blimp ceased their personal bickerings and crowded around the table. (And believe us, the verb "crowd" is singularly apt where the Senior Blimp and the Junior Blimp are concerned.)

After they had played for three minutes it was obvious that they were fast reaching a climax.

With trembling fingers the Beast reached for a card. It fitted into his hand perfectly. Gratified, he picked the seven of spades out of his hand and prepared to discard it.

As he poised the seven of spades, he felt a gentle but distinct nudge in the small of his back.

"Aha," he breathed to himself, "an ally in the house."

Looking at his opponent craftily, the Beast put the seven of spades back into his hand and instead discarded the eight of hearts.

To his vast surprise Doc promptly picked up the eight of hearts and tucked it into his own hand. Then Doc discarded, and again it was the Beast's turn to draw.

Once again he drew a card that fitted into his hand perfectly. Smiling smugly, he started to discard the seven of spades. As the card was poised in the air he felt that distinct but gentle nudge in the small of his back. The Beast paused apprehensively and made another move to discard the seven, but the gentle nudge was repeated.

The nudge couldn't be ignored this time. The Beast shoved the seven back into his hand and resolutely discarded the two of hearts.

"GIN!" screamed Doc triumphantly, pouncing on the deuce of hearts and flopping his hand on the table.

Naturally there was a great hullabaloo and considerable shouting and the Beast forked across his stake, which left him with enough to make a down payment on a streetcar ticket. And there were several speeches and the Senior Blimp presented Doc with a solid silver spittoon.

Meanwhile the Beast still was sitting there with perspiration streaming down his face and he pulled a straight-edged razor out of his pocket and decided to ascertain who had been giving him those advisory nudges.

At that precise instant he felt another gentle nudge in the small of his back, and he whirled viciously. There, sitting on a chair directly behind him, was the club cat—and the cat's tail was nudging the Beast.

The club cat was extremely fast on his feet, but as they disappeared toward the waterfront it could be seen that the Beast was gaining with every stride.

And, strange as it seems, this story is on the level.

Ching Checks the Big Apple

Toronto *Globe and Mail*
February 28, 1946

The resignation of Lester Patrick from the managership of the New York Rangers has released a flood of stories about some of the gay characters who performed for the Gotham team in its early years. Inevitably, the conversation concerning those teams turns to the Rangers in the pre-Patrick era when Conn Smythe was assembling the original squad for the proprietors of Madison Square Garden.

The first Rangers were rather lusty fellows, and they were astounded upon reporting to the Rangers training camp in Toronto to discover that Smythe actually was planning to make them train seriously. Egad, he was going so far as to stop them from chewing tobaccy on the ice!

Conn had set up his training headquarters in a little West End hotel out near Ravina Rink, and he determined to keep his athletes under strict surveillance. He imposed a strict curfew and ordered that the hotel doors be locked at an appointed hour, thus confining his brawny chattels to their quite rooms.

Out of the west one day roared that irrepressible fellow, Ivan "Ching" Johnson. Ivan, you will recall, was the large chappie who belted the bejabbers out of incoming forwards but always wore a wide and most pleasant-looking grin when performing those robust chores. Actually, his grin was a peculiar facial grimace, and Ivan wasn't entirely the gentle soul that he appeared to be. Those who played alongside him will tell that his lips curved back that way simply because he was grinding his teeth fearsomely and uttering threats to the enemy.

Johnson's great jaws gaped widely when he arrived in Toronto and heard reports of the Smythe training regime. Having suspected that Toronto might be located in an arid section of the country, he had the foresight to arrive carrying four forty-ounce medicine bottles filled to the corks with grain alcohol. After all, you never know when you're going to need something to cure a snakebite in unexplored territory.

With another intrepid member of the New York squad, Ching decided to test the efficiency of the Smythe curfew. They established their base camp in the King Edward, and in the interests of scientific research they made numerous experiments with Johnson's supply of medicinal spirits.

Along about three o'clock in the morning they summoned a hack and drove far away to the Rangers small hotel. They dismissed the hackie after he had joined them in one final chorus of "Loch Lomond," and then they assaulted the front door of the hotel.

The front door was locked. The back door was locked, too, and so were the other doors. They scaled the fire escape. The fire escape doors were locked. They sang two verses of "Bonnie Dundee" without getting any response and withdrew to hold a council of war.

"We must admit temporary defeat," said Johnson, shaking his noggin sagaciously, and the two doughty warriors wandered off toward the westernmost limits of Bloor Street in search of transportation.

Johnson's companion perceived a large red object.

"Looks like a fire truck," he said hopefully.

"Nope, it's a streetcar," said the astute Johnson.

Sure enough, it was a Bloor Street tram just about to take off on its lonely crosstown jaunt from west to east. The operator of the tram was bored and in a mood to welcome company. Johnson and his Rangers teammate swarmed aboard jovially.

"By gum, you remind me of my Uncle Elmer in Okotoks," roared Johnson as he saw the motorman.

"I have an Uncle Elmer in Spokane. He's a taxidermist," replied the motorman, shaking hands.

"Might be the same fellow," replied Johnson, reaching for another of his medicine bottles. "My Uncle Elmer's an undertaker. He spends his time stuffing stiffs, too!"

"Can you sing 'Annie Laurie'?" Johnson's companion asked the motorman.

"Shore, shore," agreed the motorman heartily, taking a snort of Johnson's medicine and coughing so sharply that he cracked the large window in front of the car. "Say, we can take down the trolley and the car will run okay on this stuff," he added, sampling it again.

The still of the night was broken by the sounds of three pleased voices singing "Annie Laurie." This was followed by "Mother Machree," "Loch Lomond" and "I'll Be Glad When You're Dead, You Rascal, You."

"Say, where are you boys going?" asked the motorman, throwing his gloves out through the door and twisting his cap around on his head until the peak was hanging down the back of his neck. The motorman leaned out the window and gave a very fine imitation of a fire siren.

"Drive us to the King Edward, bub," roared Johnson.

"You said it," said the motorman, and gave his tram full throttle. Ignoring the standard practices of the Toronto Transportation Commission he switched the tram off Bloor Street at Roncesvalles. He headed for Sunnyside and King Street. Early morning risers were startled to see a Bloor Street car going down Roncesvalles. They were even more startled when the car didn't stop for their signals and the wild strains of "Sweet Adeline" emerged from the speeding car in which three figures seemed to be huddled in the darkened front vestibule.

Two paper boys in front of the King Edward were surprised, too, when a Bloor Street tram, with its bell clanging furiously, drove up to the hotel portico. Two large gentlemen descended from the tram bellowing, "Goodbye, old pal," in delighted tones.

The motorman shoved his head out of the window and gave another excellent imitation of a fire siren. He released the brake, and the car shot down King Street in the general direction of Woodbine Park.

Neither Mr. Johnson nor his companion ever saw the motorman again, and the Toronto Transportation Commission still is bemused by some mysterious discrepancies in their schedules for that particular night. For instance, it never has been satisfactorily explained how a Bloor Street car arrived at the North Toronto station.

"Say, that bum kept my medicine bottle," yelped Johnson as the tram disappeared. "It's a lucky thing that I didn't tell him I had another one," said Johnson, reaching into an overcoat pocket and producing the last of his supplies. Arm in arm, Johnson and his teammate entered the hotel. That was the night on which guests complained about the room clerks singing "Annie Laurie."

It's a lucky thing, too, that Conn Smythe was spared the necessity of managing those Rangers. They would have driven him crazy.

Just Julia

Toronto *Globe and Mail*
March 14, 1946

JOHNNY NEEDLE-NOSE braced himself against the wind of the winter night as he entered the foaling barn and closed the door behind him. He stamped the snow from his shoes and looked across into the stall where the Blow-Back Kid was down on his knees beside the old mare.

The Kid shook his head soberly and said, "It's no use. The foal was stillborn and the mare's a cooked goose. Damn vets never are around when you want 'em. Anyhow, this snow's too deep for travelling, and even the croaker at Bellevue couldn't do anything for this old hide. Don't know why you've bothered about her all these years. She never was worth a quarter."

Johnny Needle-Nose didn't answer, but he stared at the wall for a moment, lost in thought. A pail of water was whistling gently on the pot-bellied stove that warmed the little barn. The Blow-Back Kid spat at the stove and wiped his hands on his grimy dungarees. The spittle disappeared almost instantaneously as it hit the red-hot side of the stove.

"She never was worth a quarter," persisted the Blow-Back Kid. "Damned if I can understand how a man can get married to a horse, particularly some old bum that never was worth a quarter."

You find strange people around a racetrack. Good men, bad men and men that are just plain shiftless and lazy. The best thing about racing is the horses: honest, loyal and uncomplaining. It would be difficult to classify Johnny Needle-Nose, but you couldn't call him a bad man. Sometimes it's wise not to ask too many questions around a racetrack because the yesterdays are nobody's business and it's only an even-money bet that the sun will rise again tomorrow morning.

It was nobody's business, for instance, that Johnny Needle-Nose had been an altar boy and had studied for the priesthood. You can't tell who you'll find around a racetrack. The passage of years had left Johnny Needle-Nose's face seamed and scarred, and his hair was white. As far as anyone knew, he had been around horses all his life, and now he had money and good horses, and he sat in the clubhouse while other men mucked out the stalls and walked the hots.

Johnny looked at the Kid and looked down at the old mare and lit another cigarette. As the smoke curled upward Johnny thought of the mare. Her name was Just Julia.

"She's better off dead, anyhow," said Blow-Back. "Too bad the foal didn't live, though. Looked as if he might have been a good little colt. Better than his mammy. Bet this old bag of bones never won a race."

"She won one," said Johnny, almost to himself.

There was no point in telling the Kid about it. It was many years ago, when Juarez was a roaring border town—and besides, the Kid wouldn't have understood.

Johnny Needle-Nose stood there while the life ebbed out of the old mare and he was lost until the cigarette burned down to scorch his fingers. Her name was Just Julia and the Blow-Back Kid wouldn't remember it, but she had beaten a horse named The Tuscan. He shook himself as he thought of the years that had passed since then.

He had arrived at Juarez, sleeping in a boxcar that carried Just Julia to the track. He slept in a corner of her stall, too. His was a one-horse outfit and they didn't even give him a tack room. As far as that goes, he didn't need a tack room, because by that time he didn't have anything to put into it. He didn't have anything in his pockets either, and he stole the feed for Just Julia and he galloped her himself on those bleak winter mornings. He was as close to starving as a man can be in a land of plenty. He had no friends and no enemies because, even then, Johnny Needle-Nose was a loner.

He had Just Julia because she had broken down as a two-year-old and her owners had given her to the thin-faced, long-nosed kid who asked for her. He had doctored her and babied her, and his loving treatment had restored her to a semblance of the strength and speed that was her birthright.

So he entered her at Juarez. He couldn't afford to bet on her, and he tightened her saddle girths and gave the boy a leg-up, and he crossed his fingers.

She was at The Tuscan's throat latch when they turned for home, and in the long, bitter battle down to the wire she ran his eyeballs out.

She beat him, but they had to van her off the track and she never ran again.

Johnny Needle-Nose couldn't afford to bet on her, but the purse that she won that day gave him his stake. It was one of those propitious moments that occur once in the life of every man. From that day he never looked back to the yesterdays.

He looked down at the old mare as she lay there dying. Her troubled eyes looked back at him, but there was nothing he could do. Strange, he thought, that horses, infinitely nobler than man, are denied a final hour of dignity in death.

Desperately, he thought of something that he might do for her. Suddenly a small bell tinkled distantly in his memory. He thought of a place, far away. He saw men in simple vestments. He heard the chanting of many voices.

He took off his hat and stood erect. Reaching out his foot with the tip of his shoe he knocked the hat from the head of the Blow-Back Kid, who was kneeling still beside the old mare.

The long-forgotten Latin words came haltingly to Johnny Needle-Nose's lips at first. Then they poured out of him as if it were only yesterday. He made a sign with his hands.

"What does that mean?" asked the Blow-Back Kid, his eyes on Johnny Needle-Nose while his hands groped behind him in the straw, searching for his hat.

"Nothing," said Johnny Needle-Nose wearily, "nothing at all."

And without a backward look, he went away from there.

Goodbye to Apple Annie

Toronto *Globe and Mail*
April 13, 1946

A FRAGILE BIRD-LIKE OLD LADY died yesterday morning. She died in terrible loneliness, dropping dead on the floor of her tiny apartment on Carlton Street. Civic officials, who know nothing about the countless persons whom they are called upon to cart away in the face of such sudden and inexplicable death, took her to the coroner's office.

Her name was Edith Mitchell and, although she went to her death unmarried, it is probable that she never realized the affection with which she was viewed by hundreds of thousands of Torontonians.

You knew her, too. They called her "Annie" at every sporting event. They changed the name to "Apple Annie" after May Robson made a startling success in a sentimental picture of that name.

You must remember her, walking along on her tiny legs, heckling the players, exchanging badinage with those who sat close to her and, despite her raucous comments, always cloaked in a strange unapproachable dignity.

When they took her away—small, lifeless and serene—it was almost incredible to hear that she was sixty-nine years old. It was incredible, too, to learn that she had no relatives. A nice, gentle, inoffensive old lady and they took her away and their next stop was Potter's Field.

It's impossible to imagine what her life must have been, but it's certain that her life was lonely, and loneliness is the curse of the old and feeble.

It's strange, too, how you can look at a fragile old person without worry. We've seen her at the hockey games and the baseball games. We can remember her salty comments. We can recall a catch that Roland Gladu made in the outfield for the Montreal Royals last year. It was a great catch: the grass was wet and, after a terrific run, he caught the ball and fell in a sitting position.

Apple Annie, who was sitting next to us, turned and said, "This is getting to be a lousy game. It's getting so bad that a guy can catch a ball sitting down."

Well, she won't lie in Potter's Field.

She had countless friends who helped her casually during her lifetime but who never managed to penetrate that shell of loneliness. They gave her tickets to sporting events and, in the rough, unquestioning atmosphere of sport, they let it go at that.

But she's going to have a decent funeral. It's too bad that many of us didn't do more for her during her lifetime, but anyone's past is full of regrets. Most of us are too selfish to say that extra kind word or extend that small but important helping hand.

She was a fine little lady. Her passing wrenches an important little piece out of the fabric of life. We imagine that many of those who pay her a final tribute will be those youngsters from St. Mike's whom she delighted in annoying when their team was playing.

God will give her rest: she was lonely and she deserves it.

Old Man, Old Dream

Toronto *Globe and Mail*
May 16, 1946

SOMEONE—I believe that it was the late Gerald Beaumont—once wrote about "the look of eagles." He was writing only of two-year-olds. A thoroughbred that has the look of an eagle is young and arrogantly conscious of his destiny. Horses, like human beings, aren't all born equal. Their characters are molded by environment and twisted by heartbreaking tests of speed and strength. But when they are young and scent the exhilarating challenge of the future, they lift their heads into the wind, and then, for a fleeting instant, they have the look of eagles.

If you step down the shedrow of a racetrack, you'll discover that old horses are like old men. Old horses are like old men with one important exception: old horses have stopped dreaming. Take a good look at an old man, sitting in the warm afternoon sun, and you'll see that he is dreaming.

Willie Meeker was an old man. Probably no one around the racetrack knew his exact age, but he had been one of Regret's grooms when Regret won the Kentucky Derby, and long before that, he had worn out a hundred pairs of shoes while walking hots. He knew nothing but horses, and that was quite enough for him because he loved them, and with the instinct of well-bred animals, they understood his feelings.

It was May, you see, and the sun was very warm as Willie sat on an upturned feed bucket, leaning against the tack-room door. It had been a long winter and now the sun was creeping into him and easing the ache of his bones. He whittled aimlessly on a piece of softwood, and his glance shifted across the track toward the vast rambling stands that tomorrow would be crowded with people.

Willie liked to stable his horses on the backstretch from where he could see across to the stands. All tracks looked pretty much the same to him these days, but he could remember Havana and Juarez and Tia

Juana. He could remember Churchill Downs and the big New York tracks, too, but Willie had graduated to the ranks of the gypsy owners soon after Regret won the derby, and his horses weren't the kind that ran on the New York tracks. His horses were cheap platers, and Willie's years had been spent on the leaky-roof circuits.

Willie closed his eyes and he could hear Malachi pawing fretfully in his stall. He could hear Miss Murphy bumping her feed bucket with her soft nose, too. When you had been around as long as Willie Meeker you could identify horses in the dark just by listening to the way they moved in their stalls. Willie Meeker and Malachi and Miss Murphy had been together for a couple of years now, and if you took a glance at them you could see that all three of them were going to run out of time.

Without opening his eyes, Willie sniffed the rising breeze and remembered that this had been the longest and hardest winter in his memory. It had been the loneliest winter, too. An old man's friends disappear overnight, and an old man doesn't make new friends. His oldest and best friends had gone years ago—High-Ball Kelly and Stub Barnes, and dozens more of them.

Somehow, Willie and Malachi and Miss Murphy had struggled through the winter, but Malachi and Miss Murphy looked as if they had eaten oftener than Willie. There was a reason for that: a man who has been around as long as Willie doesn't neglect his horses.

The healing heat of the sun rekindled that old spark in Willie Meeker's breast. This is the year, he thought. This is the year I've been waiting for, and I've babied and coddled these two horses and I can't miss.

He had stopped whittling, but his eyes still were closed. He could win two races each with Malachi and Miss Murphy in the first two weeks of the meeting, and then he could ship to California. He wanted to get back to California. He knew a little place that he could have for a song, and horses grew well there and the weather wasn't hard on an old man. He could win a couple of cheap races in California, too, if things didn't go wrong.

He wouldn't let anyone claim Miss Murphy though. He would run her in cheap allowance races. He had plans for Miss Murphy. Hers was aristocratic blood. No one except Willie Meeker knew much about it, but Miss Murphy's breeding combined the same blood that had coursed through little Regret. Willie would breed Miss Murphy to Beau Père or one of those other high-priced stallions and someday he would have a colt.

He could see the colt now: a chestnut with a wide blaze on his face and a gingerbread mane. The colt would be of medium size and compactly built. Straight of limb and his quarters would give a hint of his terrific power. He would have a fine head and a bold eye— that was it, "the look of an eagle."

Willie would go back to Churchill Downs again. This time it would be his own horse that ran in the Kentucky Derby. A man could win a fortune with a horse like that. The derby is worth one hundred thousand dollars to the winner. A man could live a long time with money like that. There would be no more cold winters. Why, with a little luck, a man could become a millionaire . . .

Willie opened his eyes with a start. He was surprised to discover that he had dropped his piece of wood and his hands were clenched. He was surprised to see that the sky was black and a chilly breeze tugged at his coat and rattled the stall door. May is a month of uncertain weather: those squalls come in swiftly from the lake.

Willie stood up and closed the door of Malachi's stall. He closed the door of Miss Murphy's stall and then he opened it again. He whistled to her softly and she smiled back at him. He locked the door securely.

Old Willie Meeker felt in his pockets and shuffled off toward the gate and then toward the coffee counter across the street, where an old man could buy ham and eggs and a coffee for thirty-five cents.

From the grandstand, it's a long way across the track to where the old men dream in the afternoon sun.

"Too Bad That He's Black"

Toronto *Globe and Mail*
July 9, 1946

WITH ALL DUE RESPECT to the boys in the backroom, we saw two baseball players over the weekend. They were baseball players who were too good for the International League. There's a certain sense of satisfaction in watching a man who, although he hasn't come into his maturity, shows all the signs that indicate athletic greatness in the future. Without any hesitation we give you the name of Marvin Rackley, who is playing left field for the Montreal Royals.

There, without a doubt, is a man who is destined for the big leagues. He can hit; he can field; and he is almost incredibly fast on the base paths. He has competitive spirit and, in short, he has all the qualifications for a man who wishes to reach the peak in his chosen profession. If he doesn't prove to be a star with the Brooklyn Dodgers of the National League we are prepared to eat all that remains of a singularly battered fedora.

But there is another man to whom we wished to refer. He is a black man. His name is Jackie Robinson, and he is one of the very blackest men ever to appear in public. He plays second base for the Montreal Royals and, for our money, he's a very good second baseman.

When Robinson joined the Royals a few months ago he came into the game with all eyes focused on him. He was the first Negro ever to be admitted into Class Double-A baseball. In that brief period he has proved himself a credit to his race and a credit to baseball.

We can recall that, when first he appeared, rival players and southern scribes predicted that he wouldn't last throughout one complete trip around the league. Well, he has fooled them, and it looks as if his next step is into a big-league uniform.

They said that some hot-headed southerner would spike him the first time that he was involved in a close play at second base. They said that some hot-headed southern pitcher would bean him when he stepped up to the plate. They said that he couldn't hit International League pitching because he was too loosey-goosey at the plate. To put it briefly, they said that he wasn't a baseball player of International League calibre.

Well, he has fooled them. He's very close to the top of the International League batting average. In addition, on Friday night, he made a play that was sensational. With a man on base in the ninth inning, Ben Drake hit a ball that was labelled for a single into right field. Robinson had no right to be close to the ball but he scampered out to field it. He tipped it with his glove and juggled it into the air. With the greatest grace he caught it in his bare right hand. It was a tremendous play and it ended the game.

On Saturday night, for the first time, we heard a white ballplayer give Robinson the credit to which he is due.

Herb Crompton, a gentleman who played for the New York Yankees last season, was sitting in the stands just before leaving to visit his father, who is reported dying of gangrene poisoning. Crompton watched Robinson leap on an infield hit, turn and whirl the ball to first base for the put-out. Crompton turned and grinned. "A great ballplayer," he said. "A great ballplayer—but it's too bad that he's black."

Mr. Crompton wasn't completely right. Robinson is a great ballplayer, and it's a good thing that he's black. He was an All-American backfielder when he played football for the University of California at Los Angeles. He was an honour student. He was an officer in the United States Army.

It's a hell of a thing when a lad with all those qualifications can't be treated as an equal by his white teammates—and by his white rivals. We hope to live to see the day when Robinson's critics will give him his due without mentioning his pigmentation.

Jackie R.

Toronto *Globe and Mail*
August 30, 1946

So you've been wondering about Jackie Robinson, eh? Well, he's a big, clean-cut guy with an easy smile and a firm handshake. He has the legs of a hard-driving football player and the shoulders of a wrestler, and he possesses a calm detachment that belies the fact that he is an earnest and incisive thinker. Ostensibly his only worries are that despite the fact that he is leading the International League in batting, he is in the midst of a bit of a hitting slump and he is suffering from an injured right ankle that has kept him out of several games.

From the cut of his jib, it is obvious that Robinson is a big-leaguer. Despite the fact that he has been a sensation in his first year in organized baseball, he considers himself to be far from perfect. "I'm hitting them on the handles," he said yesterday in his room at the King Edward. "A good ballplayer shouldn't do that. I guess I must be leaning too far over the plate when I take my cut at the ball."

How will he go at third base, the position at which he is expected to receive his tryout with the Brooklyn Dodgers?

"I don't know," grinned Robinson. "I never played there. I never played any position except shortstop until I joined the Montreal Royals."

The International League audiences, who expect Robinson to make the jump to the Brooklyn Dodgers on his first attempt, actually are being grossly unfair to him.

"You know," said Robinson, "I haven't played much baseball—I haven't much experience."

That was an understatement. Robinson had two years of baseball in high school. He had two more years at Pasadena Junior College and one year at the University of California at Los Angeles. Then, from 1941 until 1945, he was in the United States Army and played a total of five games. Last year he performed for the Kansas City Monarchs, the Negro professional team, and this is his first season in organized baseball. It's expecting too much these days for a man to jump to the National League with only one year of baseball in an organized league. Johnny Pesky did it, of course. He jumped from the Rocky Mount Red Sox in the Piedmont League, to a permanent place in the Boston Red Sox lineup; but Johnny had played semi-pro baseball around Portland for several years—and with a very good team—before the Boston scouts happened to notice him. If Robinson makes the grade with the Dodgers next year it will be an outstanding tribute to his own remarkable physical ability and his moral tenacity.

Robinson is twenty-seven. Football was his number-one sport and he was cut out to be an All-American at UCLA, where he played in the backfield. He left college at the end of his second year because his parents were in financial difficulties, and he took a job with the National Youth Administration. That should give you an idea of Robinson—the National Youth Administration works to make good citizens out of underprivileged children.

He played two years of professional football with the Los Angeles Bulldogs in the American League, and he suffered a broken leg that has left its mark on him.

He's married and his wife is living in Montreal. "She was with me at the training camp and she's stayed with me ever since," he says simply. "I couldn't have made it if it hadn't been for her."

Despite his calm exterior it is certain that this season has cost him something. He has lost twenty pounds since he started his first road trip with the Royals.

We'll give you another tip on Robinson: he made seven errors in the first two weeks of the season and he's made a total of only *three* since that time.

He uses a large-handled bat that permits only a minimum of wrist manipulation, but at the same time he's a fellow who places his hits accurately. Despite his fine average he has clouted only three home runs. Incidentally, he plans to play professional basketball again next winter. (This is a tip to the gentlemen who plan to operate the professional basketball team in Toronto.) He rooms alone. He's a fine young man and we hope that he makes the grade.

Mrs. Shea's Meat Pies

Toronto *Globe and Mail*
August 22, 1946

THE BLOW-BACK KID lay back comfortably on his bed.

Comfort is comparative. Some persons find it in a hotel suite at eighteen dollars per day. Others find it in the open, under the stars, or on a tick mattress in a garret. The Blow-Back Kid was comfortable and modern architects hadn't taken any extreme measures to assure his comfort. He was lying on a camp bed in a room with a low, slanting roof. There were two cots in the room; two cots and a large trunk and saddles and bridles and bottles of medicine resting on a small ledge. If you have been around a racetrack very often you would have recognized a tack room.

As usual, the Blow-Back Kid was resting fully clothed. There was a reason for that, of course. When you're up at five o'clock in the morning and messing around with horses for five hours and then indulging in the vigorous chit-chat of the profession, it's almost obligatory for a man to snatch a sleep in the afternoon. About four o'clock it's time for a man to struggle out of the hay to feed the horses. Horses, like humans, are creatures of habit, and if they aren't fed after four o'clock, they are inclined to become testy and might be suspicious of anyone who enters the stall.

The Blow-Back Kid stirred lazily and a grin creased his face as he looked across the room at Johnny Needle-Nose, who was occupying the other cot. For many years Johnny has been the Blow-Back Kid's boss. His antecedents are obscure, but Johnny has that innate gentleness that is common to persons who love horses.

The things that Johnny Needle-Nose did prior to coming around the racetrack are nobody's business and never has he volunteered any information. The Blow-Back Kid often had thought about Johnny's past but never had he dared to ask any questions. He knew that Johnny Needle-Nose had been a racetracker for more years than most people could remember. He looked at him now, lying there, wearing a pair of brown trousers and a yellow shirt.

It was impossible to guess his age. His hair was completely grey. He had a long, pointed nose, the point of which twisted down toward his mouth. Strangely enough, his mouth was small and hard. Johnny Needle-Nose was a paradox in that his hard-bitten features didn't give witness to the fact that he was the softest touch in the shedrows.

"Johnny," said the Blow-Back Kid lazily, as he saw Johnny Needle-Nose roll over on his right side to face him, "did you see in the blats the other day where Mrs. E.R. Bradley once bet on Wishing Ring when she paid better than nine-hundred-to-one? That was a pretty fair score for an old doll."

"I remember the race," said Johnny Needle-Nose. "I remember it well. I was there. It was at Latonia in 1912. Mrs. Bradley wasn't the only person who bet on that horse. There was another woman who bet on that horse—she was Michael Shea's mother."

Needle-Nose was stirring and the Blow-Back Kid knew better than to interrupt him.

"Michael Shea's mother was a woman of character," said Johnny Needle-Nose, reaching into his hip pocket for a package of cigarettes that had been rolled out of proportion during his slumbers. He pulled a cigarette out of the pack, lit it and puffed on it slowly.

"Michael was a racetracker," said Needle-Nose. "He wasn't much—in fact, he probably was less than much—but he had a mother who followed him around and looked after his socks and his laundry and, every Sunday morning, she went to church and prayed that Michael would get the hell away from the racetrack.

"She never bet, but one day she went to a small store in Latonia and she overheard a man saying that Wishing Ring would win that day. Wishing Ring didn't have a chance, but the old doll had the idea that if she could make a good score she could persuade Michael to go home and live like a human being."

Johnny Needle-Nose permitted himself a luxurious sigh and blew a cloud of smoke toward the roof of the tack room. "Whatever that might be," he added, blowing clouds of smoke toward the roof.

"Well, she bet ten dollars on Wishing Ring that afternoon. When she swept up to the cashier's wicket, she asked for a cheque for more than nine thousand dollars," said Johnny, grinning again. "She went to Michael and told him that she was going to take him home so that he could act like a normal human being."

Needle-Nose turned his face toward the wall for a second, and when he rolled over again, the Blow-Back Kid looked at him closely. The Blow-Back Kid had worked for Johnny Needle-Nose for ten years and he knew that he couldn't prod his conversation.

For once, though, he dared to intrude. "What happened to Michael Shea's mother?" he asked.

"She was wealthy," said Johnny Needle-Nose briefly. "What more could any woman ask?"

He arose slowly and walked to the door of the tack room. He pulled out another cigarette and lit it. He puffed on it and looked across the track. If you've looked across the track when the shades of evening are coming down, you know what he saw.

What he didn't see was an old lady who was picking her way carefully down the shedrow. She was the sort of old lady that you see occasionally around a racetrack. She was carrying a tray under her arm and the tray contained meat pies.

"Meat pies, sir?" she inquired as she came opposite to the door of Johnny Needle-Nose's tack room.

"I'll take two," he said, reaching into his pocket. "On the other hand, I'll take four."

She handed him the pies and, as the Blow-Back Kid peered out of the tack room at the two of them, he saw Johnny Needle-Nose reach into his left-hand trouser pocket. Johnny Needle-Nose never reached into that pocket unless he was making an important payment.

The Blow-Back Kid saw the colour of the banknotes as they came out of that pocket. They were orange in colour and orange bills are fifty-dollar bills. There were two of them in Johnny Needle-Nose's hand. Johnny Needle-Nose twisted them into a ball and passed them to the lady with the meat pies.

"God bless you, Michael," said the old lady with the meat pies.

"Bless you, Mrs. Shea," said Johnny Needle-Nose, removing the hat that, in some strange fashion, he had donned before going to the door, "and those meat pies are worth a hell of a lot more than ten cents each."

The old lady had gone away before the Blow-Back Kid looked again at Johnny Needle-Nose. Johnny was staring fixedly across the track. The Blow-Back Kid chuckled contentedly.

The Blow-Back Kid rolled over on his back and stared at the ceiling. Comfort is only a matter of environment.

Timmy O'Riordan's Last Ride

Toronto *Globe and Mail*
November 26, 1946

DUBLIN— "A GRAND HARSE," said Shamus, shoving his cap to the back of his head and leaning on the whitewashed railing of the infield. "A grand harse and a grand race and a grand day," said Shamus, appreciatively.

The horses had charged past the winning post and they were being eased to a walk a furlong beyond the wire. They turned and cantered back toward the paddock. The winner, swinging his head fretfully, pranced his way toward the unsaddling enclosure. He was a big chestnut stallion with fire in his eyes. His long, flowing tail was whipped by the autumn wind and his mane quivered as the rider guided him through the gap in the fence. The winner was big-boned but clean-limbed, and the flesh fitted snugly on his frame. "A lovely harse," said Shamus judiciously. "A champion harse. A lovely harse fit to be ridden by Timmy O'Riordan, may God rest his poor, lonely soul."

Shamus Murphy—for that is his name—is lean and slightly stooped and there are tiny, humorous lines at the corners of his bright eyes. His old clothes cling to him with an air of raffish elegance and the gentleness of his speech and the economy of his gestures carry you home three thousand miles to Johnny Needle-Nose and the Blow-Back Kid.

Someday, somewhere, the rising sun will find Shamus Murphy and Johnny Needle-Nose dozing in the same sweet-scented haystack. And they'll shake the sleep from their eyes and stamp the dew from their boots and walk down the road slowly—slowly, because rushing and jostling and pushing are only for fools.

"Timmy O'Riordan could win on that harse, even without the Little People," said Shamus. He looked out of the corners of his eyes. "Timmy once told me that it was his nurse, Bridget Flynn, who showed him how to see the Little People. She'd take him into the garden at night and, after a while, he grew so that he could see them in the broadest daylight."

Shamus tossed aside his cigarette butt and leaned down to pluck a four-leafed clover, which he stuck in the lapel of his jacket.

"Timmy was an orphan and he lived with his aunt," he said. "She didn't understand about the Little People. She was a North of Irelander—may God have mercy on her soul! She had a lovely copse of trees in front of her house and she decided to cut it down because it interfered with her view of her neighbour's garden.

"But Timmy knew that the copse was the home of the Little People. There was an old family that lived in a tree trunk, and there was a wee clearing where the Little People did their singing and dancing. So Timmy pleaded with his aunt and he took on somethin' awful and finally the old woman agreed to let the trees stand. The Little People knew about this because they heard the racket in the house and looked in to see if Timmy was in any trouble.

"Well, Timmy finally ran away from the old woman because he loved the harses and she forbade him to have a harse about the place. He wanted to be a jockey, but the truth of it was that he never really was a good jockey because he was a frail bit of a man and his heart was bad. Still, he knew the language of the harses, and the Little People always were with him.

"He rode many a winner. He rode many a winner because the Little People helped him and no one in the stands knew it and only a few guessed the truth. When Timmy was riding in a race the Little People would chivvy the other horses and hang onto their tails and frighten them by shouting in their ears. It would take a good horse to win with a whole horde of Little People playin' the divil with him.

"Timmy loved life and he spent his evenings gabbing and drinking in the Crown, and because he was such an uncommon fellow he had many a man for company. The doctor told him that he couldn't last, but he laughed at the doctor, who was a practical man who didn't know that, many years before, the Little People had told Timmy that he would have a short life and a merry one."

Shamus lit another cigarette.

"I remember his last race," he said. "He was riding a great brute named Caesar, and in the Crown the night before he whispered to me that I could bet my life on him because the Little People had told him that he wouldn't lose.

"Timmy was white and sick before that race. His heart was about through with its work. Caesar was leading by six lengths as they came to the last furlong and you could see Timmy swaying in the saddle. Caesar won, and then he eased himself as he passed the post. I could see Timmy falling, and I jumped over the fence and caught him before he hit the ground. His head landed in my arms. I said to him, 'Are you all right, Timmy man?' But he didn't answer. He was dead.

"It was right in this spot," said Shamus Murphy, vaulting the railing, stamping a piece of turf with his foot and looking back defiantly. Slowly, he came back and ducked under the rail.

"He had been dead all through that last furlong," he said. "The Little People held him upright in the saddle until after he had won the race.

"They gave him a grand funeral and the old aunt came to it and carried on somethin' fearful, crying and blubberin', and there was a lot of tosh as they buried him.

"The next morning, his grave was empty. The earth was neatly piled beside it, but the grave was empty. The Little People had spirited Timmy away to live with them."

Shamus Murphy paused and threw away the butt of his cigarette.

"I saw him last night," said Shamus. "He was sitting in his corner at the Crown. Three or four of the Little People were with him, clinging to his arms, and all of them were laughing and singing. They go there often and I sit with them. The Crown is a splendid place to talk with a ghost.

"Last night, Timmy O'Riordan told me something," said Shamus Murphy. "He told me that Light o' Morn will win this next race."

Shamus Murphy looked at the visitor who had been listening to his story. The visitor opened his pocketbook and produced two pound-notes.

"Bet this for me," said the visitor.

Shamus Murphy took the money and sauntered across the track toward the bookmaking ring. As he reached the other fence he looked back and then disappeared into the crowd.

That was the last that was seen of him. The Little People spirited him away, too.

4

1947–49

Hume Cronyn: He Coulda Been Somebody

Toronto *Globe and Mail*
February 21, 1947

Mr. Warren Stevens, a Syracuse old grad, is on hand with the intelligence that the Canadian intercollegiate boxing and wrestling championships will be staged here tonight and Saturday. It is with some regret that we learn that they have eliminated fencing from this annual assault-at-arms. We remember that McGill once had a West Indian fencer who was so proficient that he would use his foil to carve his name on an opponent's chest and even would dot the i's before he screamed "Touché!"

Touché, indeed! Why, he left his opponents mutilated to such an extent that the doctors used a sewing machine to stitch them instead of employing the standard knit-one-purl-two technique.

Ah, such wonderful memories! The mere mention of the assault-at-arms is enough to send us out in search of a red-and-white sweater and a cheering-section fez. It reminds us of our old roommate—J. Carrington Harvey, Jr.—the reversible snapback who could snap the ball through a keyhole. In fact, he *did* snap the ball through a keyhole at the end of Molson Stadium in an important game one afternoon and Coach Frank Shaughnessy fell right off the bench. What did Coach Shaughnessy say? Well, he didn't learn that kind of language at Notre Dame.

Those were the days when boys went to college early and stayed a long time. Harry Batstone went to Queen's and took every course except Animal Husbandry. It looked for a while as if they were going to have to pass an Act of Parliament to persuade him to leave school after he had graduated in medicine. The other colleges were fearful that he would decide to take dentistry as a sideline. The intercollegiate heavyweight boxing champion for several years was Don Carrick, who also was the Canadian amateur golf champion. Don finally decided to quit college after the Canadian Seniors Golf Association offered him a membership.

His successor as heavyweight champion was Frederick Bouchier Taylor. Ah, those good old days! Taylor went down to New York to compete in the United States championship at Madison Square Garden. He made a distinct impression. As soon as he appeared the New York reporters described him as "the best-built man ever to step into Madison Square Garden's ring." Fifteen seconds later they were describing him as "the best-built man ever to be carried out of Madison Square Garden's ring."

Taylor was one of the boys from our fraternity and so was a little guy named Hume Cronyn, who happens to be just about the best character actor in Hollywood these days. We remember Cronyn's arrival at college because he was equipped with a Franklin air-cooled roadster, a set of jug ears and pair of brown suede shoes. He had other qualities, of course, but those were the things you saw first.

The rest of the chaps were sitting around one day, playing mahjong and snap and whist, when a distraught freshman rushed in with the startling news that Cronyn had just won the McGill featherweight championship. Furthermore, in a display of unseemly violence, he had stiffened a couple of opponents. My, but the other chaps were so excited that they scarcely could lift a teacup for several days.

Cronyn would have been a cinch to win the intercollegiate title. However, Sir Arthur Currie had a long talk with Cronyn one morning. Sir Arthur was the president of McGill, and he told Cronyn that he was going to graduate him without the necessity of spending the next three years at college.

Cronyn thus was deprived of an opportunity to go on to great heights in the pugilistic trade. Probably he would have been a maineventer in Madison Square Garden. Instead, Sir Arthur Currie sent him out into the cruel world and the poor kid has been forced to earn a living down in nasty, hot Hollywood, surrounded by a lot of good-looking tomatoes who bother him for his autograph. Oh well, Mike Jacob's loss is Sam Goldwyn's gain!

Hundred-Dollar Jones

Toronto *Globe and Mail*
February 27, 1947

THE RAYS OF THE DYING SUN rippled across the waves of ice in the infield as Johnny Needle-Nose took a final turn down the shedrow. Carefully, he adjusted the catches on the stall doors and kicked the clinging clods of snow from his boots before he entered the tack room. A single bulb gleamed above his cot and a small electric coil warmed one corner. Needle-Nose stretched out on the cot and placed his hand over his eyes. The winter had been long and Needle-Nose was low in funds and low in morale. More important, he was lonely.

Even the Blow-Back Kid had gone south, though—true to his nickname—he'd be back with the first crocus. But there's no place on the fancy southern circuit for a man with three old eight-hundred-dollar selling platers, a short bankroll and a heavy thirst.

Johnny Needle-Nose stretched regretfully, swung himself to his feet and looked at his reflection in the mirror. He needed a shave but it was too late and too cold to do anything about it. It could wait until tomorrow. He reached into his right-hand pants pocket to count his money. Two bills came out: a ten and a one. Very carefully he folded the ten into a small, flat rectangle and shoved it into his left-hand pocket. The one went back with his right hand to its original hiding place.

It's bad enough being stranded and cold, but it's worse when you're broke. Needle-Nose was something of a loner, and he was a complex character, too. His thin face, his soft voice and his penetrating gaze often repelled more exuberant racetrackers, but he was a good man with a horse and his long, sensitive hands looked oddly out of place hanging below the cuffs of his dirty windbreaker. Needle-Nose was a loner, and he hated to borrow money.

He switched off the light, stepped out beneath the shedrow and locked the door behind him. Night had come, but it was clear and the new moon was bright. The stalls were quiet: old horses are patient and uncomplaining.

The snow crunched under Johnny's feet as he walked past the empty barns and turned toward the street lights. Mentally, he was budgeting his resources and he contemplated his dinner without any enthusiasm. Once clear of the barns, he stood on the sidewalk for a second and then picked his way over the trolley tracks to the coffee pot on the corner. The windows of the coffee pot were steamy but he could see the shadows of people inside.

The door opened easily and as he stamped on the mat he picked out a booth in the farthest corner. He nodded to the girl behind the counter and was sitting down when a booming voice greeted him.

"I thought I'd find you here," said Hundred-Dollar Jones, sitting down after reaching for his ham and eggs and coffee in the next booth. Needle-Nose ordered the same from the girl and looked across the table at Hundred-Dollar. The big man on the other side of the table was sporting a Florida tan and his camel-hair coat wasn't exactly the thing for winter weather.

"Great season down there," said Hundred-Dollar enthusiastically. "I caught that thing of Hirsch Jacobs's for a century across the board, and I had Big Jake betting for me in New Orleans. Decided to come home because the Pinkertons were getting too hot and anyhow I wanted a rest before we open up here."

Needle-Nose nodded noncommittally and plodded through his ham and eggs.

"Saw Blow-Back down there and we were talking about the time that we stiffened that beetle of Fatty Anderson's." Jones laughed uproariously. "You must have made yourself a real score on that," he added, reaching across the table to nudge Needle-Nose.

"Yeah," said Needle-Nose.

"Do you remember the time that we took that mossback of yours from Chicago to Tia Juana and kept him there for four weeks before we unloaded him?" asked Jones. "Migawd, we cracked every book on the Pacific coast. I remember that I bought myself that yellow Packard roadster and I had a gal with a shape like Theda Bara and hair like the Seven Sutherland Sisters."

"Yeah," said Needle-Nose. "How've you been going yourself?"

"Knocking 'em dead," replied Hundred-Dollar noisily. "But it isn't like the old days when we were at Juarez. I remember when you won three handicaps in a week. I'd hate to think how much money you made. You used to give us that guff about sending the dough to your mother." Jones nudged Needle-Nose again and laughed. "You always were a great kidder. You must have made a lot of money in your time."

"Yeah," said Needle-Nose.

He had finished eating and he swallowed the last of the coffee. The two cheques lay on the table and Needle-Nose reached for them. He examined them solemnly. They totalled ninety cents.

They walked toward the front of the restaurant and Needle-Nose paid the tab and they walked into the street and stood for a second beneath a street lamp.

Johnny Needle-Nose put his hand carefully into his left-hand pants pocket and felt the ten-dollar bill. The bill came out of its hiding place and Johnny handed it to Jones.

"Well, thanks," said Hundred-Dollar Jones, smiling broadly. "I really don't need it but I didn't get to the bank in time today and I might be a little short until morning. Thanks, old pal, I'll be seeing you."

Needle-Nose watched him disappear and then he walked across the trolley tracks and started for the barns. He was walking swiftly now and he was chuckling at some secret jest.

He looked up and he winked at the moon.

Tomorrow? Tomorrow would look after itself.

Whippah Billy Remembers

Toronto *Globe and Mail*
May 8, 1947

WHIPPAH BILLY WATSON, who lost his world champeenship recently in St. Louis to a cad named Louis Thesz—ah, the treachery and perfidy of those Americans!—can afford to smirk comfortably as he examines his savings account. His current situation is a far cry from the days when he wrestled in these environs as a "bootleg amateur" for four dollars a night. And it's a far cry from the day in 1937 on which he packed his belongings in a cardboard suitcase and left Toronto to seek fame and fortune in Jolly Old England.

The Whippah's start on his campaign to earn a million dollars was quite inauspicious. A promoter named Harry Joyce induced Watson and three iron-muscled companions—Pat Flanagan, Al Korman and Tommy Nelson—to accompany him to England. Strangely enough, Mr. Joyce didn't book any first-class accommodation. The wrestlers were driven to Montreal in an automobile. Then each of them paid twenty dollars to the master of a cargo vessel for the privilege of working passage to Bristol. They had to wait a couple of days before the vessel sailed, so in a financial emergency, they booked beds in a seamen's hostel at the bargain price of twenty-five cents per night. (This is the same Whippah Watson who now books hotel suites at thirty dollars per night without blinking his eyes more than twelve or fourteen times.)

When the Whippah and his sinewy mates boarded the ship they discovered that they were expected to act as chambermaids and orderlies to a cargo of living, mooing cattle. The circumstances of this voyage have left Watson with a deep distaste for beef in any form. The voyage also left him with a distaste for seafood. He developed that latter distaste while examining living forms of seafood as he leaned over the rails of the freighter.

Anahoo, the boys arrived in Bristol strictly COD and Joyce, in an excess of confidence, invited them to accompany him to his mother's home. So they discovered that Mother Joyce had exactly one bedroom in her establishment, and the hardy wrestlers bought themselves a tent and raised it in a field belonging to a neighbouring farmer.

But they reckoned without the English rains. The first night it rained so hard that the wrestlers floated down through the rows of Brussels sprouts. The farmer came to the rescue—he told them that, thenceforth, they could sleep in his chicken pen. (Yep, this is the same Whippah Watson who stays at all expensive hotels and who complains when the maids don't leave sufficient face towels in the bathrooms.)

Well, their first bouts were part of a charity show. The promoters asked them to take one-half of the proceeds. The grapplers, who were flatter than soup on a plate, grandiosely told them that they would work gratis.

They went to London on the cuff, and before they started they donned their best white flannel trousers and white sport shoes. But as they walked down toward Blackfriars they were caught in one of those London downpours, and before they reached the wrestling promoter's office their trousers had shrunk to their knees and they looked like four fugitives from a paper chase.

That was ten years ago, and now Whippah Billy Watson has the earning powers of a bank president. And really he doesn't complain about the scarcity of towels in his hotel suites. He still remembers how comfortably he slept in that English chicken pen.

During his recent travels in the southern states, the Whippah ran into Robert "Hi" Lee and induced promoter Francois Xavier Toney to import this six-foot-eight-inch Arkansan to Toronto. In so doing, Watson has confronted the Canadian people with a major food shortage. One evening recently, Mr. Lee, sitting down to a late snack, ate thirty-six eggs as an appetizer and then satisfied himself with a modest three-pound steak.

That isn't Mr. Lee's sole eating accomplishment: he eats glass tumblers and light globes and swallows burning gasoline. Interviewed yesterday afternoon, he confessed modestly that he has quit eating razor blades because they chipped the enamel from his teeth.

Mr. Lee also runs needles through the flesh of his arms and permits friends to throw needle darts into his bare back. He opens his mouth, shoves a long darning needle through one cheek, through his open mouth and then through the other cheek. One night he placed a frankfurter on the darning needle and roasted it on burning gasoline in his mouth.

He's quite a kid! He was a professional box-fighter, too, for a year before he turned to professional wrestling. "But," a reporter protested yesterday afternoon, "you're much too tall to be a box-fighter."

"Ah, no," Mr. Lee sighed reminiscently. "I discovered that they could reach me."

Requiem for Big Red

Toronto *Globe and Mail*
November 18, 1947

He died fifteen minutes past noon on the first day of November. They buried him three days later as the rays of the waning sun picked their way furtively through the gaunt autumn trees and then lay cold and pale on the rolling hills. There were no tears, no hymns, no lamentations. It was his native heath, but those who stood around him at that last simple ceremony were aliens—they were not of his kind. The huge oaken casket creaked into its resting place, and they left him there, cloaked in the dignity of death.

His name was Man o' War.

He was possessed of a nobility that is denied to man. He was scrupulously honest. He was fearless. He was great in heart and body. He was born to greatness and he claimed his heritage with a fierce pride. Take a look at the pictures of him when he had attained the age of thirty. Take a look at the gentle mouth that provides a striking contrast with the fiery eyes, undimmed by the passage of time. Look at that mighty neck; the deep, broad chest; the massive body. Look at those legs that carried him so far, so fast and for so long. Man! You're looking at a horse that was born for the ages.

The story of Man o' War has been oft told, but some of the details have been omitted in most histories. It is believed generally that he was beaten only once, by Upset in the Sanford Memorial at Saratoga. Actually, he was beaten twice. He lost to Golden Broom in a quarter-mile trial when the two horses were yearlings.

As a yearling, he was unprepossessing if one didn't notice his head and his blazing eyes carefully. He was very tall and gangling. He was thin and ungainly. It was thought he might become a good hunter, not a racehorse. Then, as a two-year-old, he contracted a fever at Havre de Grace. His temperature rocketed to 106 degrees, but the blood of Hastings and Fair Play coursed through him and outburned the fever.

His trainer, Louis Feustel, watched him closely during that illness. The morning that the fever broke, Man o' War tottered to the door of his stall, sniffed the fresh breeze and whinnied. Feustel turned away with a smile on his face. He knew that he was training a racehorse.

You've heard the rest of the story. You will remember that the jockey who rode him when he was beaten by Upset was Johnny Loftus. It has been written that Loftus was suspended after the running of that race. It has been written also that Loftus never rode him again. Both stories are incorrect. Loftus wasn't at fault in the running of the Sanford Stakes. Man o' War was a fractious, eager horse at the starting ribbon. He was pawing the ground impatiently. Even at that, he outbroke two other horses in field. He just failed to catch Upset, who had started with a burst of speed. Loftus wasn't grounded and, for that matter, he rode the horse in all his remaining races as a two-year-old.

It was an old man named Will Harbut who knew Man o' War best. The chemistry of an occasional human being is such that a horse feels the bond between them. Harbut was such a rare man.

Take a look at the picture of this old man standing with Man o' War. The horse is facing the camera, proudly but inquisitively. Harbut stands beside him, but he is looking up at the horse. The old man's wide, generous mouth is half open in a smile of genuine affection. The picture was taken last year and, if the edges of the print are blurred slightly, it is because even then the shadows were closing around both of them. Old Will Harbut turned ever slowly in his bed and died on October 3. Man o' War didn't wait long and followed Old Will within a month.

Loneliness? Who can tell? It isn't wise to scoff about things that one doesn't understand too well. Who can say that a wise old horse can't hear an old friend calling to him when the night winds whisper softly?

He stands as clean as the morning, as swift and as strong as the breeze,
Awaiting the call of the bugle to echo from Elysian trees.
He looks again at his rivals, the truest, the best of their breed,
Unfettered by saddles or bridles, untroubled by problems of creed.
They race away from the barrier, wildly outspeeding time's sands.
Their riders are will-o'-the-wisps, guiding with ghostly hands.
There's Upset and little John Grier and a dozen more of that ilk,
The bravest, the fleetest, the fines— the "tops" to ever tote silk.
It's Man o' War at the quarter; it's gallant Big Red at the half;
It's Man o' War at the mile pole breezing (oh, hear the gods laugh!).
He charges along to the finish, his coat glistening gold in the sun.

He turns and faces his rivals—another splendid victory won.
Now Old Will leads him again to the pasture, a valley without
fences or rails,
And lolls deep in the clover beside him, and spins him wondrous
tales.

Score One for the Cowboys

Toronto *Globe and Mail*
November 29, 1948

THOSE UNSOPHISTICATED HILLBILLIES known as the Calgary Stampeders met the city slicker Ottawa Roughians on Saturday afternoon and fleeced them as mercilessly as a confidence man rolls a stiff. The barefoot boys from the Alberta steppes outsmarted the Roughians in scandalous fashion and stole the Grey Cup under circumstances that should call for the immediate appointment of a Royal Commission.

It had been anticipated that the comparatively youthful and inexperienced Stampeders might suffer from nervous indigestion and other emotional malaise when exposed to a roaring and critical gathering in University of Toronto Stadium. Instead, it was the veteran Ottawans who fumbled, mechanically and mentally, in the moments of crisis.

It was Calgary's day on the football field, in the lobby and cookeries of the Royal York Hotel and in the streets of the cities and villages of the West. On Sunday afternoon the citizens of this spacious Dominion were nursing the most shocking mass hangover since Confederation, and safety engineers who examined the Royal York condemned the building because it was leaning dangerously in the direction of Lake Ontario.

The football game for the Grey Cup was contested officially in the stadium and was continued unofficially in the hotel lobby. At 5:01 p.m. the goalposts were borne triumphantly through the front doors and were erected against the railings of the mezzanine.

At 5:02 p.m. two platoons of bellboys circumspectly removed the potted palms, flower vases and anything that weighed less than three thousand pounds.

The gaudily caparisoned Calgary supporters were boisterous and noisy but well-behaved and courteously declined to ride their horses into the elevators. Any minor untoward incidents were occasioned by youthful local yahoos who suffered from the delusion that the consumption of two pints of ale and the acquisition of a pseudo-western twang entitled them to ride the range astride any convenient chesterfield.

The Stampeders won because they were the smarter team. The Roughians made all the mistakes and the Stampeders capitalized on those errors. The Calgarians were alert and aggressive, and they were tenacious on defence. If the Roughians fumbled, it was because they were gang-tackled more fiercely than they have been hit all season.

The cup was won in the quarterbacking department where Keith Spaith called an almost perfect game for Calgary. Only on two occasions could he have been accused of employing dubious strategy: once when he declined to kick for a point and again when he essayed a third-down forward pass at midfield. In contrast, the Ottawa signal-calling appeared to be panicky and uncertain when the Roughians were within striking distance of the western goal line.

At that, we would suggest that Anthony Golab, Ottawa's human tank, was the dominating figure in the game. Golab's plunging and Howard Turner's long, skittering runs were responsible for the fact that the Roughians aggregated so much yardage in midfield.

Coach Wally Masters of the Roughians probably reaches for the gas pipe every time he contemplates how the two Calgary touchdowns were scored.

Can you imagine any team scoring against Ottawa on a sleeper play? Spaith's long second-quarter pass to Woodrow Wilson Strode rattled the Roughians so badly that they paid no attention to Norm Hill, who lay flat on his face on the opposite side of the field. On the ensuing play, Hill had so much time that he could have crawled across the goal line on his hands and knees before catching Spaith's pass.

And then in the fourth quarter, Pete Karpuk of the Roughians apparently was mesmerized by the remarkable bouncings of a loose ball. While he was thus entranced, Strode picked up the ball, walked uncertainly for a few steps and sped for the Ottawa goal. He lateralled to Jim Mitchener, who was forced out of bounds on the 10.

The Roughians again disintegrated in the clutch. The stunned Ottawa linemen shifted to the right to stop two Calgary decoys, and Pete

Thodos scored easily as he galloped through strangely uninhabited territory.

The Calgary victory was the more remarkable in that Les Lear used three Vancouver juniors—Thodos, Ced Gyles and Rod Pantages—in his backfield for a considerable portion of the game. His regular fullback, Paul Rowe, crocked a knee on the second play of the game and performed only spasmodically after his injured limb had been frozen by the club doctor.

The youngsters, steadied by the presence of such veterans as Fritz Hanson, Rube Ludwig and Lear himself, handled the ball flawlessly. If they displayed any weakness, it was only when Pantages took Rowe's blocking spot on pass plays: the eager but inexperienced Pantages missed three blocking assignments on the left side of the line and each time Spaith was trapped. However, Spaith, who is a cool, sure-handed fellow, always retained possession of the ball when hit from behind.

The Calgary defensive work was magnificent. Their three American linemen—Chuck Anderson, Johnny Aguirre and Strode—played like men possessed. Coach Lear went into the game himself, and with those four doing yeoman chores, the Stampeders were in command of the situation in the final quarter. Lear used a five-man line on defence, and in the closing minutes he switched to a four-man line while he roamed between his guards.

A reporter could exhaust his supply of superlatives in describing Anderson. The big fellow was a tremendous factor in winning the game. You can't take anything away from Lear and his Stampeders. They played sixteen games this year, winning fifteen and drawing one. They took the Grey Cup to Calgary for the first time in history. They have a young team and we anticipate that we'll see them in the finals again next year.

There's no denying that the staging of the Grey Cup final in Toronto resulted in a fine old snafu. It's time that the Canadian Rugby Union realized that football has become Big Business. The admission prices weren't high enough; the stadium was too small; and the teams emerged from the game with nothing but prestige, a handful of unpaid bills and a headache.

The only organizations that profited from the game were the hotels, the transportation companies and the government liquor stores. If Toronto hopes to stage the national championships again, we should be sure to provide a stadium that can accommodate at least forty thousand spectators—and at higher prices, too. Otherwise, the teams might as well hold the game in Okotoks, Bella Coola, Ste. Rose du Lac or Clappison's Corners.

Blind Sam Fought 'em All

Toronto *Globe and Mail*
February 3, 1949

WHO WAS THE GREATEST BOX-FIGHTER IN HISTORY? Jack Dempsey? Harry Greb? Well, don't bet too much money that it wasn't a Canadian named Sam Langford!

Certainly Langford was the most remarkable figure in the modern history of the ring. He measured only five feet seven inches, but he whipped the leading heavyweights of his day and he fought until he was forty-three years of age and had lost seventy-five percent of his vision. He says that he lost his sight suddenly in the second round of a bout with Tiger Flowers when he was forty-two. Unable to see his opponent, he waited until Flowers shuffled into him—and then old Sam knocked him out with a single punch.

The American papers called him "the Boston Tar Baby," but the nickname wasn't entirely accurate. He was born in Weymouth, Nova Scotia, and grew up there, but Joe Woodman took him to nearby Boston when he was fifteen because a guy couldn't make a buck fighting around Nova Scotia.

It was only three or four years ago that Al Laney, a New York sportswriter, found Blind Sam living in a dirty, rented room. Langford was destitute but cheerful, and he told Laney that although people had forgotten and neglected him, he bore no ill will to the promoters who had cast him aside after he was of no further use to them.

Laney, however, was indignant. He wrote a series of scorching stories, enlightening the public concerning the manner in which Langford had been abandoned by the men for whom he had made money. The response to Laney's stories was instantaneous. Laney was deluged by contributions of money and a trust fund was established, a fund that will keep Sam in comfort for the rest of his days.

The people of Canada finally are getting around to paying a belated tribute to old Sam. His hometown of Weymouth Falls no longer is as prosperous as it was in the days when it was a centre of the shipbuilding, pulp and lumber industries. The people are poor and educational facilities are meagre. Someone has hit upon the idea of building a Sam Langford School at Weymouth Falls, with the money to be raised by public contributions. A priest and a Protestant clergyman head the committee, but the school will be non-denominational and the teaching staff will be provided by the municipality. We're writing this piece in the hope that some of the old-timers who remember Sam when he was at his peak will send a contribution to the Sam Langford School Fund.

Sam started fighting in 1895 and there's no telling in how many bouts he appeared because even *Nat Fleischer's Ring Record Book* didn't catch up with him until 1902, after he had been in the ring for seven years. But it was in 1902 that the fistic world heard about the boy from Nova Scotia because on December 8 of that year he whipped Joe Gans, the lightweight champion, in a non-title fight. Gans was knocked down by Langford and was forced to call on all his great defensive skill to avoid a knockout. Only a couple of weeks later Langford engaged in the first of his many fights with the late Jack "Chappie" Blackburn, who is remembered best as the man who developed Joe Louis.

Less than a year later, Sam won a "newspaper decision" over Joe Walcott, the world welterweight champion. Officially it was listed as a draw, but the scribes all the way from here to Topeka contended that Langford won.

When he was twenty-six, he fought Jack Johnson, who went on to become heavyweight champion. Although he was six inches shorter and thirty pounds lighter than Johnson, Sam dropped his man in the tenth round and all but had him kayoed. Johnson came back to win the decision in fifteen rounds, but never again could he be persuaded to meet the heavy-hitting Langford in the ring.

It was always the same with Langford—the bigger boys with reputations steered away from him. He travelled to Europe and the Antipodes, flattening any man who dared to step into the ring with him. He kayoed the famous Philadelphia Jack O'Brien and, on two occasions, he knocked out Harry Willis. It was Willis, remember, who couldn't get a bout with Jack Dempsey when Dempsey held the heavyweight title.

One of Langford's last bouts took place in Toronto when he was forty-one. Charlie Hallett brought him to the University Avenue Armouries. Hallett couldn't find an opponent for Sam, and the story goes that he grabbed an oversized Negro boy from the racetrack and gave him the name of "Young Peter Jackson."

Charlie thought that the show would be a flop and, accordingly, he declined to give Young Peter a guarantee of four hundred dollars but offered him ten percent of the gate.

The funny part of it was that Langford's name still was magic at the box office. Sam knocked out Young Peter as painlessly and quickly as possible and the racetrack roustabout was paid one thousand dollars as his percentage of the gate.

The Brothers Stuki

Toronto *Globe and Mail*
February 10, 1949

THE MOST PLEASANT SPORTING NEWS of the week is contained in a press dispatch from Edmonton. The tidings from Alberta are to the effect that Annis Stukus is one of four men who are being considered for the coaching job when the Edmonton Eskimos re-enter the Western Inter-Provincial Football Union next autumn.

We urge the Edmonton executive to hire the Loquacious Lithuanian without any further delay. He is a very competent football man and he is a hearty, uncomplicated character who would feel right at home among the uninhibited westerners.

Big Stuke—or Angus MacStukus, as he is known among his playmates—lives for the football season. He talks football in his sleep. For at least one meal each day his long-suffering wife is compelled to prepare a salad, the centrepiece of which is a chunk of jelly molded into the shape of a football. Only last week he threatened to divorce her because she didn't have the correct number of lace holes in the jelly football.

It was with extreme reluctance that Big Stuke retired from active football competition at the end of the 1946 season. However, the best orthopedic surgeons in the country had examined him and had reached the conclusion that he was their masterpiece. They had him screwed together with enough nuts and bolts to assemble a mail-order tractor. He clanked when he walked and his nose looked as if it had been designed by an architect who specialized in scenic railways.

In the best interests of the Edmonton Eskimos and Stukus, he should be offered a three-year contract. If he is hired he will be starting off with a bunch of untried youngsters and four or five Americans. Any coach would need at least two seasons to assemble, from such material, a team that would be a contender in the hard-hitting Western Conference.

We're gratuitously assuming the job of Stukus's business manager because we know that he is refreshingly naive about money matters in connection with football.

Big Stuke had been playing senior football for the Dominion champion Toronto Argonauts for three years before he discovered that players actually received money for enjoying themselves on the field. He was stunned and bewildered. His younger brothers—Little Stuke and Medium-Sized Stuke—were equally chagrined when he reported his discovery to them, and they beat him about the eyes and ears for being such a dope.

Before the 1938 season Big Stuke presented himself to the Argonaut executive and announced timidly that he thought he should receive five hundred dollars for the coming campaign.

The Argonaut management was deeply wounded by this show of professionalism.

"Do you realize what you're doing, sonny?" they asked, patting him gently on the shoulders. "You are acting in a very ungrateful fashion. Here we have been buying pretty blue sweaters for you for three years, and this is the way you reward us?"

Stukus had tears in his eyes, but he stood there, stubbornly cracking his gargantuan knuckles.

They paid him the five hundred dollars.

"I would have asked for dough before that," confesses Stukus, "but I was afraid that they wouldn't let me play football. What would I have done if they wouldn't let me play football?"

Sure, he loved football. That's the kind of football player he was, and for that reason we think that he'll prove to be a great coach.

He played most of his senior football for Lew Hayman. Those were the days when Lew was turning out great teams. (Much as we like Hayman and admire him, we think that he has slipped since he moved to Montreal—down there he has been coaching with one eye on his players and the other eye on the cash register.)

The Stuki are a thoroughly admirable family. Papa Stukus was something of a strongman and weightlifter in his native Lithuania. He deplored football and couldn't see any future for twenty-four young men who padded and helmeted themselves and butted each other into unconsciousness as they quarrelled over a small, inflated pigskin.

Consequently, Big Stuke learned his football in the strictest secrecy. He begged and borrowed a battered set of equipment, which he kept at a friend's house. By the time he reached Central Tech he was acknowledged to be one of the best kickers in the city, but his parents hadn't heard about it.

All went well until one afternoon when Central took the field for an important game. Annis was handling the ball just before the kickoff when he saw a familiar figure on the sidelines. The familiar figure was that of Papa Stukus, and he wasn't smiling affectionately at his son. Big Stuke ran right out of the park when the final whistle ended that game.

It was after dusk when he paused for breath under a street lamp and regarded the bleak future. He cadged an evening paper from a delivery boy and a small headline on the front page hit his eye. The headline read: "Stukus Stars for Central."

He folded the paper and strode toward his home. As he reached the front steps he broke into a trot. He was travelling approximately twenty miles per hour when he passed his father at the door.

"Look Pop, I got my name in the papers . . ." he gasped, thrusting the paper at his father and displaying remarkable broken-field running ability as he sprinted for his bedroom.

Half an hour later, Big Stuke emerged from his sanctuary and peeked into the dining room. Papa Stukus still was staring at the newspaper. Papa Stukus had a proud smile on his face.

Tramping loudly, Big Stuke picked up the telephone. Whistling, he dialed a friend's number. "Come on over," he shouted when the phone was answered. "We're going to hold the football meeting at *our* house tonight!"

For the next twelve years, Mama Stukus was cooking happily for hordes of hungry young football players who cluttered up her house with their muddy equipment. Papa Stukus, for his part, became one of the best grandstand quarterbacks in the business.

Even Hayman was slightly nonplussed when Big Stuke first turned out with the Argonauts. "What position do you play?" he asked, assaying the large, ham-handed youth in front of him.

"Any position," beamed Stukus.

And he *did* play any position before he was through. Officially, he was a quarterback, but he taught himself to play outside wing, all the line positions and halfback.

One day he heard that Hayman was looking for a placement-kicker.

Stuke took a ball and soon was booting it over the crossbar with a concentration and determination that indicated that no other player need apply for the job. Stukus, in addition to other chores, became the Argonaut placement-kicker.

All he wanted was the privilege of playing sixty minutes of each game. Every time that an Argonaut was injured, Stukus would begin to warm up hopefully on the sidelines as he glanced longingly over his shoulder at Hayman.

You see, Big Stuke was a self-made player. Hayman has insisted that Little Stuke was the best quarterback in Canadian football. Big Stuke and Little Stuke were equally insistent that Medium-Sized Stuke was the best line-plunger in the business.

But if Hayman ever was asked to name the best all-round handyman who had played for him in Toronto, we don't believe that he'd ponder more than two seconds before answering.

All rumours to the contrary, Big Stuke is only thirty-four years of age. It was only a few seasons ago that Bob Cosgrove staggered into the Balmy Beach dressing room and collapsed laughing.

"I've heard everything now," screamed Cosgrove. "I just met a lady who asked me if Annis Stukus and his two sons were going to play for us again this year."

Okay, you lucky Edmontonians—take him away!

Eat Your Heart Out, Fred Astaire

Toronto *Globe and Mail*
March 5, 1949

You never can tell what you're going to read in the blats. For instance, we picked up this journal yesterday morning and, in perusing the same, discovered that an eminent critic from New York has referred to one of our numerous offspring as a "born dancer."

We experienced momentary difficulty in identifying this child. Her name escaped us, but upon peering down the dining-room table we realized that she is the gabby little blonde who sits about halfway down the south side and who is identified in our mind as "No Carrots, No Cabbage, No Beets, No Spinach and PUH-LEASE Go Easy on the Gravy!"

A "born dancer," eh? Well, we would like to inform the New York critic that this is a striking example of an inherited talent. If this child has exhibited any trifling manifestations of grace and rhythm it is only a result of heredity: although we blush to admit it, her father was a terpsichorean who, by contrast, made Fred Astaire look like a first baseman with two left feet.

We took to dancing as a Litvak takes to apple strudel. We ignored the pastime in our early formative years, but when we essayed to trip the light fantastic, we mastered its intricacies in the same keen and nonchalant manner with which we had mastered double-deck pinochle and three-horse parlays.

We attended our first dancing party on the insistence of Mr. Sonny Brockwell, a fifteen-year-old Winnipeg sophisticate who wore bow ties and his father's coon coat.

"What about this dancing dodge, Jack?" we asked him as we appraised the fresh-faced little tomatoes huddled fearfully on the chairs that lined the walls of the room.

"Nothing to it," replied Mr. Brockwell. "Just keep time with the music and let yourself go. It's a cinch."

"Twenty-three, skidoo," we chortled, as Frank Wright's Country Club Orchestra broke into the stirring strains of "Dardanella." (If it wasn't Frank Wright's Orchestra, it must have been Dave Steele's or the Canary Cottage Orchestra, which was fresh from a successful nineteen-year engagement at the Pennsylvania Hotel in New York.)

Our first partner was Miss Betty Read, a little girl we remembered as a childhood playmate who, a few years earlier, had broken a mashie over our shoulders on the sixth fairway at Pine Ridge.

Grasping Miss Read firmly, we remembered Mr. Brockwell's advice to "let yourself go." Geez, what a sensation! We sped down the floor at a reckless pace, threaded our way skilfully through a row of potted palms and whirled around a bend as the metal studs in our heels raised a shower of sparks. It was warm but exhilarating work. After five minutes we knew that we had been born to dance.

"How are we doing?" we bellowed happily at Miss Read.

Receiving no answer, we glanced down and perceived that Miss Read was unconscious.

Well, two weeks passed before we attended another dance, but we had to go without Miss Read, who still was encased in a plaster cast at Misericordia Hospital.

In the intervening two weeks, Mr. Brockwell had showed us how to do the varsity drag or hobo hop, a stomping dance that was particularly suited to our somewhat athletic style. We guess that Miss Read must have been gnawing on the stumps of her arms jealously but we told her mother that we'd drop around to see her when we found time, and we took Miss Peggy Drummond to the dance.

Gee, Miss Drummond probably never will forget that night. The hobo hop was a cinch and as we danced, we could hear Miss Drummond gasping with delight.

"How are we doing?" we shouted at her midway through the first dance.

"*You're* doing all right," she whined, "but I lost my shoes at the half-mile pole."

Miss Read retired from dancing after a couple of seasons. She developed arthritis or something. We don't know whether her terpsichorean experiences with us had anything to do with it, but she married one of our friends who was the western Canada representative for Kayser Hosiery. She and her husband always entertain us when we visit Winnipeg, but in recent years they have become strangely neurotic on the subject of dancing. Sometimes late at night, when we have been exchanging colourful lies and the radio has been blaring, we have suggested to her that we should tread a few measures.

Then she begins to shake and sob hysterically and her husband reaches for a rather stout claymore that he keeps hanging on their sitting-room wall. If they weren't such good friends of ours, we'd suggest that both of them should consult a psychiatrist.

Ah, yes! We stopped dancing after a few years, too. By the time that we got around to going to nightclubs we discovered that the dance floors were too small and the music too slow. There's no point in exhibiting any extraordinary talents when the audience doesn't have space to appreciate them.

We've been attending the performances at the Canadian Ballet Festival this week. Some of the dancers are quite promising. They don't do at all badly for kids. Of course, we know that they'd feel pretty ashamed of their amateurish efforts if they knew that we were sitting in the audience.

Would anyone care to dance?

Tales of the Silver Fox

Toronto *Globe and Mail*
March 30, 1949

THE SILVER FOX didn't invent hockey, but he has been associated with the sport as a player, coach, promoter and innovator throughout the half-century in which the game has developed from corner-lot shinny into a multi-million-dollar business enterprise. Today, at the age of sixty-five, Lester Patrick still is active as the National Hockey League representative in charge of the Stanley Cup semifinal series between the Boston Bruins and Toronto Maple Leafs. As an operating official, he has outlasted all his hockey-playing contemporaries with the exception of Arthur Howie Ross, vice-president and general manager of the Bruins.

The Silver Fox has been one of professional hockey's most distinguished advertisements and the game owes him great debts. He and one of his brothers, Frank Patrick, were the pioneers who first realized that hockey is Big Business and not merely a winter pastime.

Lester was born in Drummondville, Quebec, and he was the oldest of nine children. His father, the late Joe Patrick, was a successful lumberman in Quebec and British Columbia until he retired to Victoria.

Lester began his career in organized hockey with the MAAA Juniors in Montreal in the winter of 1901–02 and when he was twenty, he went to Calgary determined to be a cowboy. Lester was tall and the cow ponies were short and within a few months Patrick had decided to be a surveyor. On his way home from cow country, he stopped off in Brandon in the winter of 1903–04 and was persuaded to play hockey there. He worked in a laundry for the handsome weekly wage of fifteen dollars.

The Brandon team was good enough to win the Manitoba championship and then had the temerity to challenge the mighty Ottawa Silver Seven for the Stanley Cup. The Silver Seven won of course but the Brandons gave them a two-game battle.

At the ripe old age of twenty-three, Lester Patrick was captain of the Montreal Wanderers when they upset the Silver Seven to win the cup in 1906. Just for the record, it is interesting to list his teammates: Doc Menard, Billy Strachan, Rod Kennedy, Pud Glass, Ernie Russell and Moose Johnson.

The Patrick family moved to new timber limits in Nelson, British Columbia, after Lester had been a member of three Stanley Cup winners, and he played in the Kootenays until the end of the 1909 season.

Financial recession hit the lumber industry in 1909 and Lester determined to play professional hockey. He offered to play for Art Ross's Montreal All-Stars for $1,200 but Ross was horrified by his financial demands and asked Lester if he thought that such money grew on trees. More in a spirit of levity than anything else, Lester told the Renfrew Millionaires that he would play for them for three thousand dollars. To his surprise, the Renfrew club met his demands and also offered to pay Frank Patrick two thousand dollars. Even by modern standards, the pay was excellent because the Millionaires had only a ten-game schedule.

It was in the summer of 1911 that the Patricks decided to introduce professional hockey to the West Coast by starting the Pacific Coast Hockey Association. Lester married that summer and, on his honeymoon trip, he investigated artificial ice rinks in the eastern United States. There's a betting item for you—the United States had artificial ice for hockey games before Canada had it. And the first hockey game on artificial ice in Canada was played in Victoria on January 3, 1912.

Then came the great era of western hockey, an era that lasted until the Patricks sold all their players to the National Hockey League in the summer of 1926. The Patricks, as we said, saw hockey as Big Business. They sold the game to new customers. They worked at it twelve months of the year, competing with vaudeville, motion pictures and every other form of entertainment in a moderate climate that, in those days, was believed to be unsuited to a winter sport such as hockey.

The Patricks were the first promoters in any sport to put numbers on the sweaters of their performers so that the players could be identified by the fans. They got the idea watching a large field of harriers competing in a cross-country race.

They amended the rules to suit themselves. They permitted a goalie to drop to the ice to stop the puck. They introduced substitutions. They introduced the blue lines in 1914. They invented the playoff system, which now has been copied by baseball.

Although he was owner and manager of the Victoria Cougars, Lester played regularly up until the beginning of the 1920s. He made a comeback in 1926 when two of his players were injured, but he retired permanently after his hand was broken by Bunny Cook at a game in Saskatoon.

Lester began a new life when he went to New York to manage the Rangers in the autumn of 1926. Now, twenty-three years later, he still is a vice-president of Madison Square Garden. In his time, he has been associated—as player or coach—with seven teams that won the Stanley Cup.

Lester doesn't believe in picking all-star teams, but he is willing to name the men whom he considered to be outstanding in the Pacific Coast and Western Canada Leagues between 1912 and 1926. He places Hughie "Eagle-Eye" Lehman in goal. His defencemen include Moose Johnson, Si Griffis, Herb Gardiner and Joe Simpson. His forwards include Dick Irvin, George Hay, Bill Cook, Duke Keats, Frank Fredrickson, Mickey MacKay and Cyclone Taylor.

At sixty-five, Lester isn't one of those men who pine for the Good Old Days, but he deplores modern hockey factories for youngsters—factories that sacrifice stickhandling ability. A brilliant raconteur, he has the story of Fifty Years of Hockey on the tip of his tongue and it will be a pity if he doesn't find the time to put that story on paper.

Ha! We fooled you! We finished this piece without mentioning the night that silver-haired Lester Patrick went into the New York Rangers net when the Rangers beat the Montreal Maroons in the 1928 Stanley Cup series.

Big Sam Hits the Road

Toronto *Globe and Mail*
July 1, 1949

The boy was leading a tired mare across the stabling area. She wore a halter, though she should have been wearing a bridle because it was obvious that she had just finished a race. She was sweating and blowing and the veins lumped out under her chestnut coat.

Johnny Needle-Nose tilted in his chair by the tack-room door and looked at the mare idly as her weary feet kicked up spurts of dust that hung in the hot summer air. Johnny squinted at his racing program and looked at the mare again, glancing, too, at the boy who was leading her.

"Joe Martin must have claimed Myrtle M. out of that race," he observed. "That means that Joe will have to get himself a new groom. Big Sam will be down the road within half an hour."

"Who's Big Sam?" we asked.

"You know him," said Needle-Nose, still looking after the mare as she disappeared round the corner of the barn. "Joe didn't get himself any bargain. She's as sore as a boil. You know Big Sam—he's that big old guy with hands like the bucket on a dragline. He'll walk by here in a few minutes, headed for the gate."

Knowing that a story always goes with it, we waited and sure enough Mr. Needle-Nose gave himself a small shot from the jug under his tilted chair and got on with it.

Big Sam had been around the tracks for thirty years—maybe forty years—and he was one of those grooms who arrived one morning and started to play nursemaid to the horses. He minded his own business. He didn't drink and, in a manner that is unusual around the racetracks, he banked his wages each week.

Those bucket-shaped hands of Big Sam's were extraordinarily powerful. Once he caught another groom rifling Sam's trunk in the tack room, and Big Sam grabbed the groom by the shoulder with one of those hands and held him while he bellowed for the track Pinkertons. When the Pinkies persuaded Sam to loosen his grip on the groom's shoulder, it was broken.

Johnny Needle-Nose remembered that when the horses shipped to Tropical and Hialeah in the winters, Big Sam nonchalantly would crush coconuts in his hands when he wanted to get at the meat of the nuts. Most powerful hands you ever saw.

The funny thing about it was that Big Sam, who never paid attention to any woman, finally tumbled for a little peroxided hasher in a coffee pot in Florida. Danged if he didn't up and marry her. He bought her a little cottage far enough from the track so that when he went home at nights he could get free of the smell of the shedrows. He turned over all his dough to her, too, and he seemed to be very happy.

Then came the summer, and Clay Copenhaver, for whom Big Sam was working, shipped his horses to Chicago for the season. The little blonde hasher didn't want to leave her Florida cottage and Big Sam went along alone. He sent her his dough each week and she wrote to him regularly. He used to tell the boys that his wife was really smart because she was investing all their money in railroad stocks and she was making profits hand over fist.

When Sportsmans closed down in the autumn, Copenhaver shipped back to Florida. The year was 1929 and the Copenhaver horses, with Big Sam as head groom, arrived in Florida about October 1.

You needn't look up your old newspaper files to recall what was happening to railroad stocks in the first two weeks of October 1929.

They had been back in Florida only three days when a couple of state troopers walked onto the track early one morning and grabbed Big Sam. The little blonde hasher had been found murdered in her cottage. The coppers said that her skull had been crushed "just as if it had been caught in a vice."

A woman in the house next door had heard the little blonde hasher scream the night before. She set the time at about ten o'clock. She said that she heard the blonde *start* to scream, and then it choked off suddenly. You might say that she suffered from an impediment in her screech.

The peculiar thing was that Big Sam couldn't possibly have been guilty. On that particular night he was sleeping in the tack room. Copenhaver had a sick horse and Big Sam never, under any circumstances, would leave the track when a horse was sick. He would stay right there, twenty-four hours a day, until the horse was better. Not only that, but the track veterinarian, who was a very respected man, remembered that he had driven his car around to Copenhaver's barn almost exactly at ten o'clock. He wanted to take another look at the sick horse before he shut up for the night.

The track veterinarian recalled distinctly that he had gone to Big Sam's tack room and had looked through the door. He had his flashlight with him and, as the beam circled the room, he could see the figure of Big Sam lying underneath the blankets. Big Sam couldn't possibly have been at that cottage, twenty miles away, at ten o'clock. And besides, he'd never leave a sick horse.

After the track vet told his story, the state troopers took the arm off Big Sam and they hung the rap on a couple of bums who had been picked up that night, sleeping in a "jungle" on the riverbank about three hundred yards from the little blonde hasher's cottage.

After the funeral, Big Sam quit Copenhaver and drifted away. Needle-Nose didn't see him again until three years later at Tia Juana.

The funny thing was that Big Sam had changed a lot. He had developed a peculiar distaste for the company of women. As a matter of fact, he wouldn't even eat in any hash house that employed waitresses.

His antipathy toward the opposite sex extended even to horses. He wouldn't take a job with any man who kept fillies or mares. This naturally cut down employment potentialities, but Big Sam was such an excellent groom that many a horseman cleaned the fillies and mares out of his barn, figuring that it was better to have Big Sam than a few female horses.

And you see, he was quitting this latest job because his employer had claimed Myrtle M.

"What did I tell you?" said Johnny Needle-Nose triumphantly, tilting the jug again. "Here he comes now. He's hitting the road."

We looked up in time to see a large old man shambling through the dust. He moved slowly but purposefully and he was carrying a suitcase and a sleeping bag about twice as big as any sleeping bag we'd seen before. The sleeping bag was almost as large as Big Sam.

"Ain't that the biggest sleeping bag you ever saw?" said Needle-Nose. "Sam's had that sleeping bag ever since I remember him. He keeps his money sewed in it now.

"Y' know," he said. "If you had a bed and put that sleeping bag on the bed and then covered it with a couple of blankets, you'd almost swear that Big Sam was in the bed."

Yeah, and if we ever catch up with that track vet in Florida, we'd like to ask him one question. We'd like to ask him if he opened the door of Big Sam's tack room that night or if he just shined his flashlight through the crack in the door. Any racetrackers we've known always latch the tack-room door on the *inside* when they go to sleep at night.

Well, we've only known Johnny Needle-Nose for twenty years. Perhaps when we've known him another twenty years, we'll be able to know when he's telling the truth or whether he's just kidding.

5

1950–51

Old Coot, Old Con

Toronto *Telegram*
November 11, 1950

The Good Kid has returned from his annual business tour of Canada and, although he isn't quite as optimistic as Finance Minister Douglas Abbott, he is reasonably confident concerning the future of the country. In his own circle, the Good Kid's opinions are believed to be more reliable than Babson's business reports or the monthly indices of the Dominion Bureau of Statistics.

The Good Kid is a carny and, in the past thirty years, he has conducted his annual business tours under the auspices of such celebrated firms as Johnny J. Jones Exposition, Rubin & Cherry Shows, Conklin & Garrett Shows and, latterly, Royal American Shows.

The Good Kid says that the current wheat crop is large but of mediocre quality and he adds that the current crop of suckers is large but of mediocre quality. Suckers, as any veteran carny will tell you, aren't confined to one particular section of the country; they bloom as vigorously in Quebec City as in St. Boniface, Manitoba.

Unfortunately, there is a widespread belief among many westerners to the effect that all easterners consider them to be suckers. There is a corresponding belief among many easterners that all westerners consider *them* to be suckers. As Ralph Allen, the distinguished editor of *Maclean's* magazine, observed after a particularly bitter East-West football argument: "What Canada needs more than anything else is Confederation."

Suckers aren't confined to any station of life. Any person is likely to prove to be a sucker if the buildup is sufficiently adroit.

Take the case of the Old Coot.

This happened some years ago in the lobby of the Prince George Hotel in Toronto, only a few blocks from where this piece is being written. It was the habit of sundry horsey characters to gather in the lobby each evening to discuss the day's affairs. The evening assemblage was composed of the most upright bookmakers and outstanding members of the gambling fraternity and associated arts.

These gentlemen discouraged strangers because after business hours, they were interested only in making friendly wagers among themselves. On the evening in question, they were discussing the lamentable fate of a three-to-five shot that had been delayed that afternoon at Woodbine.

None of them ever had seen the Old Coot before he shambled into the lobby. He wore an ancient stetson and a beaded Indian jacket and he was nudging the century mark. He looked so disreputable that the bellhop thought of giving him the heave-ho. However, the bellhop resumed his study of the *Racing Form*.

As the Old Coot came through the door, he was tugging on a long, heavy chain. There was silence and several boys cowered in fear as they expected to see a cougar at the end of that chain. But when the end of the chain came through the door, it was attached to a tiny, beaten-up spitz dog.

They did their best to ignore the Old Coot and his under-nourished spitz dog, but he sidled up to them and listened respectfully to their conversation. The chit-chat continued for some minutes before the Old Coot astounded them by asking, "Who was the greatest fighter who ever lived?"

Hoping to get rid of him, one of the boys snapped, "Jack Dempsey."

The Old Coot snorted in disgust.

The boys who were there still can't explain exactly how that it happened that, in a few seconds, all of them were bickering and finally, Bill

Long, who could outshout almost any man, insisted that Ruby Robert Fitzsimmons was the best of all fighters.

The Old Coot moved in gently. "Fitzsimmons didn't look so good the night that Jack Johnson kayoed him in 1907," he said.

"Ridiculous," scoffed Bill, who was official timer at Maple Leaf Gardens and Ontario racetracks. "Fitzsimmons was at least sixteen years older than Johnson. He would have been forty-five in 1907."

"Johnson knocked him out," persisted the Old Coot.

By this time all hands were thoroughly fed up with the Old Coot. Wishing to give him the immediate brush-off, Bill reached into his pocket and produced two fifty-dollar bills. "This," he said, "says that Johnson never fought Fitzsimmons."

"Bet!" barked the Old Coot and from his filthy clothing pulled a bundle of large, coarse notes.

Well, they all trooped to the old *Mail and Empire* building and asked Eddie Allan, the sports editor, to get out the book. Eddie produced the book and read them this shattering line: "Jack Johnson kayoed Bob Fitzsimmons in the second round in Philadelphia on July 17, 1907."

The Old Coot collected his money while willing friends led Long away, mumbling brokenly to himself. Slowly the Old Coot dragged his spitz dog across the sports department floor.

"Hey," Allan shouted after him, "how come you were so sure about that fight?"

The Old Coot turned and chuckled over his shoulder. "I was there," he said.

The Good Kid or any other well-travelled carny would have recognized him of course. It transpired that the Old Coot was a revered con man who went up and down the country with his big chain and little dog, winning bets on the long-forgotten Johnson–Fitzsimmons fight. He never tried it too often, just often enough to pay his modest living expenses.

Moral: if you're not too greedy, you can make an honest living.

Indian Jack and the Mud Bowl

Toronto *Telegram*
November 28, 1950

Jake Dunlap, an underprivileged lineman who was carrying fifty pounds of muddy excess baggage, broke up the ruddy ball game here Saturday as the Toronto Argonauts won another Grey Cup at the expense of the Winnipeg Blue Bombers.

Honest Jake was sloshing through the swamplands of University of Toronto Stadium when he was confronted by a football attached to the right shoe of Indian Jack Jacobs, the Winnipeg quarterback.

"What's the use of being beautiful as well as brilliant," philosophized Honest Jake and courageously stuck out his bare face and kissed the toe of Jacobs's boot.

The ball sagged and nearly burst as Honest Jake lapsed into a temporary coma. The ball whimpered, lay still and was recovered by Jack Wedley, another Argonaut who had been fording a stream on the 20-yard line. A few seconds later, the Argonauts scored the touchdown that gave them a 12–0 lead and the strangely inept Blue Bombers were faced with the fact that they've never been able to beat a Toronto team in seven Grey Cup trips.

The game—as they referred to it laughingly—might as well have been played in the guano-loaded hold of a storm-tossed corvette. The winds howled; the whitecaps crashed on the sidelines; and the only manifestations of nature's wrath that were lacking were forest fire and earthquake.

The spectacle must have provided a perverse chuckle for Johnny Peterson, who receives his daily quota of insults concerning the condition of his Osborne Stadium in Winnipeg. Compared with University of Toronto Stadium, dear old Osborne was as immaculate as the lawns in the Cedars of Lebanon Cemetery.

The Bombers were outplayed scandalously. For the second year in a row, quarterbacking decided the Grey Cup game. One year ago, Frank Filchock out-general-ed Keith Spaith and the Montreal Alouettes beat the Calgary Stampeders. On Saturday Al Dekdebrun out-general-ed the veteran Jack Jacobs and today the waters of the Assiniboine and Red Rivers are aflood with blood.

It would be hard to convince a Toronto audience that the Bombers dominated Western Canada football so completely in the past three months. The truth of it is that Saturday's Winnipeg team wasn't the same Winnipeg team that won the prairie championship. Somewhere in the space of twelve days they lost their poise and initiative.

They went through the motions on Saturday afternoon but they played without any lift or drive and they received uninspiring leadership from Jacobs, who had a thoroughly miserable day.

Jacobs had a total of only three pass interceptions registered against him during the regular season. On Saturday, the Argonauts intercepted two of his slovenly tosses. The sure-handed Jacobs fumbled seldom during the regular schedule, yet on Saturday he fumbled twice and those fumbles and interceptions contributed heavily to the Toronto triumph. Jacobs is the best kicker to be seen in the West, yet on Saturday he was outkicked consistently by Joe Krol.

Jacobs's chief contributions were confined to a couple of fine tackles and a running exchange of insults with the Argonaut benchwarmers, an occupation from which he appeared to derive a negative form of amusement.

Bud Tinsley, rated by many critics as the best lineman ever to appear in western Canada, was mousetrapped regularly by the eager Argonaut linemen before he was forced out of action by a twisted knee. Of the Winnipeg imports, only Joe Aguirre and John Brown covered themselves with glory as well as mud and Brown left the slot open frequently as he drifted to protect the weak side of the line.

The Argonauts displayed all things that the Winnipeg team lacked. They charged fiercely and they defended tenaciously. They showed excellent competitive spirit and they were alert. Despite the obvious limitations of the playing conditions they showed an imaginative offensive and they made no mistakes.

The Winnipegs spent most of their time in their own section of the field as if they were reluctant to risk their lives in alien territory. They threatened only once and that was in the fourth quarter when a lowly substitute named Pete Petrow replaced the mighty Jacobs. Petrow fired a pass to Bud Korchak, who made a remarkable catch. On the next play George McPhail broke through on a quick opening play, cut for the east sideline and sprinted all the way to the Argonaut 20 where Nick Volpe snagged him with a despairing tackle.

The mutterings over the field were justified in that the record crowd was deprived of an opportunity to watch Canada's greatest annual sports spectacle in a proper setting.

Neither team had a chance to display its actual ability. Your correspondent maintains stubbornly that the Argos and Bombers probably would have scored fifty or sixty points between them if they hadn't been forced to equip themselves with water wings and outboard motors.

The much-abused Canadian Rugby Union must bear the blame for the fact that Saturday's schmozzle was one of the dullest contests in Grey Cup history. For an expenditure of eight to ten thousand dollars a tarpaulin could have been provided to assure the success of the eighty-thousand-dollar sports production.

Winnipeg owes much to the generosity of eastern Canadians who rallied to their assistance when their city was inundated by last summer's floods. The Winnipeggers haven't forgotten such generosity.

As a reciprocal goodwill gesture they're starting their own flood relief fund for University of Toronto Stadium.

Andy Waits It Out

Toronto *Telegram*
November 30, 1950

THE FLOOD wasn't too much for Andy Robinson. Andy has lived around the racetracks all his life and, at the age of eighty-two, little things such as floods, famine, pestilence and death have lost their impact. This flood was different though—cold, vicious and utterly devastating. It swept smoothly and mercilessly across the countryside and even a wiry old man such as Andy Robinson couldn't expect to survive alone.

Before you hear of The Flood, you should know something of Andy Robinson who, if he couldn't beat The Flood, at least retreated with dignity and honour to fight another day.

Andy is a symbol—a symbol of the best things in the business of breeding, raising and racing horses. Andy has known horses ever since he was born in Ailsa Craig, Ontario. He has the instinctive gentleness of men who have spent their lives with horses and respect them.

Andy knows The River as well as he knows the backs of his gnarled hands. He went to Winnipeg in 1896. As far back as 1902, he had trained Loughderg, a horse that won the $2,500 autumn stake at Winnipeg, beating Moses by a lip after they had fought it out over nine heartbreaking furlongs. He owned probably the best western-breds, a rugged old gelding named Madgu Don that had the same equable temperament as his owner. In the West, they'll tell you that when another man claimed Madgu Don from Andy, the distraught old horse ran away and committed suicide by crashing head-on into a truck.

It was inevitable that Andy Robinson should return to The River when his racing days were over. Jim Speers built him a little private apartment in the winter barn at Whittier Park, just where The River elbows between St. Boniface and Winnipeg.

When old Andy moved back to spend the remainder of his life beside The River, Whittier Park had lost its glory. The once immaculate lawns were matted and tangled. The grandstand was an empty shell; the windows of the clubhouse were boarded; and the jocks' room echoed only to the clatter of forgotten ghosts.

But in the winter, there was life in the barns. As Andy lay in bed at night, listening to the steady ticking of the clock, he could hear the yearlings stirring in their stalls, restlessly awaiting their destiny. The winters went swiftly for Andy and the summers lingered as The River quietly swept past the door.

The first morning that Andy saw The River creeping over the fence at the lower eastern end of Whittier Park, he called to a couple of swipes and told them to get the horses ready for the van. He went into his apartment and telephoned for the van and then he sat down and took a long look around his little home. Looking at him from the pictures on the wall were Madgu Don and his champions from the past.

They moved the horses that night and Andy sat down with a small bottle of cough medicine and listened to the flood reports on the radio. The military commander of the district was ordering the immediate evacuation of every person from the zone. Andy simply turned off the radio and went to sleep.

The River surrounded him, under cover of darkness. It slithered under his door. Even then Andy wasn't going to leave but Harry Jeffries, the van man, came down from the high railway grade to evacuate him. Andy went out of there, through the deep water, but he went under his own power.

At the top of the railway grade he looked back. At the age of eighty-two, it isn't easy for a man to leave his only home.

By that night The River was up to the roofs of the barns. The nervous searchlights that swept the ominously silent waters that night picked out only the gaunt frame of the upper grandstand in that wilderness.

It ended of course. Eventually, The River's outburst of violence was exhausted and the waters relaxed. Andy watched the waters recede inch by inch, foot by foot, and as The River vacated his little apartment, he walked back into it. Old Madgu Don looked down at him reassuringly—the picture had been mere inches above the waterline.

Andy hitched up his radio, cleared up the mess and checked off the calendar as he prepared to wait for the winter when the horses would return to Whittier. Lonely, you might ask? How can a man be lonely with his memories?

He was there alone on the night that The Big Wind came perilously close to completing the damage caused by The River. It was the greatest cyclone in thirty-five years and Andy sat there alone in gloomy Whittier Park while the lightning struck wickedly and the thunder rocketed crazily down the jagged streaks of flame. The back wall was ripped from the grandstand and the squat barns shuddered and moaned like human beings.

There isn't much left of Whittier Park now. The jocks' room is gone. The grandstand is crumbling. The barns are desperately in need of paint.

Andy is a symbol, we said—a symbol of human indomitability in a small corner of the world where steel and wood and stone have succumbed to the battering of the elements.

The horses moved back into Whittier a few weeks ago. When Andy shuts off his radio and flips the light switch he can hear the horses pawing and the barn is warm with life. He sleeps well.

Dib, Dib, Dib

Toronto *Telegram*
January 23, 1951

WINNIPEG—It is singularly appropriate that your agent should be in Winnipeg on the eve of the annual national appeal for funds launched by the Boy Scout Association. It is appropriate, I say, because my entire association with the Boy Scout movement was confined to the city of Winnipeg and the period of affiliation was unfortunately very brief. To be specific, I never won promotion to the Boy Scouts, having flunked out of the Wolf Cubs ignominiously.

Come to think of it, the manpower situation in the St. Luke's Church Wolf Cub Pack must have been deplorable that year. I was a "ringer." St. Luke's Church was, and is, situated in Fort Rouge and I lived on the other side of town at the Royal Alexandra Hotel on the corner of Main Street and Higgins Avenue. The journey from the Royal Alex to St. Luke's on the Park Line trolley was long and perilous and the Park Line car, which had a tendency to yaw on the turns, was no conveyance for an impressionable boy with a nervous stomach. The Winnipeg electric cars of that period were disinfected with something brewed by the witches in *Macbeth*. This peculiar aroma, when combined with the effluvia of wet Buffalo overcoats on a snowy winter night, was enough to grow barnacles in your nasal passages.

I was sponsored in the St. Luke's pack by a couple of young gentlemen with whom I played hockey. The Cub master flinched as he looked at me, with my hands dangling by my knees and my eyes staring at him myopically from behind thick spectacles. Shuddering ever so slightly, he signed me up. As I said, the manpower shortage must have been acute.

The first occasion on which I disgraced the St. Luke's pack was when the late Lord Baden-Powell visited Winnipeg. All the Scouts and Cubs in the city paraded from the corner of Main and Assiniboine by way of Portage Avenue to City Park. The manly little fellows stuck out their chests and clomped along dutifully. Unfortunately, I had an unmilitary, loping gait inherited from some Cree ancestor. Furthermore, I have a tendency to march with my nose only eighteen inches from the ground, in a manner reminiscent of a bloodhound following the spoor of a rogue elephant. My Cub master professed to overlook this eyesore in his disciplined ranks but I wounded him by waving cheerfully and exchanging badinage with some of my rougher friends from the North End who followed the route of the march, hurling small boulders and chunks of coal at the columns.

After that, I was assigned to orderly room duty whenever a parade was imminent, but the handwriting was on the wall. My days in the Boy Scout movement were numbered.

It was that good-deed business that really finished me as a member of the St. Luke's pack. In order to stay in the racket, it was necessary to give the details of at least one good deed you had performed during the week. The truth of the matter is that when the other Cubs were out piously performing their good deeds I was sitting at home slothfully in the Royal Alex, reading copies of *Chums* or the *Boy's Own Paper.* At other times, I was reading the past performance charts in the Winnipeg *Turf Digest,* which My Old Man had secreted behind his bound volumes of *Blackwood's Magazine.*

Additionally, I had fallen under the spell of an older boy named White, who also lived in the Royal Alex. White had a .22 rifle and we enlivened dull afternoons by leaning from a fourth-floor window and shooting out lights in the bedrooms of the Alberta Hotel just down the block.

In any event, White taught me one thing I certainly couldn't have learned in the Wolf Cubs. He showed me how to extract the nickels out of the coin boxes in the pay telephones in the lobby of the Royal Alex.

Naturally, such an exhausting schedule gave me little time for good deeds. I was forced to rely upon my imagination when the Cub master asked me to report on my weekly good deed.

"This afternoon," I would lisp, "I helped a blind woman to cross the street at the corner of Broadway and Sherbrooke."

Each week I reported that I had helped a blind woman to cross some dangerous intersection. The Cub master's approbation turned to suspicion. He began quizzing me concerning the exact hours and locations of my good deeds. He checked the civic census to obtain accurate figures on the blind population of Winnipeg.

Some mealy-mouthed little snitch finally peached on me. The Cub master learned that, at the precise moment when I was supposed to have been helping a blind woman across the corner of Higgins and

Main, I had been observed entering the Monarch Theatre carrying a bag of humbugs and a peashooter.

Mercifully, very little was said about it in the newspapers. They just stripped me of my green-and-yellow neckerchief, made me turn in my pathfinders badge and cast me out into the cruel world.

I went downhill swiftly after that.

I spent a couple of years playing the piano in that place in Port Alberni, and then I sank to the abysmal depths of the newspaper profession.

I am sure that the Boy Scout movement would have made a better man of me. If I had played the game at St. Luke's, I'd probably be a wealthy stockbroker by now.

Mr. Chick, Meet Mr. Goose

Toronto *Telegram*
April 7, 1951

MONTREAL—HOCKEY PLAYOFFS are becoming rather cut-and-dried affairs. Even the characters who write about hockey players seem to have lost their zest. Your agent looked around the press box the other night and we saw the same crew of characters who were writing about hockey and other sports ten years ago. They were the same guys but somehow they appeared to be a bit older and a bit greyer and a bit grimmer. Strange that they should look like that, because there wasn't a guy in the crowd who wasn't born with a song in his heart.

Sportswriters are the perennial adolescents of the writing world and, if that is a charge, it is one to which your agent would plead guilty.

Looking down that line of austere characters, correctly attired in their navy blue overcoats and homburg hats, there wasn't a guy in whose head we couldn't have found a large hole. There was, for instance, the very sober chappie who in his palmier days used to bite his initials, without any warning, in the arms of chorus girls who happened to sit at our restaurant table.

We couldn't help recalling the Toronto–Detroit series when first we were exposed to Onkel Jonkheer DeGeer, a little guy who had been fired out of a cannon from Mars and just happened to land on earth.

He walked into our apartment one morning with a see-gar jutting from one corner of his kisser and the imps of hell jutting from his eyes. The next thing we knew, we were down in Toronto's Chinatown purchasing a large and vigorous goose, which we wrapped in a newspaper. A few minutes later we were being borne upward in the Royal York Hotel elevator, loaded with citizens of some considerable importance.

The goose was concealed beneath the folds of newspaper but, in the manner of his kind, he chose that moment to say, "Quack! Quack! Quack!"

Until the day we die we will recall the spectacle of DeGeer solemnly removing the cigar from his mouth, staring at a thoroughly respectable dowager who was built on the generous proportions of Mae West and saying sternly, "Madam, were you responsible for that unseemly noise?"

Well, we spirited the goose into the suite of Red Dutton who at that time was the president of the National Hockey League. We shoved the goose into Dutton's bathtub, gave him three or four inches of water in which to swim and then drew the shower curtain to hide him.

It was some hours later that Mr. Dutton went into his bathroom to shave. He was lathering his face when suddenly he heard, "Quack! Quack! Quack!" from behind the shower curtain.

The maid on that particular floor was treated to the spectacle of the president of the National Hockey League, clad only in his underwear shorts, pursuing a very startled goose down the corridor. Fortunately for herself, the chambermaid gave a small scream and fainted dead away.

Well, your agent gave the maid a shot of Benzedrine, rescued the goose and hid it in the bathroom of John Digby Chick, the very large and very dignified president of the American Hockey League.

John Digby had been out with the boys and he didn't arrive in his room until a very late hour. He was giving himself a small final libation of hair lotion when he heard, "Quack! Quack! Quack!" from his bathroom. Mr. Chick picked up the bottle of hair tonic, threw it out the window and vowed that he'd never touch the stuff again.

Some minutes later, Mr. Chick felt it expedient to perform his nightly ablutions and he strode into the bathroom.

He was perusing a copy of *Time* magazine when the goose reached around the corner of the shower curtain and bit him on his portly thigh.

Summoning what was left of his dignity, Mr. Chick stalked to the phone and asked to be connected with the house detective.

"Come up here immediately," said Mr. Chick. "There's a goose in my bathtub."

The house officer, who was a serious-minded member of the hotel's criminal investigation department, referred the call to the assistant manager on duty.

"Come up here!" screamed Mr. Chick. "I have a goose in my bathtub!"

"Now, now, Mr. Chick!" laughed the assistant manager indulgently. "You go on to bed and everything will be tip-top in the morning."

"Listen," said Mr. Chick patiently, "if I had a blonde in my room, there'd be three house detectives here in fifteen seconds. Now, all I'm asking you to do is get a goose out of my bathtub."

Well, the upshot of it was that the assistant manager and two house officers removed the goose from the bathtub and the assistant manager ate the goose for lunch the next day.

And looking down the line at our confreres the other night, we wondered about this and we wondered if the grave is so close that all of us have forgotten how to laugh.

One-Day Wonder

Toronto *Telegram*
April 10, 1951

SPRING CAUGHT UP WITH THE HOCKEY SEASON this year and the sun was crackling over Woodbine the other morning at a time when, in the downtown section of Toronto, men and women were yapping and yawping for hockey tickets. It was one of the first dry days and Johnny Needle-Nose was taking advantage of the fine weather to scrub his good old leather tack industriously with saddle soap. The Blow-Back Kid peered mournfully from a stall door—a stall that quartered one of their three patched-up pieces of equine crow-bait.

Blow-Back shaded his eyes to peer at a two-year-old being guided through the Gap by a fair-haired youngster.

"Good seat on that punk," mused Blow-Back. "And a good pair of hands, too. I watched him galloping a couple of Whitey's yesterday morning. Looked as if he'd been horsebacking ever since the day he was foaled."

"Hmmm," answered Johnny Needle-Nose noncommittally, continuing to rub the beautiful leather.

"Someday I'm going to pick me up a punk like that Joe Culmone and teach him the trade," said Blow-Back, jingling the change in his pocket. "Then I'll sell his contract to some wealthy outfit and retire to the South Seas and live surrounded by beautiful dancing girls and bananas."

"Hmmm," said Johnny Needle-Nose. "You'd never grab yourself a Culmone. You'd probably grab yourself one of those One-Day Wonders like Charlie Thompson."

"I recognize the face but I don't know where to put it," said Blow-Back, squinting into the sun to watch another set of horses coming in from a late gallop.

"The kid who rode Behave Yourself in the 1921 Kentucky Derby," explained Needle-Nose. "You know, the egg who beat his boss out of a five-hundred-thousand-dollar bet."

So it was thirty years ago next month that an excited youngster on a fast horse cost his employer a fortune and, after a brief hour of spurious glory, disappeared from the major racing scene.

In the spring of 1921, the late Colonel E.R. Bradley had two candidates for the running of the Kentucky Derby. The colonel loved to win a wager and secretly he and his trainer, Derby Dick Thompson, had been testing the two candidates. The better of the two, in all their trials, was a handsome black colt named Black Servant. Bradley, Thompson and their farm manager, Barry Shannon, were convinced that Black Servant was the best colt they'd ever handled.

Throughout the spring Bradley wagered heavily on Black Servant in the Winter Books. He wagered so extensively that, on the day of the race, he would collect five hundred thousand dollars if Black Servant won.

In accordance with the custom of the Bradley establishment, they entered two horses in the race. They entered Behave Yourself to act as the pacesetter for Black Servant. Bradley hadn't bet a nickel on Behave Yourself.

Then fate and Charlie Thompson stepped into the picture.

Lawrence Lyke, the riding star of the Bradley Stable, was assigned to pilot Black Servant. Thompson, who was little more than a second-string exercise boy in the Bradley establishment, was given the mount on Behave Yourself.

Derby Dick carefully gave instructions to both boys in the paddock before the race. Thompson was told to set a fast pace on Behave Yourself while Lyke was to keep within striking distance on Black Servant.

Little Thompson whipped his mount away from the barrier and Behave Yourself was a runnin' hoss that afternoon. He widened on his field as they swept down the backstretch and, even when they turned for home, he showed no signs of chucking it.

Perhaps Lyke—on Black Servant—became desperate. Perhaps little Thompson was over excited. In any event, both boys went to the whip and they ding-donged through the stretch with Behave Yourself still inches in front as they passed the finish line.

Colonel Bradley was a gambler who prided himself on the fact that he never betrayed emotion. No one knows for certain the thoughts that went through his mind as he leaned forward in his chair and watched his own horse, Behave Yourself, beat him out of five hundred thousand dollars in bets.

Smiling grimly, he accepted the applause of the great crowd that greeted another Bradley Derby victory. After all, Bradley bred his horses in Kentucky and the Hardboots were ready to overlook the fact that Bradley hadn't been born in the state.

No one knows for certain, either, the emotion with which Bradley congratulated his young jockey after the race. Then, in a final ironic gesture, Bradley gave Charlie Thompson a cheque for five thousand dollars as a bonus for winning the race.

"What became of that chucklehead Thompson?" said Blow-Back, turning his trouser pockets inside-out fruitlessly after Johnny Needle-Nose finished the story.

"Hmmm?" murmured Needle-Nose, giving the saddle a final rub. "Oh, he's probably living down in the South Seas, surrounded by dancing girls and bananas."

My Old Man

Toronto *Telegram*
June 16, 1951

Tomorrow is Father's Day, but if my children neglect to give me a Cadillac convertible I shall be willing to forgive them. After all, I've never given much to My Old Man, unless it was a severe headache. Come to think of it, things always were the other way around: My Old Man was giving and the rest of us were receiving.

There was pleasure in receiving, too, because all of us realized the purely generous and affectionate motives behind the giving. Things worked out that way. My Old Man comes from what is popularly described as "poor but honest Irish stock." My Old Man never had time to play because he went to work too young and he worked too hard on his way to the top. But he wanted the rest of us to have all the things he had missed. Looking back on it now, I realize that I inherited my love of sport from him and, if there are times when he regrets that I became a sportswriter, he has only his own indulgence to blame for that.

I remember him playing soccer with me in our yard on Donald Street in Winnipeg. Once I broke his little finger when he tried to stop a shot. He took me to watch the Falcons and on Saturday afternoons we went to the Mercantile and Commercial Hockey League doubleheaders. Then there was the Big Four League that embraced the CPR, the CNR, Eaton's and Hudson's Bay.

Even now he never says much at sporting events. But one night the CP was playing the CN and, because My Old Man was a CP man, we were even quieter than usual. Then the CP team scored four goals in two minutes and My Old Man jumped up and lifted his hat and cane in the air and shouted "Hurray!"—and sat down again quickly. Just like that!

He could do wonderful things. Suddenly, I would be sent off to Regina alone, in the care of the sleeping-car conductor, and one of My Old Man's friends would meet me and I'd be watching the Regina Caps play the Vancouver Millionaires for the western professional hockey championship. When I was away at school in Victoria, wires would arrive from his office in Winnipeg, and I'd be watching the Victoria Cougars beating the Montreal Canadiens for the Stanley Cup, or I'd be on the night boat headed for Vancouver to see the Allan Cup finals.

Then there were those business trips on which he took me. They were business trips but somehow we'd arrive in Detroit just in time to see the Tigers play the Philadelphia Athletics. When we reached St. Louis, who should be playing there but Babe Ruth and the New York Yankees? We'd arrive in Chicago with the Washington Senators. It was just coincidence that Charles "the Old Roman" Comiskey had sent us tickets for the baseball game.

It just so happened, too, that My Old Man had some cough syrup secreted on his railway car. It was a type of cough syrup that the Old Roman wasn't able to obtain in those days of the Volstead Act. My Old Man heard that Mr. Comiskey's cough was bothering him, so he sent him a bottle of syrup. The next day we received a lifetime pass to Comiskey Park.

I can't remember exactly when My Old Man first took me to the racetrack but I can tell you all about Jingo and Prairie and Olds Eight and Lucky Hayes. Once we were on a business trip to Victoria and My Old Man sent a friend and me out to Willows Park with instructions to bet two dollars on each of his selections. The name of the first horse was Trulane and it paid $237.45 and the next horse was Quiparo, which paid $36.

It was My Old Man who first showed me Saratoga in the morning. He got me up and we went out to the track and sat alone in the rambling old stands while the sun climbed over the elms and the colts galloped past in ones and twos, scarcely disturbing the birds that perched on the white-painted inner rail. He didn't ask me to leave but just sat there watching me while I watched the horses. I know I'll never forget that morning.

I like to remember another thing after My Old Man reached his business goal. After lunch each day, his chauffeur would usher him into the back seat of the car. As the gears meshed smoothly and coasted down Côte-des-Neiges, the chauffeur would reach on the seat beside him, pick up a copy of the *Daily Racing Form* and courteously hand it back to My Old Man, who would read all the way to his office.

He's retired now and the afternoons are long and sunny. I know where he'll be this very afternoon. He'll be sitting at Blue Bonnets and I can see him looking out contentedly because, even if they aren't the best horses in the world, they're horses.

Tomorrow's Father's Day and there's no point in me sending a tie or a book or a telegram. If My Old Man happens to see this, I'm sure that he'll be glad enough to know that I've remembered all these things.

I said that he wanted us to have all the things he missed. But the way I feel about it is that he never missed anything that was worthwhile.

Poppa Tongay's Great Idea

Toronto *Telegram*
June 28, 1951

COME ON, KIDDIES, eat up all your nice mushy slumgullion and old Uncle Jim will tell you a true story about the cute little Tongay children, who went all the way across the Atlantic Ocean to swim the great, big, bad English Channel.

Now Poppa and Momma Tongay have two of the sweetest, prettiest children you'd ever care to see. The younger is named Kathy and she is only four. The older is named Bubba. (Pardon me—I'll come right back to the microphone as soon as I find something to settle my stomach.)

Well, the older is named Bubba, which is a cute pronunciation of the word "brother." It comes out that way sometimes if you're not wearing your teeth. Bubba (ugh) is only five years old.

Poppa and Momma Tongay taught Kathy and Bubba (ugh) to swim when they were just tiny tads. ("Tads" is a cute abbreviation for tadpoles or baby frogs.) Of course there is no frog in the Tongay tads. No *sir*—and no canary, either.

Well, kiddies, the Tongay tads took to water just as a Litvak takes to apple strudel. Poppa Tongay started to teach them to swim when they were just old enough to drink their own bathwater. (Florida bathwater, like everything else in Florida, is of course better and more expensive than in any other part of the world. Not just *ordinary* bathwater—No siree!)

Before you could say "Wilbur Maloney is a mealy-mouthed little snitch," the Tongay tads were swimming up and down their jolly old bathtub as fast as fast can be. They uttered merry cries and bumped their little heads against the faucets but they didn't give a darn.

Poppa Tongay bought a pair of goldfish and put them in the tub to swim races against Kathy and Bubba. (Hmmm, I must be getting accustomed to that name.) But the goldfish were no match for clever little Kathy and Bubba and soon the goldfish were whimpering and crying for mercy. The goldfish usually were all tuckered out after three or four laps.

Kathy and Bubba outgrew their bathtub. They were kicking each other in the stomach when making their racing turns. So Poppa Tongay tried them out in a few neighbouring rivers and lakes. They were swimming several hundred yards, long before they could talk, but this is only natural because it is almost impossible to learn to talk if you swallow several gallons of water every time you open your mouth.

They spent so much time in the water that they couldn't go to sleep in their own little beds each night unless Momma Tongay sprinkled them gently with a garden hose.

One evening, Poppa Tongay was sitting in his chair in front of the television set when a great idea struck him. Gee, it was funny how the idea struck him, kiddies. The water from Momma Tongay's garden hose in the tads' bedroom upstairs loosened the plaster on the ceiling and a big chunk of plaster fell and hit Poppa Tongay right on his head—kerplunk!

Poppa Tongay wiped the plaster out of his ears with a cheery laugh. (If you ain't seen Tongay employing a cheery laugh to wipe plaster out of his ears, you ain't seen nothing.)

"Gee, that gives me a great idea," he said, snapping his fingers. "I'll take Kathy and Bubba across the ocean to swim the great, big, bad English Channel. Oh boy. Oh boy. Will we make money? We'll get our pictures in the papers and in the newsreels and maybe on the television. Look at what that Shirley May France did last year. She got her picture in the papers for *not* swimming the English Channel. Of course, Shirley looked better than Kathy or Bubba in a bathing suit."

And so, kiddies, that's why little Kathy and Bubba Tongay went all the way across the wide ocean.

Won't those little Tongay tads have peachy fun?

Well, old Uncle Jim, who was a sourpuss right down to here, isn't so sure that the Tongay tads will have peachy fun.

The English Channel is considerably rougher than the Tongay family bathtub and considerably rougher than the water around Florida's Everglades. The only time old Uncle Jim tried the Channel, he was on a big boat that bucked and sunfished and whinnied and hollered like a western cayuse. Doggone it, kiddies, old Uncle Jim didn't feel like eating for three or four days.

Of course, Poppa Tongay won't mind because *he* won't have to swim the Channel. He'll be following Kathy and Bubba in a boat and he'll be eating bananas and drinking hot coffee to keep up his strength.

Do you know what old Uncle Jim hopes, kiddies? Old Uncle Jim hopes that a great big nasty shark leans over the side of Poppa Tongay's boat and grabs him by the leg and pulls him into the Channel and eats him all up into little eensy-weensy pieces. That's what Uncle Jim hopes.

Yes, I do. Yes, I do.

6

1958–61

The Great Hawaiian Football Fix

Toronto *Globe and Mail*
February 1, 1958

A GENTLEMAN SLIGHTLY AWASH IN THE GRAPE floated past me at the Sports Celebrities Dinner last Monday night and complained that he lost a wager of five hundred dollars when the Detroit Red Wings defeated the Montreal Canadiens 4–2 in a hockey match that had been played the previous Saturday evening. The gentleman insisted loudly that the game had been "in the sack" for the Detroiters before the teams skated onto the ice. This came as a great shock to me as I didn't know that the hockey rinks were equipped with parimutuel machines. And most certainly no respectable bookmaker would be engaging in the highly illegal practice of accepting wagers on hockey games.

Please don't get the impression that I paid any attention to the gentleman's demands for the immediate appointment of a Royal Commission to investigate the activities of the National Hockey League. Although I have gambled—legally and illegally—for thirty years and have suffered many grievous misfortunes as a result of these ventures, I am convinced that 99.9 percent of all athletic events are on the up and up. (I must remember to tell you about Irish Davy and Big Bear.)

Scott Young was reminding me recently that, not so many years ago, several of our mutual friends were involved in a "fixed" football game in Honolulu. (In the following recountal, fictitious names will be used, to protect the innocent.)

The residents of Honolulu were relatively unsophisticated as far as football was concerned, when a team known as the Honolulu Warriors performed in that city shortly after the Second World War. However, the Hawaiians went batty over the Warriors and regarded them as the greatest football machine ever to be assembled.

The Warriors were scheduled to conclude their season by playing the All-Stars, a pickup team composed mainly of semi-professionals from the United States mainland. Several days before the game, the Warriors were approached by the representative of a Honolulu gambling syndicate. He addressed them along the following lines: "Red-blooded fellow Americans, these Honolulu citizens are so buggy that you are certain to be at least two-to-one favourites in the game. We suggest that you should lose this game. You can become very wealthy by betting on your opponents. You will be able to purchase chateaux in the south of France and you will spend the remainder of your lives surrounded by beautiful dolls. We will arrange to make large bets for you on the opposing team."

The Warrior players hadn't managed to save any money during the season. The gamblers' proposition was attractive. It was so attractive, in fact, that the Warrior players robbed their piggy banks and bet their *own* money on the All-Stars. The gamblers, of course, were very honourable men and lived up to their pledge to wager on the "fixed" game.

The Warriors did their best to lose the game but the All-Stars, who had spent the entire previous night training industriously in a bar, offered little in the way of co-operation.

The game was pointless for twenty-five minutes until the All-Stars fumbled behind their own goal line. The Warrior right guard had charged across the goal line and recoiled in horror when he saw the ball lying on the ground in front of him. He circled the ball in the manner of a reluctant seagull. The Warrior left guard also had charged across the line. He attempted to stop but collided with his teammate. The right guard fell on the ball for a touchdown.

The score: Warriors 6, All-Stars 0.

Panic-stricken, the Warriors obligingly missed the convert by kicking the ball into the line of scrimmage. Throughout the remainder of the game, the Warriors quarterback threw forward passes directly at All-Star defenders. The All-Stars, still reeling after their night of pleasure, were so inept that they couldn't intercept the ball. The Warriors deliberately missed tackles but the All-Star ball-carriers fell, exhausted.

Final score: Warriors 6, All-Stars 0.

The irony of it all is that the Warriors emerged as heroes. The Honolulu citizens swarmed out of the stands, tore down the goalposts and bore the Warriors players triumphantly to their bus. The Honolulu spectators couldn't understand why the players seemed so dejected in their hour of victory.

As a final twist, the Warrior players who were going to their homes in the United States after the game were forced to ask for a police escort to the boat. Professional gamblers occasionally become very narrow-minded when they lose large bets.

The moral of this little story: never bet on "fixed" football games.

It happened, honest! You can look it up in the newspaper files.

Then there was the case of our old friend, Irish Davy Ambersley and the horse that was running in a steeplechase at Chicago many years ago. Big Bear was the *only* starter and, just for the heck of it, the bookmakers laid a price of one-to-one-hundred that Big Bear wouldn't complete the course.

Irish Davy always had longed to bet on a sure-pop cinch, so he bet two hundred dollars himself to win two dollars.

Big Bear fell at the tenth jump and broke his neck. He broke Irish Davy, too.

The Rocket's Red Glare

Toronto *Globe and Mail*
April 19, 1958

It will be quite appropriate if the goal that wins the Stanley Cup is scored in Boston on Sunday night by that incomparable performer, Maurice Richard. Even in the twilight of his career, it is quite evident that Richard is the greatest individual star ever to appear in the National Hockey League. Before tucking themselves between the sheets each night, owners of hockey clubs should utter a few words of thanks for the fact that the flaming brilliance of Maurice Richard has maintained hockey's popularity in an era when other spectator sports were beginning to feel the financial pinch.

You will note, I trust, that I used the words "greatest individual star" when describing M. Richard. Very carefully, I avoided the use of the phrase "the greatest hockey player."

There are purists who will tell you that Gordie Howe is the peer of Richard as a hockey player. Some years ago, Lloyd Percival, the Toronto muscle detective, conducted a series of tests that proved to Percival's satisfaction that Howe's physical ability was greater than Richard's.

All of which probably is true and all of which, as far as I am concerned, is for the birds. Give me Maurice Richard and I'll fill every hockey rink in North America. Give me an entire team of Gordie Howes and I'll have the greatest hockey team in history—but how would they do at the box office?

None of this is intended to disparage Gordie Howe, who is a magnificent hockey player. I have seen many others who could be rated ahead of Richard on technical ability. Just to mention a few, I would name Bill Cook, Eddie Shore, Aurel Joliat and Howie Morenz.

I remember, years ago, my father telling me that if he could select just one player around whom to build a team, he'd take King Clancy of the Ottawa Senators. Conn Smythe must have been of the same mind because Smythe always has said that his best deal was the purchase of Clancy for the Toronto Maple Leafs. Technically, there were better defencemen than Clancy. But Clancy had colour and fire and dash and provided inspirational leadership on the ice.

For a parallel with the case of Richard and Howe, it is necessary to take a look at baseball when Babe Ruth and Lou Gehrig were teammates on the New York Yankees. Manager Miller Huggins always said that, on a day-to-day basis, Gehrig was the better ballplayer. But it was the mighty Ruth who drew the spectators into the ballparks. Ruth was the Maurice Richard of baseball—he could hit the big ones.

Mild-mannered old Connie Mack was appraising Ruth one day. "My, my," said Mr. Mack admiringly, "even when Ruth strikes out, he scares you to death."

Ruth's individual brilliance is credited with saving baseball after the

Black Sox scandal. He inspired some of sports' most colourful legends. Hard-pressed television commentators seldom fail to mention the afternoon that a Chicago Cubs crowd was heckling Ruth during a World Series. Ruth, grinning at his tormentors, pointed toward distant right field and hit the next pitch into the bleachers for a home run.

Richard has been professional hockey's greatest single asset in the past sixteen years. His name has attracted hundreds of thousands of new spectators. To be truthful, the most recent converts to hockey know little of the niceties of the game. At least twenty-five percent of them don't realize that the puck is in the net until the goal judge turns on the red light. The work of Howe, a perfectionist, often is lost on these new spectators. However, even a casual television fan can appreciate Richard, whose every appearance includes the violent promise of thunder and lightning.

Many Torontonians, including this columnist, were slow in accepting Richard. In his first two seasons, the shy, moody Richard seldom played good hockey on Toronto ice. In later years, he has explained that he detected a strange air of hostility in Toronto. This hostility probably stemmed from the fact that the conservative Toronto hockey audience resented Tommy Gorman's publicity campaign in which the ebullient Thomas proclaimed that Richard was greater than Howie Morenz.

In re-examining Maurice Richard's accomplishments in the National Hockey League, it is necessary only to mention one department: Richard has broken up ninety-eight games by scoring the winning goal. No other player has come close to such a record for bringing a hockey contest to a spectacular conclusion.

Richard has broken the professional scoring records. He has been the centre of countless controversies. He lost the Stanley Cup for Montreal one year by clouting Bill Ezinicki and Vic Lynn in a playoff game. He was suspended for the next game and Toronto went on to eliminate Les Canadiens. Maurice won another Stanley Cup for Montreal by flattening Ted Lindsay with a single punch. The Detroit Red Wings never recovered from that kayo.

Colour is the prime necessity in professional spectator sports. As far as colour is concerned, this man stands head and shoulders above the throng.

Coaches and managers say that Gordie Howe is a better hockey player. Well, the coaches and managers, with all respect, can have Gordie Howe. The cash customers will take Maurice Richard!

Sport of Kings—and Paupers

Toronto *Globe and Mail*
June 7, 1958

SO YOU WISH TO KNOW who'll win today's ninety-ninth running of the Queen's Plate, eh? Well, you've come to the correct department, Jack, because horse racing is one branch of sport in which your balloon-bellied, bandy-legged correspondent is an expert. Just sit down over there and don't move a muscle while I tell you all about my painful operation. As far as I can ascertain, I have the unique and disastrous distinction of being the only working newspaperman ever to start a horse in the King's Plate.

This incident that, even now, causes me to grimace as if assailed by tic douloureux, has been forgotten by all other human beings with the exception of certain officers of the Bank of Montreal. These bankers write to me on the fifteenth of each month, just to refresh my memory.

One other person *might* remember the incident. He is a little chap named Pete McCann who was associated with the late Dr. R.K. Hodgson in training my horse Leonforte. I suppose, though, that working with Leonforte was the peak of McCann's career because McCann slid downhill rapidly after that and, the last I heard, he was training horses for someone. I think that the name was Taylor.

Leonforte was a gift to me from my father. My dad, who was the kindest, most patient and most indulgent of parents, deluded himself into believing that if I raced a horse of my own, I would break my unfortunate habit of pawning his household chattels to wager on horses owned by others. (If my mother still is wondering what became of her grand piano, it's in the window at McTamney's.)

As a yearling, Leonforte was placed in the care of that delightful gentleman, Doc Hodgson. For a one-horse stable, we had our share of high-priced help. Doc received noisy daily advice from myself, agent Johnny Finn, jockey George Courtney, and Willie Morrissey who was advisor-without-portfolio. The only person who couldn't make himself heard amid the clamour was McCann.

Leonforte proved to be a very good two-year-old and he went into winter quarters as one of the favourites for the 1947 running of the King's Plate.

If you examine the record books, you will see that there were two divisions of the Plate Trial in 1947. The first division was won by Leonforte. The second division was won by Tularch.

Tularch happened to be owned by the late George McCullagh, who also happened to own the *Globe and Mail*. By a hilarious coincidence, I happened to be a lowly employee of the *Globe and Mail* and Mr. McCullagh was my sole means of support.

The gruesome possibilities of this situation didn't disturb me in the slightest. Oh, I confess that I was mildly amused when I noticed that my employer was packing a Colt .45 the week before the running of the King's Plate. Now that I look back on it, I suppose that I should have been disturbed when three companies turned down my applications for life insurance during that same week.

I have preserved my financial ledger for the first half of 1947 and I shudder now as I read the disbursements. Some of the items are as follows:

Training fees, Leonforte: $1,650.00
Special feed, Leonforte: $280.00
Medical bills, Leonforte: $300.00
Artist's fee for sketch, Leonforte: $25.00
New set of silks: $30.00
Shoes, Leonforte: $48.00
Shoes, J. Coleman: $3.98
Food and shelter, J. Coleman: $127.00
Shirt, J. Coleman: $2.98
Medicine to steady nerves: $60.00
Rent for grey top hat and tailcoat, J. Coleman: $20.00

I was bubbling over with good spirits—very good spirits—when I strode into the Woodbine paddock on Plate Day to give my final instructions to jockey Courtney.

When the paddock judge called "riders up" I turned to jockey Courtney and addressed him solemnly, "The dignity of man must be upheld this afternoon," I said. "All men are equal on the turf and under it. My horse must beat Mr. McCullagh's horse. We must show the world that in this democracy of ours the worker has the same opportunities as his master. Beat Tularch and all Canada will sing your praise."

Jockey Courtney was leaning against the side of the stall, picking his teeth with a piece of straw. He asked mildly, "You been into the sauce again, Jim?"

Ignoring the ignoble rejoinder, I grasped him by one leg to boost him into the saddle. "On to victory, bold Cossack," I cried, boosting him so enthusiastically that he went clear over the horse and nearly fell over the partition into the next stall.

Well, Leonforte *did* beat Tularch in the 1947 running of the King's Plate. Leonforte finished twelfth. Tularch finished fourteenth.

The race was won by Moldy, owned by Colonel R.S. McLaughlin, the chairman and president of General Motors. I was glad to see Colonel McLaughlin win because it is quite likely that he needed the money.

Jimmy and the Good Kid

Toronto *Globe and Mail*
August 23, 1958

A FEW WORDS THIS WEEKEND concerning two of our old friends who, despite tremendous physical handicaps, never have lost their burning desire to live.

It was just twenty-five years ago on August 4, 1933, that a filly named Skirt fell at Connaught Park and broke her neck. The jockey who rode Skirt that afternoon was little Jimmy Darou. For the past twenty-five years, Jimmy has been a paraplegic, paralyzed below the waist. On the twenty-fifth anniversary of the accident, we received a letter from him in which he wrote, in part: "I haven't a regret in the world . . . I had twenty-five years of gathering together the greatest array of friends a man ever had . . . Do you think that I have made a success of my life?"

When Jimmy was confined to life in a wheelchair, it was a couple of racetrackers who helped to set him up in business. They got him a service station in Montreal West. He whirled about in his wheelchair, filling tanks with gasoline and checking the oil. He lived in a little apartment above the service station, exercising continually with weights and performing gymnastic feats on a horizontal bar.

He has been successful in business. He has been a partner in a newspaper and an automobile agency, but always he has kept that service station where, alone, he faced the first desperate days of his own rehabilitation program.

It was at the end of the war that he found his real job in life. A doctor summoned him to Montreal Neurological Institute to visit another man who, as a result of war wounds, would spend the remainder of his life in a wheelchair. The patient was in deep depression. Little Jimmy's indestructible cheerfulness got through to the patient. It had its effect on scores of other paraplegics who returned from the war. That first visit to the Montreal Neurological Institute set up a chain reaction that has given many another shattered man the will to live.

And he asks, "Do you think that I have made a success of my life?"

It was just six years ago that another old friend named the Good Kid suffered his first stroke. The Good Kid had strokes as often as some people have colds in the head. Several of his strokes were recorded on the seismograph at the Dunlap Observatory. Two strokes are fatal in many cases, but the Good Kid has baffled the medical savants. The first stroke knocked him off his pins permanently, but the stout heart still is beating strongly and the tubby carnival-man's wry sense of humour hasn't been dimmed.

Each night our telephone rings at precisely 7:15 p.m. It is the Good Kid, calling from his sickroom. We know the questions in advance: "Have you heard from your daughter Ann? How's your boy doing? Have you heard from your brother in Montreal?" The cheerful voice stills any impatience that might be caused by these same questions, repeated each night, month after month.

The Good Kid was a carny. He worked for a dozen carnivals, notably Johnny J. Jones Exposition, Conklin & Garrett Shows, Rubin & Cherry Shows, and Royal American Shows. Thousands of persons throughout Canada and the United States know him only as the Good Kid. Once we asked a mutual friend if he knew the Good Kid's real name. "No," replied the mutual friend, "but he has a brother named Percy Piffles." (Just for the record, his name is Louis Drillick.)

We spent a thousand nights talking with the Good Kid. We remember when a doctor told him he would die if he didn't give up whisky. So for the next year, the Good Kid drank a bottle of Harvey's Bristol Cream sherry each night—at ninety cents a drink.

There was the night when the Good Kid mentioned a character named Pushcart.

"Who is Pushcart?" we asked.

"You must remember Pushcart," scoffed the Good Kid. "He's Squinchy's brother-in-law."

The Good Kid on finance: "A guy is born either to be a lender or a borrower. Personally, I've always been a poor lender."

The Good Kid on drinking among Polish people, of which he is one: "Them Polacks are all the same. If they take one drink, they buy a through-ticket."

In the six years since the Good Kid was flattened, it has been a racetracker, to whom all of us refer as Fishy, who quietly has conducted a campaign to keep the Good Kid in comfort. The Good Kid wasn't really a racetracker. He was a bettor and a very unsuccessful bettor at that. But Fishy and the Good Kid's family have looked after him. In hospital, each week, he is given five dollars in dimes so that he can make telephone calls.

There he is, a lonely but perpetually cheerful little man calling out to his friends, just a voice on the telephone.

This week, after six years, Fishy received a letter. The letter read:

> Dear Sir: Please find enclosed a cheque for $330 in your name from the boys in the front end of the Royal American Shows for the benefit of Louis Good Kid. I understand that you have been the main source of help for him. Please convey my own personal regards to Louis and, not knowing you personally, I salute you for what you have done and what you are doing for one of the nicest guys I remember in this business. Harold Denike.

Let's see, now—$330 will permit the Good Kid to make 3,300 telephone calls.

A Prince of a Pooch

Toronto *Telegram*
January 3, 1959

Dogs were mentioned prominently in a dispatch from West Berlin that was printed in last night's editions of the *Telegram*. Apparently, the post-war canine generation in West Berlin is hopelessly neurotic. When a West Berlin dog owner goes on a trip and leaves his pet in a boarding kennel, he must agree to send postcards to the dog at regular intervals. The dog owner must agree further to sleep with the postcard next to his body before mailing the message to his pining canine. One sniff of the card and Fido rolls over and goes to sleep, content in the knowledge that his master still loves him.

Things are coming to a pretty pass when dogs are bedded down with Nembutal and postal schmaltz.

Our family shared bed and board with some unusual dogs in my youth, but none of those four-footed companions could have been classed as neurotic. When my St. Bernard, Prince, became a bit crotchety in his old age, he would sleep more soundly if he took a good slug of scotch or a couple of martinis at bedtime. When I was a very small boy, I wasn't permitted to go to bed at night until I had removed the pits from the olives for Prince's martinis.

Before owning Prince, we had a series of four Airedales, all of which bit me. The West Berliners probably could make something out of that, but my father pardoned the dogs on the reasonable grounds that I was a particularly repulsive child. Also, there was some suspicion that in each case I had taken the first bite.

Of course, Prince was no ordinary dog. He was listed officially as a St. Bernard, but somewhere in his ancestry, there was a trace of bison or muskox.

We were living in Calgary at the time and when my older brother received a Shetland pony as a gift, I screamed so fiendishly that my father went right out and bought Prince from three dishevelled Indian braves who were staggering home to the reservation after sampling the white man's concepts of civilization. Prince was only a puppy but within six months he was as big as the Shetland pony. When Prince was a year old, a whimsical uncle bought me a saddle for him and I would race

Prince against my brother on the pony. We beat the pony one day and the Shetland never was worth a quarter after that. We had to send him out to a farm for the remainder of his life.

Prince insisted upon sleeping in the house with the children. Eventually, he grew too large for our Calgary house so we had to buy a bigger house in Winnipeg. The railway refused to ship Prince on the regular train and he travelled in a cattle car with seven Aberdeen-Angus steers. Prince arrived in Winnipeg okay but the steers were in bad shape.

Prince acted as a combination watchman and nursemaid.

He used to give my younger brother and me our nightly bath. He would test the water with one paw and dump us into the tub, then scrub our backs and refuse to let us emerge until we had washed out ears. On those occasions when the laundryman failed to deliver the towels, we dried ourselves on Prince's luxuriant coat.

He was the biggest, smartest, toughest dog ever seen in Winnipeg. Once, Jack Taylor, the Canadian heavyweight professional wrestling champion, visited our home. He wrestled Prince on our lawn and Prince pinned him twice within five minutes. Prince took all the kids on our block to school each morning and brought them home safely. When the policeman at the corner of Main and Broadway wished to sneak off duty for a quick drink, Prince directed the traffic for him and did a good job. At that, I think he was smarter than the cop. When Winnipeg's policemen and firemen quit during the General Strike of 1919, Prince pulled a chemical wagon to the famous fire that destroyed the stables of the Hudson's Bay Company.

I'll never forget the weekend when disaster struck. We came home from Keewatin on Monday morning after leaving Prince in charge of the house. We found a man sitting in a tree outside the front door. He was a substitute postman. Prince hadn't recognized him and had kept him there since Saturday morning.

Despite Prince's heroic services in the Hudson's Bay fire, he was banished to Francis, Saskatchewan, where Uncle Bert was the station agent. Uncle Bert later invented a fanciful story of Prince's demise. He said that the dog had become very attached to the station cat and, when the cat died, Prince was heartbroken and crawled under the station platform and died, too. Bosh!

The true story is that Prince was becoming a bit dotty when he was shipped to Francis, Saskatchewan. His eyesight and his hearing were failing and he took to plastering the walls of his kennel with pin-ups of such uninteresting dolls as Mary Miles Minter and Pola Negri.

One night, Prince was sleeping on the station platform when he heard a train approaching. He looked up and saw the headlight in the distance. Believing that some one-eyed enemy was attacking his home, Prince charged down the track toward the oncoming train. Eyewitnesses say that the train was travelling fifty miles per hour. Despite his age, Prince was travelling forty miles per hour. They met head-on.

Poor old Prince finally had overmatched himself.

But Prince was mighty in death. The force of the collision derailed the train. They had to call out the wrecking crew from Regina. Uncle Bert probably had a heck of a time explaining *that* to the superintendent.

Grey Cup Memories

Toronto *Globe and Mail*
August 22, 1959

After more than twenty-five years of sportswriting, this correspondent contends that no other sport can match the thrilling moments that are provided by horse racing and rugby football. Accordingly, we are grateful to Lewis Edward Hayman, who has booked night games and Sunday afternoon games for his Toronto Argonauts this season. Thanks to Mr. Hayman's brilliant planning, your correspondent now can attend football games without playing hooky from the racecourses.

We trust that Mr. Hayman and his Argonauts will have an eminently successful season and we hope that this year's action will provide us with a few more imperishable memories, such as:

> The first Grey Cup game that we covered: Montreal 22, Regina Roughriders 0. The late Eddie James inspiring an overmatched Regina team with his line-plunging at the beginning of the second half. He carried the ball the length of the field in six carries, broke into the clear near the Montreal goal line and fumbled when he took a glancing blow on his frequently broken right arm. The wild-eyed finish of the game when Red Tellier of Mon-

treal knocked George Gilhooley unconscious—an action for which Tellier received a life suspension.

Sitting in the wire room at the Edmonton *Bulletin* the afternoon in 1935 when Winnipeg won the first championship for the West. And the wire went dead just when Hamilton was attempting to tie the score in the closing minutes of the game. And we were gnawing our fingernails clear up to the elbows for fifteen minutes while we awaited repairs on the wire.

The bitterly cold afternoon in Ottawa in 1939 when Orville Burke slipped on the ice-covered field and fumbled a punt in the last minute. Winnipeg recovering the ball and Art Stevenson kicking the winning point. The ball went clear out of Lansdowne Park. Unfortunate Orville Burke fumbling in 1941 when Bernie Thornton tackled him around the throat. And the ball bounced right into the hands of Winnipeg's Mel Wilson, who lateralled to Bud Marquardt for a touchdown. And Winnipeg won a gasser 18–16 when Ottawa's George Fraser missed a "gift" field goal in the final two minutes.

If these reminiscences have a western flavour, it results from the fact that your correspondent always wagered on the West. (Nope, we weren't in Toronto when Red Storey had his famous Grey Cup afternoon in 1938.)

Riding the day coach for forty-eight hours from Vancouver to Calgary and return just to see Winnipeg and Calgary play a regularly scheduled league game. Or Adelman, the old Winnipeg centre, who had to tuck his ample paunch into his pants before each scrimmage play so that he could see the ball before snapping it to the backfield. And the delightful little Mobberley brothers, who felt that they had been cheated if they failed to land at least one punch in every scrimmage.

And the day that we almost were discharged from the Vancouver *Daily Province* for spending too much time in promoting the organization of the first professional Vancouver team. And being wise enough to leave Vancouver for Toronto before the bills were presented.

Pete Karpuk missing a lateral in the game between Ottawa and Calgary in 1948. And the ball lying there for precious seconds while the players minced around it. And Woodrow Wilson Strode finally picking it up and running it close to the Ottawa goal line before being shoved out of bounds. And Pete Thodos scoring the vital Calgary touchdown on the next two plays. The two Sarcee Indians, imported by Calgary to cheer for the Stampeders. And how they cheered loyally on every play. After the game, they were still sitting in the old covered stand at Varsity Stadium. Finally, one chief turned to the other chief and asked quietly, "Who won?"

The greatest individual performance we've seen: Jack Jacobs in the third game of the 1953 western finals in Edmonton. Jake finally was sent into the game late in the third quarter when his Winnipeg team was hopelessly beaten, and big Jacobs inspired the Winnipegs to three touchdowns, passing brilliantly and playing with that fierce, hot-eyed leadership that he could display when the mood was on him. And then Claude Arnold, the Edmonton quarterback, pulled one of the all-time "skulls." His team still had a narrow lead in the final seconds and they had the ball deep in Winnipeg territory. Inexplicably, Arnold decided to throw a forward pass. It was intercepted by Dave Skrien, who sprinted to midfield and lateralled to Tom Casey, who went all the way for Winnipeg's winning touchdown. But it was the brilliance of Jacobs that completely unnerved the Edmonton team in the final quarter. Keeping Jacobs in the defensive team—and on the bench—in the early part of that game probably had much to do with costing George Trafton his coaching job at the end of the season. Trafton and Jacobs hated each other and made no secret of their hatred.

Eddie Grant—now living in Oakville—calling back a Winnipeg touchdown in the 1937 Grey Cup game in which the Argos nosed out Winnipeg 4–3. And Eddie being forced to go home to Winnipeg in an attempt to earn a livelihood by selling life insurance. No wonder he moved east.

The all-time thriller, when Edmonton scored a rather flukey win over Montreal in 1954. The incredible break when Chuck

> Hunsinger threw away a lateral a few yards from the Edmonton goal line and alert Jackie Parker picked it up and shambled the length of the field on his fallen arches. And Johnny Bright, running alongside Parker as Sam Etcheverry began a futile pursuit. And that breathtaking split-second of indecision while Bright pondered whether to throw a block on Etcheverry. We've often wondered how the game would have ended if Bright had yielded to that impulse.

This should be a fine season. We trust that the athletes will add a few more items to this collection of football memories.

Stooperman

Toronto *Globe and Mail*
April 22, 1961

Racetrackers, generally speaking, are the world's most sophisticated group of sporting spectators. However, each year, hundreds of thousands of new patrons are exposed to the sport in North America as new tracks are built in those districts where horse racing has been legalized for the first time.

A case in point is Sunland Park in New Mexico, just across the state line from El Paso, Texas. Thirty-five years ago there was racing at Juarez, which is situated in Mexico but just across the international boundary from El Paso. In those intervening thirty-five years, the El Paso turf aficionados have died out and the operators of Sunland Park have found it necessary to embark upon an educational program. The public was invited to morning clinics at the track and, at those sessions, members of the publicity department, trainers, jockeys and racing officials answered questions dealing with the sport.

The majority of questions dealt with the slang and idiom of the racetrack. It was only a few weeks ago that our tennis expert, Perry Footfault, shambled into the office with last season's grass stains still showing on his white flannel trousers. Perry, a diffident chap until he has consumed his third double martini, asked us to define the word "stooper," which he had heard was indigenous to the racetrack.

A stooper, of course, is a gentleman who shuffles around the grandstand and paddock areas with his gaze directed at the ground. He is looking for cashable parimutuel tickets that have been discarded by careless and excited winners. Astonishingly, many spectators throw away winning tickets in the excitement of bellowing encouragement to the horse of their choice.

Experienced stoopers memorize the numbers of all winning tickets and they can spot them instantly when they see them lying on the concrete or grass. When a ticket is lying face down, a stooper can flick it over deftly with the toe of his shoe. A good stooper seldom breaks stride on his forays into the betting rings. There is an unconfirmed rumour some stoopers wear shoes with paper-thin soles and they can feel the numbers on the tickets with the bottom of their feet.

Astounded that Perry Footfault should ask such an elementary question, it occurred to us that some other common racetrack words may confuse the spectators. Accordingly, we have compiled a partial glossary of familiar racetrack terms:

Steward: The man who serves the wine in the turf club. Usually he wears a red mess jacket and carries a silver chain around his neck.

Horse: A condition that results from contracting a slight colt in the throat.

Colt: An irritation of the head or chest (sniff! sniff!).

Gelding: The process of applying a coating of gold paint (i.e. gelding the lily).

Mare: A civic official who presides over the city council. Seldom is elected for more than one term.

Filly: A particularly delectable cut of meat. At its best when served medium-rare.

Quarter pole: A man who is three-quarters Irish and one-quarter Polish.

Form chart: An item-by-item listing of Gina Lollobrigida's measurements.

Morning line: The breakfast-table explanation that a man offers to his wife after he hasn't come home until four o'clock in the morning.

Finish line: Sometimes known as the Mannerheim line where, in the first winter of the Second World War, the Finns held out courageously against assaults by a superior Russian force.

Starter: First course of a big meal. Shrimp cocktail or lobster cocktail are recommended.

Public address announcer: That blind so-and-so up on the roof who never can locate your horse during the running of a race.

Owner: The sucker who pays the bills for feeding and training the horses.

Trainer: An imaginative spinner of fairy tales that he tells to wide-eyed owners when their horses fail to win.

Groom: The fall guy at a wedding.

Jockey: A small man who drives a very large Cadillac.

Apprentice jockey: A small man who drives a Vauxhall.

Past-performance chart: A list of previous convictions that the Crown prosecutor reads into the court record before the judge pronounces sentence.

Mudder: A repulsive corruption of the word for female parent.

Maiden: If you don't know, you're not old enough to be reading this newspaper.

Racing secretary: A long-limbed, quick-witted female stenographer who can outrun her boss.

Next question, please!

Sweet Victoria Day

Toronto *Globe and Mail*
May 20, 1961

This newspaper has commissioned Mr. James Coleman, the eminent scholar and historian, to write a series of articles dealing with the background and origins of Famous Canadian Holidays. The current installment is entitled "Victoria Day—Is It Worth It?" This series is designed to enlighten the young people of Canada, and to inspire them to grow up to be big and strong and noble and just a bit crafty.

VICTORIA DAY is just as Canadian as maple syrup or pemmican, though there is a general misconception that it was named for a lady of German blood who became Queen of England.

The truth of the matter is that this great national holiday was named in honour of Miss Victoria Day who was the cashier at the old Regal Theatre in Winnipeg. (The name of the theatre has been changed, in this inspirational article, to obviate the possibility of a lawsuit.)

In any event, children, there was an old saying in garlic-conscious Winnipeg that "You can see *The Birth of a Nation* for one dollar at the Metropolitan Theatre, but at the Regal you can see *The Breath of a Nation* any time for ten cents!" (Editors' Note: Ha, ha! We get it.)

Victoria Day was one of the early Canadian martyrs. She was all-Canadian, true blue and several yards wide. She had hair that was the colour and consistency of sweet clover honey. She was an immense lady whose foundation garments were constructed for her by the Vulcan Forge company. The entire upper portion of her body rested on the counter and filled the cashier's cage from wall to wall.

Winnipeg was full of horrid little boys in those days and most of them went to the Regal Theatre on Saturday afternoons to see Elmo Lincoln, Ruth Roland and Tom Mix. Many of those little boys were expert marksmen who enlivened the afternoon by shooting lead pellets at the gentleman who played the piano in the dark theatre. Whenever the music stopped abruptly—as the pianist dropped unconscious—Victoria Day would emerge from her cashier's cage, turn up the theatre lights and confiscate all slingshots and peashooters.

When the pianist had been restored to consciousness and had made quite a speech about how he was going to hammer the whey out of the next nice little boy who skulled him while he was playing "Light Cavalry Overture" the lights would be dimmed and Ruth Roland would make another desperate effort to escape from her ropes as she lay on the railway tracks.

Precisely at this juncture each Saturday afternoon, Johnny McKinley, an eight-year-old roué, would butt his cigarette on the head of the boy in front of him and would slide from his seat, saunter up the aisle and disappear into the tiny washroom.

Several minutes later there would be terrible cries from the washroom. Children would leap from their seats and bang on the back door of the cashier's office crying, "Johnny McKinley's stuck again! Hurry, Miss Day—Johnny McKinley's stuck again!"

Panting and perspiring, Victoria Day would emerge from the cashier's cage and wrench open the door of the washroom, intent on rescuing Johnny McKinley.

The ruse never failed. Johnny would have perched a water bomb on the ledge of the door and, when the door was yanked open, the bomb landed—kerplunk!—on Miss Victoria Day's head.

One Saturday afternoon, a nine-year-old boy attempted to improve on Johnny McKinley's old wheeze and was going to put his mother's electric iron on the ledge of the washroom door. Outweighed and outreached, Johnny McKinley knocked out the older boy's teeth.

The truth of the matter is that Miss Victoria Day put up with Johnny McKinley because he was a red-blooded, all-Canadian boy, though there were times when he appeared to be a louse.

Johnny always was smarter than the rest of us. We used to have our annual school picnic and sports day on the Victoria Day holiday. A special streetcar took us from the school along Portage Avenue to Assiniboine Park, with all the nice little kids leaning out the windows, yelling and screaming. On the return trip, Johnny always took the very front window for yelling and screaming. Smarter than the rest of us, he *knew* that it was wise to have the front window—and it was a four-to-five bet that some kid, after the ice cream and peanuts and excitement and sun, would become ill while yelling and screaming from the rocking streetcar window on the way home.

Then there was the Saturday afternoon that Johnny McKinley climbed into the ventilating shaft.

Miss Victoria Day was in her cashier's cage when the nice little kids banged on her door and screamed, "Johnny McKinley's stuck in the ventilator! Hurry, Miss Day—Johnny McKinley's stuck in the ventilator!"

Miss Victoria Day scurried down the aisle to the ventilator and stuck her head and shoulders into the shaft. Meanwhile, Johnny had scrambled right up the shaft and emerged on the roof of the building. But Miss Victoria Day couldn't break loose—that old sixty-inch chest of hers was firmly wedged in the sixty-inch shaft.

That ended the show for the afternoon. The pianist took off his steel helmet, turned up the lights and chased all the nice little kids out of the Regal Theatre. We heard later that they had to use an acetylene torch to cut her loose.

And that, children, is the reason that we have a Victoria Day holiday in Canada each year. Enjoy your holiday, and if you go to a show on Monday afternoon, don't shove the cashier into the air-conditioning unit.

Don't let the school teachers feed you all that twaddle about Victoria Day being named for Queen Victoria's birthday. This is the only newspaper that prints the truth—the other papers are *afraid* to print it.

Farewell, Beloved Agony

Toronto *Globe and Mail*
July 8, 1961

THIS IS ONE OF THE DARKEST DAYS in the history of Canadian transportation. The Agony-Stricken Limited, the special train that has carried racetrack patrons from Toronto to Fort Erie for the past sixty-two years, has been derailed permanently by the heartless, unsentimental realists who operate the Canadian National Railway.

The slide-rule economists who estimate the deficits for Canada's government-operated transportation systems acknowledge that they have surrendered in the face of competition from the bus companies. The surrender has been abject and complete. The Agony-Stricken Limited, a raffish relic of the golden age of North American transportation, has dislodged the fillings from the teeth of its passengers for the last time. Before the summer has run its course, the grass between the steel rails on the Fort Erie siding will be hip-high.

In a belated attempt to assuage the grief of veteran rail travellers, the Canadian National is giving some thought to donating one of the battered and exhausted steam locomotives to the Fort Erie Jockey Club. The cab of the locomotive will be planted with perennial flowers and the huge water tender will be used as a crematorium. Several older four-horse parlay players have willed their bodies to the jockey club with the request that their ashes should be sprinkled in the infield lakes.

Thus ends a glorious and colourful chapter in Canada's history. Fact now will become legend, passed from generation to generation by word of mouth. With a heavy heart I hasten to transcribe some of the facts to fragile newsprint. There is a faint hope that some public official may deem it appropriate to clip this column and place it in an urn that may be discovered when the people of Mars or Venus overrun our own small planet.

The story of horse racing in this country has been linked inextricably with the story of railroading. Now the only remaining link is the Racetrack Special that transports the horses and horsemen from city to city on the Canadian Prairies: Calgary to Edmonton, Edmonton to Saskatoon, Saskatoon to Regina, and Regina to Winnipeg or Calgary.

Admittedly, western Canada's Racetrack Special invariably has caused some hand-chafing among straitlaced railway officials.

Officially, the train's cargo is confined to racehorses and approximately one hundred trainers and grooms. The conductor, who has counted one hundred passengers boarding the train at Calgary, always is surprised to count 425 passengers disembarking at Edmonton. In the mysterious ways of the racetrack, 325 touts, camp followers and impoverished wagerers have managed to conceal themselves beneath the bales of straw in the horse cars.

In 1861, a special train carried thousands of passengers to the Carleton racecourse on the outskirts of Toronto for the second annual running of the Queen's Plate.

The races were run off very slowly that afternoon. Forty minutes before the running of the final race, the conductor of the special train decided that he was going to be late for supper. Without consulting anyone, he ordered the train to depart for Toronto, leaving thousands of disgruntled ladies and gentlemen to walk home along the tracks.

In 1868, the Queen's Plate was raced at Newmarket. The Grand Trunk Railway ran a special train of thirty coaches over the short haul from Toronto to the Newmarket racecourse. However, on the return trip, hundreds of alcoholically inflamed and enthusiastic racing patrons climbed on the roofs of the coaches for the perilous journey to Toronto. The Grand Trunk complained that their conductors hadn't been able to collect any fares from the passengers on the roofs.

Ah, but the Agony-Stricken Limited deserves a story to itself!

The Agony-Stricken Limited was the only tram on which free Aspirin tablets and crying towels were distributed to the passengers after they had experienced a harrowing afternoon in the parimutuel jungles at Fort Erie. The conductor was named Charon and he wore white robes and carried a scythe in one hand. Several importunate morticians rode the train each afternoon and they distributed their business cards, courteously of course, to sufferers who appeared to be prospective clients.

In the old days of the coal-burning locomotives, the pièce de résistance of the daily menu on the Agony-Stricken Limited was cinder sandwiches. The reason that racing patrons in Ontario have such good teeth is that the charcoal that they consumed along with their cinder sandwiches had a beneficial effect on their choppers.

There was one conductor, who shall remain nameless, who herded his passengers from the train at Fort Erie each afternoon and then rushed right behind the wickets in the parimutuel sheds to sell six-dollar combination tickets to the same passengers. The train couldn't leave for Toronto each evening until the racetrack officials had checked the conductor's cash and then frisked him to be sure that he wasn't taking home any samples.

That last paragraph reveals a clue to the death of the Agony-Stricken Limited. There was only one train each day, and the passengers couldn't leave for home until after the last race. This worked a hardship on the wagerer who, along about the third race, had tapped-out on a beaten favourite. This unfortunate wagerer would have to spend the remainder of the afternoon sitting in sulky inactivity or exchanging insults with the tame deer in the Fort Erie Jockey Club's private zoo.

The bus companies put the Agony-Stricken Limited out of business by catering to the passenger who was likely to go broke early in the afternoon. The bus company, with scores of buses at its disposal, would send its first bus home to Toronto as soon as it was loaded, occasionally as early as the fifth or sixth race. You must give full marks to the bus companies: only yesterday they announced that all bus passengers will be given free Aspirin tablets and crying towels on return trips from Ontario racecourses. Imitation is the most sincere form of flattery.

Something noble, something fine and brilliant has disappeared from our lives. Never again will we see the Agony-Stricken Limited arriving twenty minutes behind schedule, at the Fort Erie racecourse. Never again shall we see the passengers jumping from the still-moving coaches and risking decapitation or loss of limb as they sprint toward the welcoming parimutuel machines.

The Agony-Stricken Limited has arrived late for the last time.

Sic transit gloria mundi.

Long Fall from a High Horse

Toronto *Globe and Mail*
September 23, 1961

Puss N Boots, the swimming horse, returns to action at Woodbine this afternoon. This will be the first official public appearance of Puss N Boots since he provided the aquatic sensation of the Canadian horse-racing season on the closing day of the Fort Erie summer meeting. While leading the field, about two hundred yards from the finish line, Puss N Boots jumped the inner hedge on the grass course, dove into one of the infield lakes and had an exhilarating six-minute swim.

The old-time Greeks, who were notorious liars, had a story about a flying horse named Pegasus that was reputed to have clocked a mile and one-quarter in 2:01 3/5 around those sharp turns in the Pantheon. Those old history books reveal that the Greeks were bookmakers even before they got into the restaurant dodge.

The Greeks never were content to stick to the facts and they invented a crazy and tragic story about this flying horse Pegasus.

His regular jockey was a chap named Bellerophon. Now according to the story, Proteus, the King of Argos—no relation to those characters who play football against the Ottawa Roughians on Sunday afternoon—had a wife named Anteia. It seems that this Anteia was one of those nutty dames who go down to the paddock and wink at the jockeys before each race.

Anteia made quite a play for Jockey Bellerophon, but he repulsed her, telling her that it was shameful for a married woman to be betting the crown jewels at the racetrack and, besides, he was in strict training to ride Pegasus in the Olympus Handicap.

Piqued because a mere jockey had given her the frigid clavicle, Queen Anteia went to her husband King Proteus and leaned a story on him to the effect that Jockey Bellerophon had been attempting to play footsie with her. King Proteus, who was all-powerful in Greek racing circles, promptly banished Jockey Bellerophon and his flying horse Pegasus to the leaky roof circuit. Bellerophon and his horse managed to keep body and soul together by fighting dragons and other monsters in hick towns, far from the luxurious racecourses of Mount Olympus.

The payoff to the story is that Pegasus and Jockey Bellerophon sneaked back into town one night. Bellerophon, pretending that he was carrying a torch for Queen Anteia, persuaded her to take a cool ride in the evening. Pegasus, making like a jetliner, was soaring about twenty thousand feet above Athens with Bellerophon showing the sights to the queen. When Anteia leaned far out of the saddle to take a closer look at the Acropolis, Bellerophon gave her a good heave and she fell twenty thousand feet to her death. (It's surprising that Alfred Hitchcock hasn't used *that* plot in one of his Sunday night family comedies on television.)

Personally, I think that the old Greek story about Pegasus the flying horse is a fake. In the days before the introduction of the saliva test, I saw some horses that were very "high" but I never heard of one that managed to reach a height of twenty thousand feet. Although there are many jokes about nearsighted racing officials, it would be very difficult to sneak a pair of wings into the paddock. I know a couple of old-time trainers who discovered to their sorrow that it was impossible to sneak in even a tiny one-cell battery.

The hilarious aquatic adventures of Puss N Boots at Fort Erie received international publicity—even the *Diley Mile* of London, England, published a picture of the incident—but he wasn't the first racehorse to take an unscheduled swim.

Jockey Maurice Griffin was riding a horse in a race at Lansdowne Park in Vancouver about twenty years ago. Nearing the finish, the horse fell over the inner rail into a deep water-filled ditch that circled the inner circumference of the entire track. Griffin, who was an excellent swimmer, beat the horse to the finish line by two lengths.

Then there was the case of the New Zealand horse Moifaa that was being shipped from the Antipodes to England to run in the Grand National Steeplechase of 1903. The ship was sunk in a hurricane while passing through the Mediterranean and Moifaa was swept overboard but managed to swim to the shore of one of the Greek islands.

The horse was found by some Greek fishermen and, after some incredible adventures, was restored to his rightful owner, G.H. Gollan, and was shipped to England almost six months later. He missed competing in the Grand National of 1903, but he won the 1904 running of the world's greatest steeplechase.

There is little likelihood of Puss N Boots winning another Olympic gold medal for swimming at Woodbine today since the race in which he is entered is being run on the main track. In order to get into the infield lakes, he would be forced to leap one fence and two hedges.

However, the management of Woodbine summoned trainer Frank Merrill yesterday afternoon and asked him if he would be willing to run Puss N Boots over the grass track next week in a special race.

"Yes," sighed Merrill, "providing that you'll permit my jockey to ride five pounds overweight so that he can wear an inflated life jacket."

Reg Anderson, Merrill's foreman who will bring Puss N Boots to the paddock, threatens to fracture the rules of racing by appearing in full skin-diving kit. Anderson recklessly plunged into the lake after Puss N Boots at Fort Erie and he was in eighteen feet of water before he remembered that he didn't know how to swim.

"This is one hell of a note," Merrill moaned yesterday as he acknowledged that he has been embittered by his association with Puss N Boots. "I was North America's leading trainer for three years, but no one remembers *that.* They just think of me as the trainer of that damn fool swimming horse."

7

1967–69

The Vindictive Mr. Muldoon

Southam News
February 6, 1967

MONTREAL—The Curse of the Muldoon has finally been retired. The Chicago Black Hawks are going to win the National Hockey League championship for the first time in history.

With only twenty-four games left on their schedule, the Black Hawks have the NHL championship clutched firmly by the gozzola. The Hawks really wrapped up the ruddy old pennant when they came from behind to earn a draw with the Montreal Canadiens at the Forum on Saturday night. When Les Canadiens can't maintain a third-period lead over the Hawks on Montreal ice, no other team can be expected to offer more than token opposition throughout the remainder of the season.

Seldom have Les Canadiens skated more brilliantly. Yet the Hawks permitted Les Canadiens to skate themselves to near exhaustion, then Eric "the Albatross" Nesterenko calmly rammed the tying goal down the throats of the gasping Montrealers.

One little mistake was the difference between the two teams: Jean-Guy Talbot deserted his left-defence post to throw a completely unnecessary bodycheck at Lou Angotti. Then Angotti flipped the puck to

Nesterenko, who glided solemnly through the unprotected zone and flipped the puck between goalie Charlie Hodge's legs.

And now one of the hardiest of all sporting legends must die. The Curse of the Muldoon finally has lost its potency after forty years.

The legend is that Pete Muldoon, the first coach of the Black Hawks, invoked an Irish hex on them when he was canned at the end of the 1926–27 season. Accompanied by two leprechauns, the Muldoon strode into the office of Major Frederic McLaughlin, owner of the Hawks. The Muldoon pulled a red crayon from his pocket, drew a mysterious symbol on McLaughlin's expensive wallpaper and intoned these words in a sepulchral voice: "This team never will finish in first place."

Well, the Black Hawks have been members of the NHL for forty years and *never* have they finished in first place.

There are no living witnesses to the confrontation but Chicago hockey historians insist that when the Muldoon and the leprechauns strode from his office, Major McLaughlin said only the following words: "Well, I'll be damned." Obviously, he was.

Hockey coaches aren't superstitious and accordingly, each of the coaches subsequently hired by Major McLaughlin scoffed loudly when informed of the Curse of the Muldoon.

Not superstitious, eh? The record book reveals that twenty different men have coached Chicago since the Muldoon was sacked—and not one of them managed to guide the hockey team into first place. Actually, there have been twenty-four coaching changes in Chicago, but only twenty individuals were involved. Several men, such as Dick Irvin and Bill Tobin, served more than one term in the Black Hawk cellblock.

The Black Hawks set an NHL record by hiring three coaches in a single season, 1932–33. The unfortunate gentlemen were Godfrey Matheson, Emil Iverson and Tommy Gorman.

Gorman, being a superstitious Irishman, wasted little time in Chicago. The Hawks finished second in Tommy's first full season, 1933–34, and miraculously went on to win the Stanley Cup. Gorman didn't wait around Chicago to receive congratulations. He rushed away to Montreal, where he won another Stanley Cup with the Montreal Maroons the very next season.

Billy Reay, the incumbent Chicago coach, is as superstitious as they make 'em, but fortunately he takes a scientific view of superstitions.

"The curse obviously was extremely potent when the Muldoon invoked it in 1927," Mr. Reay was saying recently. "However, the Muldoon never envisioned an era in which kooks would be setting off hydrogen bombs all over the world. I feel quite sure that the atomic fallout from these hydrogen bombs has dissipated the strength of the Muldoon's curse."

There could be only one set of circumstances under which the Chicago Black Hawks could blow first place this season: Stan Mikita and Bobby Hull would have to come down, simultaneously, with mumps.

Migawd, what a horrible thought. Surely the Muldoon wouldn't be so terribly vindictive.

The World Before the Tube

Southam News
March 3, 1967

This column isn't written for the general public. Actually, it is written for my eight-year-old son, so that he may have some personal record of the Canadian sports world before television.

WHEN I WAS YOUR AGE, the one big national sport in Canada was hockey. It was particularly so in western Canada where I lived. Hockey was the one thing that gave us a feeling of being associated with the rest of Canada. Eastern cities—such as Montreal, Toronto and Ottawa—seemed terribly remote to a small boy on the Prairies. There wasn't even network radio in those days, only a few local stations to which you listened on something called a crystal set, equipped with earphones.

Every kid on the Prairies knew the names of all the hockey players. Then, as now, you could buy chocolate bars that contained pictures of hockey players, but the players were members of western pro teams: Duke Keats and Bullet Joe Simpson of the Edmonton Eskimos, Dick Irvin and George Hay of the Regina Caps, Herb Gardiner and Red Dutton of the Calgary Tigers, Bill Cook and Newsy Lalonde of the Saskatoon Sheiks, Cyclone Taylor and Mickey MacKay of the Vancouver Millionaires, and Frank Fredrickson and Happy Holmes of the Victoria Cougars.

Few prairie kids ever mentioned the humiliating fact that an American team—the Seattle Metropolitans—had won the Stanley Cup in 1917, defeating the Montreal Canadiens. We figured that the Seattle victory must have been some scurvy Yankee trick. We figured, "Don't mention it, and the whole world will forget about it."

In Winnipeg, our heroes were the Winnipeg Falcons, who had won the first Olympic hockey championship in 1920. The Falcons were Manitoba-born Icelanders—with the notable exception of defenceman Huck Woodman—and although we didn't know the name of the prime minister of Canada, we regaled one another with stories of Frank Fredrickson, Slim Haldarson and Mike Goodman, the little Falcon winger who could skate backwards faster than anyone could skate forward. I never saw him do it actually, but I believe it.

The professional teams of western Canada travelled by train in their own private coach in those days, and often they were away from home for several weeks. The teams travelled the CPR because the CPR wisely had obtained the portering services of Pinky Lewis, a famous gentleman from Hamilton. Mr. Lewis not only was porter on the special railway car, he acted as trainer, masseur and travelling psychiatrist for the western teams. My first exposure to Stanley Cup hockey was in Regina in the spring of 1922 when, to my consternation, the Vancouver Millionaires eliminated the Regina Caps, who employed such Winnipeggers as Dick Irvin, George Hay, Ambrose Jason Moran, Spunk Sparrow and Rabbit McVeigh. The Caps outskated Vancouver, but they couldn't beat the Vancouver goalie, Eagle-Eye Lehman. Imagine, a goalie named Eagle-Eye!

In 1925, I was attending school in Victoria and the Montreal Canadiens came out to play the Victoria Cougars for the Stanley Cup. I knew that Victoria would win because the Cougars had Winnipeggers Frank Fredrickson, Slim Haldarson and Jocko Anderson in their lineup.

The West won, of course, three games to one. I was introduced to Leo Dandurand and Odie Cleghorn in the Empress Hotel. I was quite surprised to find that the easterners were nice, well-dressed men smoking expensive cigars and smelling of aftershave lotion.

The next year was the crusher! The Victoria Cougars went east to play the Montreal Maroons for the Stanley Cup. There was no direct radio broadcast, but the Victoria radio station was receiving brief reports by telegraph. We sat with our earphones, listening to the crystal set.

It was terrible. The Maroons were beating us because some fellow named Nels Stewart was scoring goals while lying flat on the ice. I knew that Victoria was finished when Babe Siebert of the Maroons body-checked Jocko Anderson and broke Jocko's hip. I took off my earphones and went to bed.

That was the beginning of the end of professional hockey as a national sport, on a genuine coast-to-coast basis. That spring, the Western League disbanded and most of the players were sold to the new NHL teams in the United States.

Some years later, I was attending McGill University and Red Dutton, my hero, provided me with tickets for all the home games of the Montreal Maroons and the Montreal Canadiens. One night, at a Maroon game, Mr. Dutton introduced me to Babe Siebert.

I was stiffly polite when I shook hands with Mr. Siebert. It was a long, long time before I could forgive Mr. Siebert for breaking Jocko Anderson's hip.

The Revenge of Angus Smudge

Southam News
March 10, 1967

OTTAWA—You are certain to have seen him sitting in the hotel lobby if you have attended a Canadian curling championship on any occasion in the past twenty years. You know to whom I am referring: short, stocky, bald-headed, with a stogie hanging limply from the middle of his mouth. He's wearing a plaid jacket sagging with the weight of enamelled curling badges that he has collected in every city and every province in Canada.

The thing about him that always has intrigued me is the sheer malevolence with which he eyes any woman who walks through the hotel lobby unescorted. Never does he speak to anyone or bother anyone; he just sits there quietly, giving those broads the old fish-eye.

I was watching this old guy in the hotel lobby yesterday when Bill Good came along and stood beside me. Bill Good has attended every Canadian curling championship since Ken Watson was in diapers.

Bill Good gauged the direction of my reportorial glance and said,

"You're wondering about that old geezer, eh? Well, he's Angus Smudge, from Armpit, Saskatchewan. His story is one of the genuine tragedies of championship curling."

I took another look at Angus Smudge sitting in a comfortable chair with his cigar drooping from his month, and I said to Good, "Why does be hate broads? He's too old to waste his time hating anything."

"Obviously, you've never heard the sad story of the famous Smudge rink from Armpit, Saskatchewan," said Good. "Come up to my room and I'll tell you there. I'm not going to tell this type of story in a hotel lobby—it embarrasses me to watch a strong man weep in public."

Angus Smudge was a prosperous farmer in the Armpit district, and he had three stalwart sons named Adam, Alex and Andrew. Angus was a curling nut and he had his three sons curling chamber pots as soon as they could stand up by themselves. When the boys were older, Angus built his own curling rink behind the pigpen and he imported two sets of expensive granites from Scotland.

From morning until night during the long Saskatchewan winters, the four male members of the Smudge family practised curling until they became, undoubtedly, the finest curlers in world history.

The Smudge boys grew up knowing little of anything other than curling, reading, writing and arithmetic. Because it was very cold in the Armpit district, all the children habitually wore heavy, lumpy clothing and the Smudge youngsters reached their late teens without really recognizing the difference between boys and girls.

Well, Angus Smudge and his three sons won the Saskatchewan championship in their very first bonspiel. They stoned the opposition and swamped the defending Saskatchewan champions 17–2 in the final match.

The Smudge rink went on to Winnipeg for the Canadian championship and they were regarded as the greatest cinch in the history of curling.

They were staying in one large bedroom at the Royal Alexandra Hotel in Winnipeg and, on the opening morning of the bonspiel, Angus Smudge left his three sons standing in the hotel lobby while he went down to the basement to have his brogans shined.

The three Smudge boys were standing in the lobby gawking at the sights when three exceptionally well-stacked young ladies emerged from an elevator. They were chorus girls, members of a touring American company that was playing at the Walker Theatre.

"What are those?" Adam Smudge asked his brothers as his eyes popped from his skull.

"I believe that they're something called girls," said Andrew Smudge tentatively.

"Wowie! What're we waiting for?" yelped Alex Smudge, and the three boys rushed out of the hotel in pursuit of the exceptionally well-stacked young ladies.

The Saskatchewan rink, naturally, was forced to default all its matches in the Canadian championship. Angus Smudge never again saw his three sons. Adam is driving a hack in Detroit. Andrew is a croupier in a casino in Lucaya in the Bahamas. Alex is selling gold stocks over the telephone in Toronto.

Old Angus Smudge, who became incredibly wealthy when both oil and potash subsequently were discovered underneath his two-thousand-acre Armpit farm, attends every Canadian curling championship and takes his own strange revenge on the female sex.

Yesterday, after hearing Bill Good's story—and weeping predictably—I went down to the lobby and watched Angus from behind a pillar.

After a wait of thirty minutes, a well-proportioned lady sauntered through the lobby. An innocent man was walking about two strides behind her. Angus Smudge pulled out a slingshot, put a lead pellet in the breech and let fly.

There was a loud "splaaat" followed by a scream from the lady, who put a hand to her injured stern.

The lady wheeled and slapped the gentleman who had been walking behind her. As her screams reached a crescendo, the house detective materialized to break up an incident that rapidly was assuming the proportions of a riot.

Smiling grimly, Angus Smudge concealed his slingshot inside his jacket and shuffled away to board an elevator.

Vengeful, wily old Angus Smudge had struck again.

Battle of the Bulge

Southam News
April 7, 1967

TO THE CHAGRIN of all lean, trim, clean-living, diet-conscious athletes, gluttony will be glorified when the "world heavyweight curling championship" opens today in Toronto. Thirty-two rinks—each group of four men totalling more than one thousand pounds—will waddle out of the starting gate this evening. No curler is permitted to compete unless he weighs at least 220 pounds.

This bonspiel, which is being advertised nationally as the Battle of the Bulge, is the brainchild of Sam'l Shopsowitz, a Toronto delicatessen food processor who personally is built on the racy lines of a rhinoceros. As often is the case with jolly fat men, Shopsowitz long has cherished a wild, secret desire to be an athlete. Although his personal wealth matches his corpulence, gladly would he have traded every dime in return for the ability to hit a home run or to score a Stanley Cup winning goal while cheers from the packed stands thundered down on his curly blond locks.

In a belated bid for athletic glory, Sam'l Shopsowitz has decided to skip his own rink in the "world heavyweight curling championship." His rink includes the current world curling champion, Chuck Hay of Scotland, who arrived in Toronto via trans-Atlantic jet yesterday afternoon. Shopsowitz also has signed Hec Gervais, the former world champion from Edmonton.

In his selection of rink mates, Shopsowitz hasn't been able to get away from his own preoccupation with food. Hay, who weighs 225 pounds, is a potato farmer in Scotland. Gervais, whose original 295 pounds have dwindled away to 235, is a potato and chicken farmer in Alberta. The fourth member of Shopsowitz's rink is a fellow named Jackie Parker, who played football or something in Edmonton a few years ago before he moved to Toronto where "football" is a dirty word. In the unlikely event that one of the four faints from malnutrition during the tournament, Wally Crouter, a slightly chubby Toronto radio broadcaster, will rush from the bench as a substitute sweeper.

"I doubt that we'll win," whispered Chuck Hay, shortly after his arrival from Scotland, upon meeting his skipper for the first time. "I don't know how this chap expects to curl a stone—obviously he hasn't seen his own toes since he was two days old."

Shopsowitz, whose curling weight fluctuates between 295 and 365 pounds, won't be the heaviest athlete in this week's bonspiel. Leo O'Connor, who curls lead for a CBC rink entered from Ottawa, weighed in at 375 pounds. O'Connor has failing health, obviously—a few months ago he weighed 450 pounds.

A stickler for sports protocol, Shopsowitz decided that he must be arrayed in a plaid costume as a competitor in this bonspiel. He dispatched his emissaries to track down a sample of the Shopsowitz tartan. Since the Shopsowitz clan originated in the highlands of Poland, the Royal College of Highland Heraldry in Edinburgh didn't have a facsimile of the Shopsowitz tartan on file.

Shopsowitz promptly designed his own family tartan, which he describes as "green matzo balls rampant on chicken schmaltz, with swatches of yellow mustard."

Since no Toronto firm was equipped to produce a plaid costume of Mr. Shopsowitz's size, the contract was awarded to the Manhattan Tent and Awning Company of New York. Said an official of the New York firm, "We haven't been tempted to produce anything of these dimensions since the occasion on which we were commissioned to provide a marquee for an outdoor reception at one of those Kennedy family weddings."

One of the features of the bonspiel is the "training table" that Shopsowitz is providing for all competitors at the Tam O'Conner Curling Club. "This is one bonspiel in which we guarantee positively that every entrant will gain weight," a tournament official said last night.

"And you should see the centrepiece on the training table," he added, stifling a burp of anticipation. "It's a huge curling stone—made of chopped liver."

This will be one Canadian championship bonspiel in which the consumption of bicarbonate of soda undoubtedly will exceed the consumption of undiluted whisky.

Tears on Heartbreak Lane

Southam News
June 5, 1967

NEW YORK—Cool Reception stumbled on the very threshold of the equine Hall of Fame. The Canadian-bred colt, a flame-haired chestnut with a heart as large as a pumpkin, almost ran himself to death in Saturday's Belmont Stakes.

Cool Reception demonstrated why the word "thoroughbred" is employed to describe a person that combines only the most commendable of qualities. Cool Reception, a thoroughbred in the best sense of the word, ran the final two hundred yards of the Belmont on a broken right foreleg.

They say that there is no lasting fame to be gained from finishing second; only the name of the winner is remembered by the public. But Canadian horsemen always should remember Cool Reception, who struggled home on three legs to finish second to Damascus, North America's champion three-year-old, in America's greatest annual horse race.

Cool Reception's racing career is finished. The cannon bone of his right foreleg was fractured completely. If he were a horse of lesser quality, the veterinarians probably would order his immediate destruction. However, he is reported to be insured for $250,000 and every effort will be made to save him for stud duty if the New York veterinarians agree that he can be saved. Cool Reception will be shipped to the Valecrest Veterinary Hospital near Hamilton, where an attempt will be made to pin together the two sections of fractured bone.

If you witnessed Saturday's race, you can understand why those of us who write purple prose refer to the home stretch as "heartbreak lane." Cool Reception grudgingly was yielding his lead to Damascus just inside the furlong pole when the Canadian colt suddenly lost his smooth running action. He may have come apart as a result of sheer weariness or the leg actually may have snapped at that point. No one knows for certain and Cool Reception can't talk.

Jockey John Sellers, who rode Cool Reception perfectly, hurried into the riders' quarters to watch the rerun on television. He pointed to the screen as Damascus and Cool Reception passed the quarter pole almost on even terms.

"Something happened to him right there. He couldn't strike out properly after that," said Sellers.

Damascus was the odds-on favourite of the crowd of 52,120 and, in the general rejoicing, few persons noticed that Cool Reception never returned to the finish line to be recognized by the stewards. Hobbling on three legs, Cool Reception was being led, slowly and compassionately to his stall in barn eleven.

A man is lucky to get his hand on a truly great horse once in a lifetime. The racetrackers who clustered around Cool Reception's stall averted their gaze sympathetically when trainer Lou Cavalaris unashamedly wiped the tears from his cheeks. There was that magnificent big horse standing on three legs—his eyes uncomprehendingly expressing pain and misery.

Cavalaris had sent Cool Reception into the Belmont prepared to run the race of his life. The colt was tuned beautifully; in the paddock, he was calm and he exuded perfectly coordinated power.

He ran perfectly, too, until Damascus and tragedy overtook him in the final two hundred yards. He raced smoothly in third place for seven longs, moved to the leaders Prinkipo and Favourable Turn even while Sellers was restraining him gently, and he took the lead easily furlongs from the finish. Proud Clarion, the Kentucky Derby winner, took a run at him, but Cool Reception put him away at the head of the stretch. Struggling home courageously on three legs, Cool Reception still was too much horse for the Kent Derby winner, who finished almost two lengths behind him.

Cool Reception's career is finished, and there is no telling how great he might have proved to be. Suffice to say that, in his final race, he ran the swiftest mile-and-one-half ever recorded by a Canadian-bred horse. He deserves to be ranked with the very best Canadian-foaled thoroughbreds of the modern era, in the same grouping with Northern Dancer, George Royal and Victoria Park.

Now Cool Reception never can have his name inscribed on the honour roll of horses that won the Queen's Plate, Canada's oldest and most famous race. At the risk of being exiled permanently, I would like to suggest timidly that finishing second in the Belmont Stakes is a more prestigious accomplishment than winning the Queen's Plate.

The running of the Queen's Plate at Woodbine on June 24 is anyone's race with Cool Reception being removed from the lists. The winner of this year's Queen's Plate will be acclaimed by his supporters, but it will be a hollow victory—because the best horse in Canada won't be able to answer the call to the post.

Spud Does Right by a Friend

Southam News
June 21, 1967

IN THE ARGOT OF THE BACKSTRETCH, Spud Murphy has gone to a faster track. When Little Spud died in his tack room at the Stampede grounds last weekend, the Calgary *Herald* printed his picture on the front page—a unique tribute to a gentle, unassuming racetracker.

What manner of man was this, rating a front-page obituary in a city of three hundred thousand? His lifetime accomplishments were unspectacular. He amassed no material wealth; in fact, he was close to flat broke in 1962 when a good horse named Brother Leo came along to provide him with a modicum of financial security. But Spud Murphy had become a personage in the West because, willingly and unashamedly, he always shared the only things that he had to give—his friendship and laughter.

Harold Murphy was strictly a racetracker. He was one of the vanishing breed of gypsy horsemen, so-called because he was an owner and trainer who lived right in the same barn with his horses. And although he was known on every Canadian racecourse from Sidney, Vancouver Island, to Fort Erie, Ontario, his home base was the Stampede grounds in Calgary. Spud's tack room at the Stampede grounds was known as "Murph's Turf Club." And because he was no stranger to the racetrack hustler's occupational malady—the miss-meal cramps—he was a generous host to drifters who bedded down in the barns to escape the bitter cold of the Alberta winter nights.

Murphy was immensely proud of his Irish stews, which he prepared in his barn. Spud's recipe for stew was fifty pounds of beef and five pounds of mushrooms. Many a drifter was strong enough to ride the rods all the way from Calgary to balmy Vancouver after Spud had fed him.

Spud, who played senior hockey for the Calgary Bronks despite the fact that he was only five feet four inches tall, was hustling on western Canada tracks thirty-five years ago when he came into possession of his first horse.

One afternoon at Winnipeg, he and a playmate named Kinky King each put a buck into the pot to buy a two-dollar quinella ticket on the day's last race. Spud had a date with a blonde and, instead of waiting for the last race, he went downtown to take the blonde to a supper club known as the Cave.

Later that evening, Spud was shooting the blonde a line of Irish blarney at the Cave when Kinky wandered in.

"How much do you want for your half of the quinella ticket?" Kinky asked silkily.

"No sale," replied Murphy promptly.

It transpired that their winning quinella ticket was worth $550. The two partners bought two horses, Time Ball and Matilda Jane. They paid three hundred dollars down and they went on-the-cuff for three hundred dollars. They shipped their steeds to Calgary and Time Ball won, first crack out of the box. They won a total of six races before the season ended, and they sold their two hay burners for six hundred dollars.

There are, however, more downs than ups in the racing business and Spud Murphy's first taste of prosperity was short-lived. Spud always managed to make a decent living, but he wasn't to know real prosperity again until Brother Leo came into his life. Brother Leo earned about fifty thousand dollars for Spud, who later sold the horse for twenty thousand dollars. Spud was sixty then, and he realized that the time was propitious to put a little something aside for a rainy day.

You wonder why so many people liked Spud Murphy? Well, he didn't set the world afire, but he had quality.

Once, during the Depression years, Spud was barnstorming with an old horse named Joe Geary. The horse was a cripple, but he was as honest as they come. On the last day of the Winnipeg autumn meeting, Joe Geary broke down hopelessly and there was Spud—absolutely stony broke—with his one-horse stable out of commission.

Spud went to a friend of ours. "A fellow has offered me one hundred bucks for Joe Geary," Spud says. "But I'm not going to take the money because I don't think that this man will give old Joe the home he deserves. He'll probably try to patch up Joe and bring him back to the races next season. Joe would be better off dead."

Spud looked at our friend and continued, "I want to borrow twenty dollars. I won't be able to pay you before next summer."

Our friend peeled off twenty dollars. Spud went to a veterinarian and paid him twenty dollars to have Joe Geary put down as painlessly as possible. Then Spud buried Joe Geary in the infield at Whittier Park. He buried Joe close to the rail so that the old horse always would hear the hoofbeats in the years to come.

And Spud Murphy—without a nickel to his name—hitched his way home to Calgary to spend the long cold winter in that familiar barn at the Stampede grounds. That's where Harold Murphy died last weekend.

Kissing the Trolley Wire

Southam News
July 29, 1967

WINNIPEG—It was singularly appropriate that some organizational genius should have selected the old Royal Alexandra Hotel as press headquarters for the Pan-American Games.

Pan-American Games, eh? Well listen, buster. The old Royal Alex has been the scene of some truly exciting games that never could have been included in the official program for any Olympiad.

At supper last night, Gordon Walker of the Toronto *Globe and Mail* was recalling that Sam Lyle brought his Edmonton Eskimos football team to Winnipeg for a November playoff game about ten years ago. The temperature was below zero in Winnipeg and the snow was howling out of the northeast. The Eskimos couldn't find a clear field to hold their final pre-game scrimmage. The management of the Royal Alex solved Coach Lyle's problem. The management permitted the Eskimos to stage their final scrimmage in the hotel's Crystal Ballroom, which is almost as large as the football field at Winnipeg Stadium.

Ha, that ain't nothing. The Royal Alex had been an athletic training ground long before Coach Sam Lyle came on the scene. When I was a small boy, there were ten kids of approximately the same age whose parents were permanent guests in the hotel. On wet afternoons, we amused ourselves by kicking field goals over the hanging crystal chandeliers in that same ballroom.

We played hockey—with a tennis ball and real hockey sticks—on the marble floors of the basement lobby and this noisy activity caused at least two assistant managers of the hotel to request premature pensions after they suffered recurrent heart attacks. My brother and I staged daily bicycle races along the wide corridors of the fifth floor, making a complete circuit of the hotel. We never killed a paying guest though we ran down a Boston bull terrier that was owned by S. Franklin Pierce, the hotel manager.

By a happy coincidence, on this particular visit I am occupying room 636. This room once was part of a suite occupied by Dr. Green and his two sons. The two Green boys had a .22 calibre rifle. On dull days, they would amuse themselves by resting their gun on the windowsill and shooting out light globes in the illuminated advertising sign on the roof of the Alberta Hotel just down the street.

The resident genius among us ten charming children who lived in the Royal Alex was a friend of mine named T. Jeffares Porte, Jr. His parents gave him a chemistry set for Christmas and he manufactured small bombs, which we called "geysers."

We would conceal these geysers in the toilet bowls in the public bathroom on the lower level of the hotel. Then we would hide until some innocent citizen entered one of the cubicles. When the innocent citizen flushed the toilet—whoosh!—the bomb would explode and the water would be blown all the way to the ceiling of the washroom. The innocent citizen would emerge in a very damp state and, sometimes, in a shocking rage. Boy, we learned some pretty fancy language before the hotel management ordered us to stop manufacturing those geysers.

There isn't enough space here—fortunately—for me to write the entire history of my life in the Royal Alexandra Hotel. Suffice to say that, as I think of these things, I am sitting here, cracking my knuckles and cackling like an old fool.

Years after the geysers, when I was a wet-eared young reporter on the Winnipeg *Tribune*, there was a profane newspaperman named Gillespie who lived just down the hall from here in room 642.

At the time, we were distilling our own gin and we mixed it with potent Ontario wine. The resultant concoction, due to its lethal impact, was known as "Kiss the Trolley Wire."

Well, one night, a bunch of us were drinking Kiss the Trolley Wire in room 642 with Gillespie's inamorata, a nice girl named Mary. Suddenly, this Mary leaps to her feet, points at Gillespie and yells, "You do not love me anymore—I'm going to kill myself!" With which, she opens the window, swings her legs through the opening and sits on the ledge, high above the street. Gillespie goes over to the window, bangs it shut and locks it.

It was thirty degrees below zero in Winnipeg that night and Mary was wearing an evening dress. When finally we rescued her from the window ledge, Mary was a solid block of ice.

We took out our cigarette lighters and attempted to thaw the ice in which Mary was concealed. Someone suggested that we could speed the thawing process by dousing Mary with a bottle of Kiss the Trolley Wire. Fortunately, cooler heads prevailed. Those cooler heads reminded us that Kiss the Trolley Wire must be reserved for national emergencies, such as drinking.

Mary lived to love again but often I've wondered what became of her. I think that I'll walk down the corridor to room 642 and see if she's sitting on the window ledge.

Big Atch's Hush Puppies

Southam News
November 23, 1967

REGINA—The Calgary Stampeders began to fall apart when Terry Evanshen's left ankle snapped after he made a brilliant catch off a pass from Peter Liske at the Calgary 49-yard line.

Four minutes remained to be played in the third quarter and Calgary was leading 9–8 as Evanshen made a leaping catch directly in front of two Saskatchewan Roughriders, Dale West and Bob Kosid.

Almost simultaneously, West hit Evanshen around the shoulders while Kosid hit the 180-pound receiver around the knees. As the bodies fell in a twisting, squirming heap, Calgary's Lovell Coleman skidded into the pileup.

One man—Evanshen—didn't arise from the heap. He was carried from the field on a stretcher. Later, on crutches, he emerged from the Calgary dressing room and watched the final three minutes of the game from a grandstand runway.

The loss of Evanshen, Canada's leading pass-catcher in 1967, appeared to stun the Stampeders. On the very next play, Liske was thrown for a five-yard by Ron Atchison. Then the Stampeders panicked. On the next play, the Calgary snapback failed to put the ball in Liske's hands. The ball slithered on the frozen field and Henry Dorsch recovered the fumble for Regina on the Calgary 49. Seven plays later, Jack Abendschan calmly kicked the 18-yard field goal that gave Regina an 11–9 victory, sending this Western Canada championship series into a decisive third game in Calgary Sunday afternoon.

The treacherous field conditions and a stiff northwest breeze turned last night's game into a defensive battle in which the resourceful Roughriders outhit the Stampeders.

The trend was indicated in the opening quarter when the Roughriders made three interceptions—two by Dale West and one by Kosid—of Liske's passes. And when Calgary was making a desperate charge in the final minute of the game, it was Henry Dorsch's interception of another Liske pass that assured Regina's well-deserved win.

They play the wackiest football in Regina. However, the weather held down the crowd to 12,456 persons, most of whom were reasonably sane. The crowd was so unusually demure, as a matter of fact, that only once was the Calgary quarterback forced to appeal to the referee to silence the yammering that was interfering with his signal-calling.

But you take a guy like Ron Atchison, Regina's defensive lineman who is completing his sixteenth professional season. Because of the tricky field conditions, players on both teams tested five or six different types of footwear before the game. Most of the players settled for steel cleats. However, after the first ten minutes of play, Atchison threw away his cleats and donned his street shoes—a pair of ten-dollar suede Hush Puppies with rubber soles. He played the entire game in those low-cut Hush Puppies, which were taped to his feet. Then after the game, Atchison dressed calmly and went home in the same pair of shoes in which he had played the game.

"Aw, that's nothing," scoffed a writer, who has covered Atchison's entire career. "I saw Ron when he first turned out to play for the Saskatoon Hilltop juniors—he wore a pair of knee-high rubber boots."

Atchison may set a trend for icy fields with his unorthodox footgear. Twice, he burst through the Calgary line to dump Liske for losses in crucial situations.

Ronnie Lancaster, the little Regina quarterback, isn't Liske's equal as a passer, but he had George Reed banging away for big yardage gains along the ground and in key situations Lancaster passed magnificently.

Calgary was leading 3–1 just before halftime when Lancaster rolled all the way to the west sideline before heaving a 40-yard pass toward Al Ford. A catch appeared to be impossible because three Calgary defenders—Frank Andruski, Larry Robinson and Ron Stewart—were converging on Ford. But the ball flew straight into Ford's hands for the touchdown, which gave Regina an 8–3 lead at halftime.

Evanshen was a major factor in the Calgary cause before he was injured. In the third quarter, he made a sideline catch at the Regina 47. At that instant, Ted Dushinski, an overzealous Regina defender, gave Terry a totally unnecessary elbow in the face. The resultant penalty gave Calgary a first down on the Regina 32 and, four plays later, Evanshen caught a touchdown pass that provided Calgary, momentarily, with a 9–8 lead.

The Regina cause was aided in the fourth quarter by the fact that Calgary punter Jim Furlong lost his touch and got away three lamentably feeble punts. However, Evanshen was out of action at that point and the Regina team was putting up such a resolute defence that I doubt that three *good* kicks by Furlong would have changed the outcome of the game.

Nevertheless, I wouldn't bet my house and lot on either team in the final game of this bruising series.

Sir Benjamin's Church

Southam News
January 5, 1968

Among this season's collection of incoming Christmas cards was one from Lady Stockley. The dear lady had written on the card: "Just a reminder of the happy times."

The thousands of residents of the towering City Park apartments, directly behind Maple Leaf Gardens in Toronto, are blissfully unaware that they are living on the former site of the world's most unusual gymnasium. The gymnasium was housed in an old church that had been abandoned by parishioners who had transferred their spiritual meditations to a more imposing temple.

In its Canadian context, Sir Benjamin Stockley's gym in the abandoned Toronto church certainly was as famous as Stillman's Gym on Jacobs Beach in New York City. Sir Benjamin made no apologies for opening a gymnasium in the old church. "The basis of the spiritual life is an 'ealthy mind in an 'ealthy body," Sir Benjamin said frequently as he gulped a glass of milk liberally laced with Canadian rye.

Jack Dempsey sparred in Stockley's gym. Joe Louis trained there when he was still an amateur fighting out of Detroit. Conn Smythe sent his Toronto Maple Leaf hockey players to Stockley's, where Sir Benjamin bullied them into condition. Overweight Toronto policemen were sent to Sir Benjamin, who clobbered them with invective until they were as slim as Audrey Hepburn.

Sir Benjamin was a former carnival boxer out of Birmingham, England. Always, he called the city "Burning-ham." He had two handsomely cauliflowered ears to attest to his rough apprenticeship.

The old church was Sir Benjamin's home as well as his gymnasium, and the walls of his commodious living quarters were decorated with an astounding collection of sporting memorabilia: old prints of boxers, boxing gloves, swords, hammerlock pistols, knives, hockey sticks and several shrunken heads from South America. For a couple of years, a racing sulky was suspended from two beams high above the dining-room table.

At nights, Sir Benjamin's quaint establishment was the centre of Toronto sporting gossip and, despite his chronic state of impecuniosity—"We're 'aving more blooming suppertimes than suppers"—he was a free-pouring host. Casual passersby must have wondered why so many gentlemen who emerged from that darkened church late at night clung to one another for support.

When he became bored with conversation, Sir Benjamin had a unique method of dismissing his guests. Grabbing a sword from the wall, he would crash it on the dining-room table, roaring, "Time, gentlemen! Time, please! Don't you have no bloody 'omes to go to?"

One night, residents in the area of the old church jammed the police switchboard with phone calls as they complained about "roosters crowing in the middle of the night." Investigating officers traced the sounds to Sir Benjamin's church belfry, where he had hidden twenty-four gamecocks he had rescued while the provincial police were raiding a private party near Hamilton.

"You should have seen me jumping from a second-floor window with twenty-four chickens," Stockley cackled. "We didn't hit the ground—the chickens flew me all the way home to Toronto."

He was the world's greatest sucker for auction sales. Any time that an auction was staged in Toronto, Benny was certain to come home with more sporting junk to hang on the walls of the church. One day, cheerfully inflamed with the grape, he came home with not one, but three polo mallets that he had picked up at an auction. A friend was sitting in the dining room watching Sir Benjamin nailing the polo mallets to the overcrowded wall.

"What the hell's the matter with you?" demanded the friend. "You're flat broke and you buy three polo mallets."

Sir Benjamin took a sip from his glass of milk and rye and replied solemnly, "You never can tell when you'll need an extra polo mallet." Eaton's, which owned the property, eventually took a dim view of Stockley operating his crazy gymnasium in the old church. Under slight duress, Sir Benjamin vacated and moved to his country estate, right next to E.P. Taylor's Windfields Farm. Sir Benjamin used to refer to E.P. as "my h'impoverished neighbour."

I took Gabby Hartnett, the Chicago Cubs World Series hero, to the country estate one night at Sir Benjamin's invitation. But by the time we arrived, Benny had overindulged and he had forgotten the invitation completely.

"This is Gabby Hartnett," I said, attempting to make the introduction to our foggy host. "You must remember Gabby Hartnett—he was the world's greatest catcher."

"'e can't be," Sir Benjamin said thickly, pointing to his own fist-battered lugs. "I'm the world's greatest catcher. If you don't believe me, just take a look at them ears."

When Sir Benjamin died, they came from all walks of life to attend his funeral. E.P. Taylor, Benny's "h'impoverished neighbour," occupied a front pew.

But there was one final Stockley touch to the obsequies. While the minister was right in the middle of the eulogy, a gaunt man walked in from the street. The man didn't wear a jacket or a tie. His suspenders were outlined against his damp white shirt, for it was a humid afternoon. And while the minister continued to talk, this man walked slowly to the front of the chapel and looked down at Benny in the casket.

And then the man shook his head very sadly and turned around and walked slowly out into the street.

Upon Sober Reflection

Southam News
April 19, 1968

EDMONTON—You can talk about Terry Sawchuk, Johnny Bower, Glenn Hall and Gump Worsley, but the most remarkable goaltending performance in the history of professional hockey was given right here in Edmonton. If you wish to have confirmation of this statement, you may consult Clarence Sutherland Campbell, the president of the National Hockey League.

Sure, I realize that Terry Sawchuk has registered 101 shutouts in the course of his National Hockey League career. But did you ever hear of a professional hockey goalie registering a shutout while he was lit up like a New York theatre marquee? Yeah that's what I mean, buster—bombed!

Red McCusker hasn't been elected to the Hockey Hall of Fame, but as surely as the good Lord created little apples, Red deserves a special niche amid the cloistered hockey memorabilia.

My plane flight from Toronto to Edmonton, where I am attending one of those sports dinners tonight, bridged many years of memories. The Western Canada Professional Hockey League is forgotten now. Clarence Campbell, who was the referee on the occasion when Red McCusker guarded the bridge in the manner of bold Horatius, was a member of a prominent Edmonton legal firm in those days. Most of Campbell's partners became adornments of the Alberta bench while Campbell went on to the presidency of the NHL.

I write these words with affection and respect for Red McCusker, who was a genuinely great goalie.

On the occasion in question, Red was a victim of circumstances. It was utter imbecility for a professional hockey league to schedule an afternoon game in Edmonton on New Year's Day. There was a great tradition that *everyone* in Edmonton got stoned on New Year's Eve in the Depression years. It was the one night of the year when the entire population forgot its helpless financial impoverishment.

Red was more unfortunate than most of us. He was an alien in a cold forbidding land: he was playing hockey for Edmonton while his wife and children were living on the Pacific coast. Red was living in a tiny room in the Selkirk Hotel at the corner of Jasper Avenue and 101st Street, and he was very, very lonely. As he thought of his distant wife and children, Red attempted to assuage his loneliness with a couple of jugs of oh-be-jolly.

Along about midnight on New Year's Eve, I was sitting in Constantinos Johnson's cafe on the main floor of the Selkirk Hotel. Suddenly, there was a terrific crash in one of the hotel rooms directly over our heads. I looked nervously at Hank Dyck, the Edmonton Eskimo left-winger, who was sitting next to me.

"Red's trying to phone his wife on the coast," Dyck said mildly. "I guess he ain't getting a very good connection."

Indeed, this was the case. Irked by the incompetence of the Alberta government telephone system, Red had ripped the telephone from the wall and he had dropped the offending instrument on the floor from his height of six feet.

The Portland Buckaroos and the Edmonton Esks skated onto the ice shortly before two o'clock on New Year's afternoon. Immediately, it was apparent that something was amiss.

Red McCusker didn't skate to the Edmonton net with his customary purposeful strides. Instead, Red clung to the sideboards and pulled himself along until he was opposite the Edmonton goal. Then, steadying himself on the shoulder of an Edmonton defenceman, he made slow progress to the net and stood there, clinging to the pipes as if they were the gunwales of a life raft.

From the opening faceoff, Ronnie Martin of the Buckaroos carried the puck toward the Edmonton net. Simultaneously, Red McCusker skated out of goal toward the advancing Martin. Red was waving his stick above his head with both hands, and he was shouting loudly.

The startled Martin shot the puck harmlessly into a corner of the rink and fled for the Portland bench. Later Martin told me, "Red was screaming, 'Don't come over this blue line, or I'll cut off your head!' He meant it, too."

Well, that opening play established the pattern for the game. Red stood, leaning precariously against the pipes, daring the Portland attackers to come close to him. Inspired by Red's noisy valour, the Esks checked the pants off the Buckaroos.

The Buckaroos were forced to fire most of their shots from the Edmonton blue line. Whenever a Portland forward made the mistake of boring in, Red left the net and tackled him in the manner of a football linebacker.

It was an incredible performance. The final score was Edmonton 1, Portland 0. Red McCusker had registered a shutout.

McCusker left the ice to a standing ovation. However, his teammates didn't surround him, pummelling him and mussing his hair. His teammates gave him a very wide berth. By that time, Red was beginning to suffer from the grandfather of all Alberta hangovers—and his teammates remembered that, even at best of times, Red's temper had a very short fuse.

Rebel's Last Drive

Southam News
September 5, 1968

THE GOOD MEN are dropping off like flies. First, Bill Beasley died in Toronto and then Rebel Mowat died of a heart attack in an Irish sightseeing bus while he was on the final leg of a world tour. In this era of dull conformists, we can ill afford to lose two such richly colourful individualists.

Bill Beasley was a paradox. Outwardly, he was a genially cynical gamblin' man, but beneath that crust there was a thick layer of Puritanism. I knew him from the time when he bought his first racing filly. Her name was Everness and she was one of the first daughters of Whirlaway. Bill Beasley was a good man and a kind man—and I always admired the dashing manner in which he "bet with both hands" to back his judgment.

Bill Beasley would have liked Rebel Mowat, though unfortunately they never met. After all, Bill wasn't the type to take a ride in a sightseeing bus to smell the flowers at Butchart Gardens in Victoria, British Columbia.

It was ironic but strangely fitting that Rebel should have died while he was a passenger in a sightseeing bus, travelling around Ireland. Rebel had been a *driver* of sightseeing buses in Victoria throughout his adult life. The good Lord obviously decreed that Rebel should leave as a passenger.

In all probability, Rebel Mowat was the most famous sightseeing bus driver in the history of Canada. Every tourist who visited Victoria and took a trip to Butchart Gardens retained a vivid memory of the rotund, cheery bus driver who described the sights of ultra-British Victoria in the incongruous accents of his native Brooklyn.

Egad, what a character he was! I knew him from the time I was a small boy attending boarding school in Victoria. Rebel drove a hack out of the Empress Hotel for Barney Olsen. Rebel's fellow hack jockeys were a gentleman named Beanie and another 350-pound gentleman named Winnipeg Chilton.

Rebel was simply a natural-born disturber. He attempted to promote the vulgar game of baseball in stuffy Victoria where cricket was *the* game. To attract customers to his first baseball game, he announced that he would parachute to the pitcher's mound from an airplane. "At least five thousand people will show up," he told me at the time, "hoping to see me get killed."

Rebel even was too much for the Canadian army in World War II. However, I wish to take this opportunity to deny the base canard that Rebel was discharged from the army transport service because he failed to pass a driver's test.

Rebel's version of the affair was that he had been incarcerated for some very minor offence at the army camp in Debert, Nova Scotia. Upon his release, he became slightly inflamed with the grape and decided to free his former fellow prisoners. He purloined a jeep and drove it full tilt into the front door of the gaol hut. He demolished both the jeep and the gaol. The army high command decided that their expenses could be reduced sharply if Rebel was returned to civvy street.

Rebel was the unchallenged master of the put-down. There were frequent occasions on which he put down Ralph Rogers, the importunate, publicity-loving heir to a chocolate fortune.

Ralph, who occupied a permanent suite in the Empress Hotel, courted publicity as a hunter. One day, carrying his .303 rifle, he returned to the Empress and three porters lugged in the body of a black bear that Ralph said he had shot in neighbouring Sooke. The bear was carried into the hotel's kitchen and it was hung on two steel hooks in the walk-in refrigeration room.

For the next three days, Ralph bored every guest in the hotel by taking them individually into the hotel's cold room to admire his trophy of the hunt.

Rebel Mowat carefully plotted Ralph Rogers's put-down.

On Sunday evening, the Empress lobby was full of the usual old dowagers as Billy Tickle's string trio played the customary post-prandial concert of Chopin and Mozart.

Ralph Rogers was sitting with a group of elderly ladies when suddenly a small, dirty boy walked into the lobby from the street. The small, dirty boy walked right up to Mr. Rogers and—on a signal from Rebel—Billy Tickle's trio stopped playing abruptly.

"Mr. Rogers," cried the small, dirty boy in a shrill piping voice as all of the old ladies in the hushed lobby turned to them with interest. "My dad says that the bank okayed the cheque for one hundred dollars that you gave him when you shot our pet bear. But my dad wants you to return the bear's collar and chain."

Oh Rebel, Rebel! Don't go too far away. Do you remember the time that you took a busload of lady tourists to Butchart Gardens? And you were showing the old ladies the flowers, but one of the old ladies—an old doll from Boston—was enchanted that the granite walls of the quarry in Butchart Gardens provided a perfect sound chamber for your voice?

And the lady said breathlessly, "My! What marvelous acoustics!"

And you said, "That's right, lady! But you should have seen them last week when they were in full bloom!"

Jolly Green Giants

Southam News
November 15, 1968

PILE OF BONES, SASKATCHEWAN—THE RAUNCHY ROUGHRIDERS are unlike any other professional football team in the world: the Roughriders don't even have lights for their practice field. "Who needs 'em?" retorted Coach Eagle Keys when a visiting eastern reporter looked around the field and remarked on the curious absence of floodlights. "When it gets dark, we know that it's time to quit practising."

Kookiest outfit I ever saw, those Roughriders. When the driver unloaded me at the grandstand of the Regina Exhibition Grounds, I walked across the racetrack to the infield. I could see shadowy figures running through the dusk. A football was being flung vigorously and large, roughly clad men were pursuing it.

To add to the atmosphere of unreality, a standardbred pacer was jogging around the half-mile racetrack. The driver, sitting jauntily on his sulky, ignored the noisy football players in the infield. The football players also ignored the solitary horseman, though he could have been a secret agent of the Calgary Stampeders, who will assault the Saskatchewan sodbusters on Saturday afternoon.

"Your blood is a bit thin for this sort of thing," said kindly old Coach Keys as he noticed the eastern reporter shivering in the gathering darkness. "You'd better go up and see Sandy in the dressing room. You won't miss anything out here. We're just running Calgary's plays—but Calgary runs 'em better than we do."

The eastern reporter promptly discovered another peculiarity of the Saskatchewan Roughriders. The Roughriders are the only professional football players who must walk *upstairs* to the dressing room. The Regina team's dressing room is located at the top of a long flight of stairs on the second floor of the racetrack grandstand.

The reporter could smell food as he entered the well-furnished and well-lit dressing room. Sandy Archer, the Roughrider trainer, was boiling chicken soup. Laid out on the rubbing tables were neat rows of soda crackers and a couple of jars of marmalade. Without ceremony, Sandy gave the reporter a cup of steaming hot chicken soup.

The reporter sipped and smacked his lips. The reporter complimented trainer Archer on the quality of his cuisine.

"You should have been here last night," said Sandy hospitably. "We had hot dogs."

Wotta football team. Hot dogs in the dressing room, and no lights on the practice field.

This misleading air of casual affability pervades the entire Saskatchewan Roughrider football organization. The players, when they clumped up the stairs, resembled a group of construction workers just getting off shift. Eagle Keys's two assistants, Jim Duncan and Jim Spavital, were bundled in heavy, hooded parkas and they wore fleece-lined flight boots.

Unlike other teams, the Roughriders don't even bother to attempt to hide the fact that their star rookie halfback, Silas McKinnie, hasn't recovered entirely from a sprained ankle and sundry knee injuries.

Noting that the eastern reporter was watching McKinnie limping around the dressing room, Coach Keys merely drawled, "It's a good thing that we finished in first place. Silas wouldn't have been ready for a playoff game last Sunday. He may not even be ready to go on Saturday afternoon. If Silas isn't ready, we'll just have to use ol' George to run back the kickoffs." Ol' George is George Reed, Saskatchewan's indefatigable fullback.

Despite all these superficial signs of indifference, the raunchy Roughriders really are ready for the first game of the Western championship.

"These daily practices become a bit boring for the players when we haven't played a game in almost two weeks," conceded Coach Keys. "But I don't think that the long playoffs are going to hurt as much as some people might suspect."

There was a slight twinkle in Keys's eyes as he continued.

"You've probably forgotten that we finished in first place in 1968. Well, after a two-week layoff, we came on like gangbusters. Our series with Winnipeg lasted only two games. Then we went on and beat Ottawa in the Grey Cup game."

Unless there is an abrupt climatic upheaval within the next thirty-six hours, the weather conditions will favour Calgary's passing in Saturday's first game. The weather throughout the Prairies is astonishingly clement and beautiful—not a speck of snow on the ground and the sun is beaming benignly.

Eagle Keys never made any secret that he would prefer to play Calgary on a frozen, windswept field.

"I know that Pete Liske won't have any trouble *throwing* the ball on an icy field," says the Eagle slyly. "But some receivers may have trouble *catching* the damn ball."

Hired to Be Fired

Southam News
September 26, 1969

LIFE IN THE WORLD OF PROFESSIONAL SPORTS is full of little ironies. Jim Champion was the only man who offered Jackie Parker the opportunity to be an assistant coach in the Canadian Football League. Now Jim Champion has been fired, and Jackie Parker is his embarrassed successor as head coach of the BC Lions.

Although Parker cherished ambitions to become a head coach, he never suspected that it would be necessary for him to walk over the still-breathing body of one of his best friends. And Vancouver has become the graveyard of football coaches, gaining a dubious distinction that had been earned by Calgary and Toronto.

Calgary began a trend in 1953 when the Stampeder executives fired Les Lear, who had coached the team through the five previous seasons. In the next nine years, the Stampeders had six head coaches: Bob Snyder, Larry Siemering, Jack Hennemier, Otis Douglas, Steve Owen and Bobby Dobbs.

Not to be outdone by those western upstarts in Cowtown, the executives of the Toronto Argonauts made a strong bid for ignominy when they fired Frank Clair before the 1955 season. In the next ten years, the Argonauts had six head coaches: Bill Swiacki, Hampton Pool, Steve Owen (the old boy certainly covered ground), Lou Agase, Nobby Wirkowski and Bob Shaw.

It is interesting to note that neither Calgary nor Toronto won their divisional championship during those years of recurrent upheavals in the coaching department. It is interesting to note, too, that the Stampeders and the Argonauts usually were polite enough to wait until the end of a football season before firing the coach. The one exception was Hamp Pool's dismissal by the Argos during the 1959 season.

Vancouver, of course, prides itself in being unique among Canadian cities. They do things differently in Vancouver—even in football.

The last four coaches who have been dismissed by the BC Lions have been fired in mid-season. Those unfortunate gentlemen were Clem Crowe, Wayne Robinson, Dave Skrien—and Jim Champion.

Canadian football must be a hell of a great game because it has survived, and indeed it has flourished, despite the muddling interference by some of the amateurish executives who operate the professional teams in some cities.

I recall interviewing Gentle George Trafton on a national television network some years after he had been fired by the Winnipeg Blue Bombers. I asked George, who insisted that he had mellowed in the years since his dismissal, whether he had any belatedly kind words for the Winnipeg football executives.

"Aw, shucks," Gentle George roared genially, "the Winnipeg executive is okay—but it could be improved by four or five fatal automobile accidents."

An epidemic of sadism swept across the western Canada plains in the early 1950s, infecting football team executives. The reaction to this epidemic was unusual: the executives suddenly decided it was a good idea to fire all coaches who won the Western Canada football championship.

The following list of events is submitted for your consideration:

> 1950: The Winnipeg Blue Bombers, coached by Frank "Butch" Larson, reached the Grey Cup final. Larson's reward: he was dismissed almost immediately.
>
> 1951: The Saskatchewan Roughriders, coached by Harry "Blackjack" Smith, reached the Grey Cup final. Smith's reward: he was fired almost immediately.
>
> 1952: The Edmonton Eskimos, coached by Frank Filchock, reached the Grey Cup final. Filchock's reward: he was fired as soon as the team returned to Edmonton.

> 1953: The Winnipeg Blue Bombers, coached by George Trafton, reached the Grey Cup final. Trafton's reward: he was fired as soon as the team returned to Winnipeg.

"I made a terrible mistake by finishing in first place in 1953," Gentle George Trafton used to cackle. "If I just had been content to make the western playoffs every year, in second place or third place, I might have been coaching in Winnipeg until I was older than Amos Alonzo Stagg."

Sir Sidney Mole

Southam News
October 3, 1969

CANADIAN HORSE RACING lost another of its legendary characters when the Flea died three days ago in Vancouver. His square handle was Sidney Mole but he referred to himself grandiloquently as "Professor Mole" or "Sir Sidney Mole."

I first met the Flea back in the days when he was playing a three-handed game with two other West Coast characters known as Yum Yum and Noodles. It was Massie White, the dapper little racetrack chart-caller, who gave Sidney his nickname. Said Massie, "I call him the Flea because, always, he's in my hair."

In addition to his racetrack duties, Massie was the night manager of the Burrard Club, which later moved into posher quarters and was renamed the Pacific Athletic Club. Massie simply "inherited" the Flea one night. From that evening on, the Flea regarded Massie White as his personal patron, lawyer, spiritual adviser and banker. It was rather a one-sided deal because Massie always worked regularly, whereas the Flea's employment record was spotty.

Sidney Mole was a tubby, yappy Englishman who appeared to be in a perpetual state of indignation. While expostulating noisily, his jowls trembled in the manner of agitated jelly.

Sidney broke down a few years ago, and it was necessary to retire him to stud in a nursing home. He became a chronic victim of a rheumatic disease, which he described as "Arthur-itis."

I made a point of telephoning him at the nursing home on most of my frequent newspaper trips to Vancouver. His voice rising to a crescendo, he would fulminate against the injustice of his invalidism.

Occasionally, however, he would con one of the nurses into taking him to the racetrack. The last time I saw him was approximately one year ago, in the clubhouse at Exhibition Park. As usual, he was grumbling happily. He was irked because he had been outhustled for his favourite chair.

"I was heading for my chair, right under the closed-circuit television set, when some old broad outruns me. I know that it's time for me to hang up my tack when old broads can beat me out of the gate."

Sir Sidney Mole has gone to a faster track now, and I like to think of him as he was in his younger days, when he had plenty of early foot.

Massie White got him a job as a messenger for the parimutuel department. After each race, the Flea would climb to the press box and would address Massie as follows: "Boss, weed me off a few more sheets of Spanish!" Banknotes were "Spanish" in the Flea's lexicon.

On Sunday mornings, we would head for the Longacres track in Seattle, where Joe Gottstein provided Sunday afternoon thoroughbred racing. Sidney, who never learned to drive, always bummed a lift to Seattle.

He was always prompt though. When his lift hove into view, Sidney would be standing at the curb on Granville Street clutching a small brown paper bag.

That paper bag contained Sidney's personal tea. "Them Yanks don't know how to make a cuppa," Sidney would say disdainfully. Then, in the clubhouse at Longacres, he would command the waitress bring him a pot of hot water—and he'd brew his own tea. Britons never, never will be slaves!

Sidney was a virtuoso on the harmonica. And one night during the racing meeting at Colwood Park on Vancouver Island, the racing buffs and assorted camp followers were staging a swinging party in a suite at Victoria's old Strathcona Hotel.

The Flea's current inamorata was a stout lady who worked in a Victoria steam laundry. While the party raged around them, Sidney was sitting on the floor, serenading this sudsy siren. The lady was sitting in a chair, starry-eyed, while Sidney wooed her with his harmonica music.

One of the roisterers in the suite was a boxing promoter who had staged a fight show in Victoria earlier in the evening. This promoter was carrying a punch—the type of punch with which trolley conductors punched holes in paper transfers. The promoter had been using the gadget to punch holes in the complimentary tickets that he had issued for his fight show.

Sidney's entire attention was concentrated on his music and the Queen of the Steam Laundry.

The boxing promoter, bombed out of his mind, pulled the ticket punch from his pocket and drilled a tiny hole in the soft lobe of Sidney's left ear.

Uttering one squeal of pain, the Flea leaped to his feet and skulled the promoter with his large harmonica. The promoter was knocked cold.

The Flea looked down at his unconscious adversary and blurted, "If that bastard has any plans to become a music critic, he ain't going to last long on the job."

With which, Sir Sidney Mole sat down on the floor again and calmly resumed his musical wooing of the Goddess of the Washtubs, who hadn't even blinked her wide, glassy eyes during the violent interruption. And all around the mutually enchanted couple, the party roared on . . . and on . . . and on.

Hidden Hoot York

Southam News
November 5, 1969

It will be singularly appropriate if the Saskatchewan Roughriders represent western Canada in the Grey Cup game in Montreal on November 30. The last time that a Grey Cup game was played in Montreal was 1931, when the Roughriders were clobbered by the Montreal Winged Wheelers 22–0.

The snow was rump-high on a tall Indian and 5,112 spectators, who sat semi-paralyzed by cold in Percival Molson Memorial Stadium at McGill University, represented total gate receipts of $5,286. I looted my piggy bank that day to make a bet on Regina and I've been waiting thirty-eight years to get even.

Adding injury to insult, Red Tellier of Montreal kayoed George Gilhooley of Regina when the two teams were walking off the ice-covered field after the game. Tellier claimed that Gilhooley had been squirting tobacco juice in his eye throughout the long, cold afternoon. Gilhooley's head struck a hummock of solid ice and he was rushed unconscious to the Montreal Neurological Institute, where he spent the next five days.

This year, the western Canada team will arrive in Montreal on a jetliner. For six days they will be quartered in an expensive hotel; they will eat steaks as large as a man's chest; and money will be plentiful! But in 1931, Regina was becoming a disaster area in the grip of the most devastating financial blight of this century. The Roughriders managed to come east only because Dr. Emmett McCusker, who later went on t the House of Commons, personally mortgaged himself to the Imperial Bank for one thousand dollars to pay the train fares.

The Roughriders travelled to Montreal in a tourist-sleeper. As was customary in those days, Coach Al Ritchie had more players than railway tickets. The extra players usually hid beneath berths when the train conductor came into the car to conduct a head count. Coach Ritchie would engage the conductor in noisy debate while the players scurried about, seeking hiding places.

Hoot York, a ticketless fan who later became a professional hockey goalie, remained hidden beneath a berth all the way from Regina to Fort William before he was overcome by a fit of sneezing. The conductor, sighing regretfully, ordered York to leave the train in Fort William.

The 1931 Roughriders hadn't played a game for four weeks when they arrived in Montreal. And by then, they were quite familiar with transportation problems.

They had travelled to Winnipeg on November 7 to play the Winnipeg St. Johns for the Western Canada championship. When they arrived in Winnipeg the morning of the game, they discovered that they had left two trunks containing every bit of their football equipment lying on the CPR station platform in Regina.

They went onto the Wesley Park field that afternoon wearing the uniforms of the Winnipeg Winnipegs, who had been eliminated a week earlier by the St. Johns. Despite the ill-fitting equipment, the Roughriders whomped the St. Johns 47–5.

This year, thousands of western Canadians will converge on Montreal for the Grey Cup game. In 1931, only five Regina fans travelled to Montreal. They were Dr. McCusker, Dr. Beattie Martin, Bill Button, J. Russell Smith and W.R. MacKenzie.

The Roughriders hadn't bothered to scout the Montreal team. Two downy-cheeked McGill University students, Max Bell and Bert McGillivray, conferred with Coach Ritchie on the sidelines just before the kickoff and told him what they knew about the Winged Wheelers. Coach Ritchie scratched his chin thoughtfully and, with his toe, diagrammed two new Regina plays in the snow while his players peered over his shoulders.

Although the final score was 22–0, the Roughriders gave Montreal a rugged battle in the first forty minutes, until Eddie James committed a tide-turning fumble when he dropped the ball after he burst through the Montreal line. After that fumble the Roughriders made only one more defiant move—they ripped the pants off Warren Stevens, Montreal quarterback and passer. The players of both teams formed a protective ring around Stevens until he was led from the field, clad discreetly in a long red blanket.

My childish illusions were dented that afternoon. Up until then, I thought that referees were sacrosanct individuals who scorned any off-field contact with athletes. So an older youth took me down to the Windsor Hotel where the Regina players were quartered in two or three large sample rooms.

The Regina players were doffing their wet, dirty uniforms. And there among the nude Regina players stood the gentleman who had refereed the game. Furthermore, the referee was clad only in his socks and shoes and a black derby hat—not another stitch of clothing—and was calmly smoking a big cigar.

Merely to set the record straight, 1931 *wasn't* the first year in which the forward pass was used in a Grey Cup game. The Regina Roughriders used the forward pass in the Grey Cup game of 1929 when the Hamilton Tigers beat them 14–3 in Hamilton.

Believe it or not, the Regina forward passes were thrown by their *centre,* Jersey Campbell. Campbell would snap the ball to a backfielder. Then he'd pull out of the scrimmage line and the backfielder would toss the ball to him laterally. Campbell would hurl the ball downfield, *left-handed.* Tie that one if you can! A left-handed centre who threw forward passes in a Grey Cup game.

8

1970–73

The Duke's Fourth Trombone

Southam News
June 17, 1970

My forty-one years with Duke Ellington:

As I was driving to the office yesterday morning, I heard a band playing Bert Lown's old signature song, "Bye Bye Blues," on the car radio. The incongruity of a 1930 theme song being played on the radio in 1970 convinced me that the time has come for me to end my double life.

Although I have had a long and happy career in the world of sportswriting, I have had a longer and happier career in a private dream world. For the last forty-one years, I have been occupying the fourth chair in the trombone section of Duke Ellington's famous band.

If this revelation comes as a surprise to veteran readers of these columns, they will be relieved to know that it comes as a surprise to Duke Ellington, too. Over the last forty-one years, the Duke has been blissfully unaware of my presence on the bandstand.

I was a spindle-shanked little gossoon in 1929 when the earphones of my Zenith super hetrodyne emitted some captivating sounds that altered the course of my life. Those sounds were Duke Ellington's band playing "Ring Dem Bells." When I heard Cootie Williams's trumpet growling counterpoint to the surging melody of the reed section, I was hooked, inextricably.

Every man has indulged in some harmless private fantasy. Some men dream idly of living in a tropical island paradise, their only companions consisting of Sophia Loren, Angie Dickinson and Anita Ekberg. Other men dream of wearing a Green Bay Packers uniform and running 100 yards through the entire Los Angeles Rams team for the game-winning touchdown. Other men dream of winning ten thousand dollars at the races and paying off the mortgage.

My forty-one-year secret excursion into the wonderful world of imagination has injured no one, though understandably it has irritated my wife. She insists upon asking silly household questions when I am on the bandstand. Invariably, she grabs nervously for her bottle of sedatives when my answer is something like, "Okay, Larry, this is mine. I'll take the next eighteen bars in E-flat." Never has she realized that in such circumstances, I am talking to Lawrence Brown, who has always occupied the first chair in the Ellington trombone section.

Getting into the Ellington band was quite a problem for me because I don't know a note of music and I never have played a musical instrument. I decided that my instrument would be a Selmer gold-plated trombone. Armed with this tailgate slush pump, I have been making beautiful music for forty-one years. When I joined the Ellington band, Freddy Guy was playing guitar, Sonny Greer was on the drums and a man named Braud was playing bass fiddle. Duke, of course, was on piano. The reed section was composed of Otto Hardwick, Johnny Hodges, Barney Bigard and Harry Carney. The trumpeters were Rex Stewart, Cootie Williams and Wallace Jones. The trombones were Lawrence Brown, Juan Tizol and Joe "Tricky Sam" Nanton.

We've done some pretty good stuff over the years: "Mood Indigo," "Sophisticated Lady," "I Let a Song Go Out of My Heart," "C Jam Blues," "Take the A Train," "Cotton Tail" and "I'm Beginning to See the Light," just to mention a few of our major hits.

I haven't always been entirely happy in the band. Billy Strayhorn upset me a bit when Ellington took him into the group. Strayhorn's convoluted arrangements were occasionally too complicated. For a while, I considered defecting to the big bands of Benny Goodman or Glenn

Miller, but I stayed because I knew in my heart that Ellington would eventually get back on his original beam.

My older children learned never to interrupt me when the radio or the hi-fi was going and I was working with the Ellington band. They used to look at me curiously as I sat alone in the living room. But they grew up, married and went away, remembering their father as a mild eccentric.

One eleven-year-old son is still left in the house. He barges into my dream world occasionally to blurt, "Hey Dad, I'm stumped. How do you do this problem in long division?" And I lower my Selmer trombone from my lips and I growl at him, "Fake it, sonny, fake it!"

Well, the fantasy has ended now. As I listened to the car radio this morning, I realized with a pang that the big bands are just about gone. It's time that I devoted myself completely to the newspaper business, to accumulate enough loot to keep my family in reasonable comfort in my old age.

There's one wry reason why I'm not going to regret ending my musical career: in all my forty-one loyal years of service to Duke Ellington, there wasn't even one occasion on which he asked me to stand up and play a solo. When I go home tonight, I'm going to take my Selmer gold-plated trombone and I'm going to hang it on a hook in my clothes closet. No one will notice the trombone hanging there, gathering dust, because really it has never existed.

Goodbye, Duke!

When Western Hockey Ruled

Southam News
September 25, 1970

VANCOUVER—The hockey clock has turned its full cycle for me. On March 22, 1926, I saw the last Stanley Cup playoff game that took place in this city and I am looking forward to big-league hockey's official return to Vancouver when the NHL season opens here on Friday, October 9.

Strangely enough, the last major league game to be played here didn't involve a Vancouver hockey team. The contestants were the Victoria

Cougars and the Edmonton Eskimos. The natural ice in the Edmonton arena had been melted by early spring weather and the Eskimos were forced to go to the Pacific coast for their two-game total-goals series with the Cougars.

The Cougars won the first game 3–1 on Victoria ice and the final game in Vancouver ended in a 2–2 tie, giving the Cougars the semifinal series by an aggregate 5–3.

I don't remember too much about that final major league game in western Canada because I was only a kid in knee britches. However, I recall that Edmonton blew its last opportunity when Duke Keats, the terrible-tempered centre of the Eskimos, slugged referee Carl Battell and received a match penalty.

Each team had a total of only nine players and yet six of the eighteen players in that last western series were elected to the Hockey Hall of Fame. Edmonton's contributions to the Hall of Fame were Keats, Eddie Shore and Barney Stanley. Victoria contributed Frank Frederickson, Frank Foyston and Jack Walker. All six joined NHL teams in 1927, after the Western League disbanded. In fact, fifteen of the eighteen went into the NHL.

As a native western Canadian, my hackles still rise in indignation when hockey historians write patronizingly of the old Western League. Hell, we had the *best* league. And we had the biggest arena, too! Vancouver's double-decked wood arena could handle crowds of close to twelve thousand. Frank Patrick, the only genuinely far-sighted innovator in the history of hockey, built his Vancouver rink about 1910. The cities of Montreal and Toronto didn't have comparably sized rinks until fifteen or twenty years later.

As kids, we took hockey very seriously in western Canada. In our estimation, the only good easterner was a dead easterner. Actually, the first Stanley Cup playoff game that I witnessed involved the Vancouver Millionaires in the 1922 semifinal against the Regina Capitals. I was only a little boy and we lived in Winnipeg but my father arranged for me to be sent on the train, alone, to Regina. The sleeping-car conductor was my reluctant babysitter. When we arrived in Regina, my father's good friend, A.E. Whitmore, picked me up and took me to the game between Vancouver and the Regina Capitals.

The Capitals were my heroes because they had six Winnipeggers in their lineup. Regrettably, two of my Winnipeg heroes—Ambrose Jason Moran and Emory "Spunk" Sparrow—were the goats of that series. They got drunk in Vancouver and they missed the train to Regina, finally arriving twelve hours after their Regina teammates. They played lamentably. Vancouver won 4–0 and the total goal series 5–2 and Moran further disgraced himself by barging into the referee's room between periods and punching that surprised official on the snout. Regina might have won the series if Moran and Sparrow had eschewed the demon rum. However, Vancouver had a pretty good hockey team with players such as Eagle-Eye Lehman, Mickey MacKay, Jack Adams—yeah, the same old Jolly Jack who managed the Detroit Red Wings for so many years—Art Duncan and Alf Skinner. The Millionaires went on to Toronto, where the St. Pats defeated them in the Stanley Cup finals, three games to two. Undoubtedly, the easterners cheated: Babe Dye scored nine goals for Toronto and Adams scored six for Vancouver.

I saw western Canada's last Stanley Cup triumph in 1925. You may wonder how I did so much travelling in knee pants, but the fact is that my father had sent me from Winnipeg to a boarding school in Victoria. The Victoria Cougars were playing host to the Montreal Canadiens in the 1925 series and my father arranged for H.J. Wilson, the manager of the Empress Hotel, to take me to the three games that were played in Victoria.

It was a best-of-five-games series—won by the Cougars in four games—and the second game was played in Vancouver. Somehow, my father arranged for me to be in Vancouver too. I was sent from Victoria on the afternoon steamer, SS *Princess Charlotte*, and a kindly porter from the Hotel Vancouver accompanied me to the rink. Later, he put me aboard the night boat for Victoria. I told you that all little boys in western Canada instinctively abhorred eastern athletes. On the afternoon before the final game, Mr. Wilson introduced me to Howie Morenz, Sprague Cleghorn and Leo Dandurand as they were entering the dining room of the Empress Hotel. I was appalled by the discovery that they were friendly, courteous gentlemen. I couldn't even boo them with any real enthusiasm later that night when they were being hammered 6–1 by the Victoria Cougars. I was a stinking traitor: I found myself feeling just a little bit sorry for Les Canadiens.

The next season ended major league hockey in western Canada.

The Victoria Cougars went to Montreal to meet the Montreal Maroons in the 1926 Stanley Cup finals. My father was visiting Victoria for my school's Easter holidays and each night we listened in his hotel suite to the fragmentary hockey reports on the local one-lung radio station.

It was a terrible denouement. Babe Siebert of the Maroons broke Jocko Anderson's hip in the opening game and I sensed that we were doomed. When Montreal finally won the series, three games to one, I switched off the radio with tears in my eyes.

My father put one arm gently around my skinny shoulders and said, "Don't let it upset you. It's only a game." It took me some years of growing to understand his remark. Kids bled pretty freely in western Canada.

I wish that my father had lived long enough to see major league hockey return to western Canada. Frank Patrick once told me that my father offered to form a syndicate in 1926 to keep the Western League in operation instead of selling the players to American cities. If Mr. Patrick had listened to him, we might not now be preparing to welcome major league hockey's return to western Canada—major league hockey might never have *left* western Canada!

The West Comes East

Southam News
November 26, 1970

ON THE GRIMLY DARK AND DANK AFTERNOON of Sunday, November 21, 1948, a motley group of cowpokes boarded a bus at the Pig and Whistle Inn on the shores of Lake Ontario about thirty miles west of Toronto. In those days, the Pig and Whistle consisted of a central dining hall surrounded by tiny cabins with two beds in each cabin.

They *must* have been cowpokes because certainly they didn't resemble the Metropolitan Opera's corps de ballet. They came in the wildest assortment of shapes and sizes: tall, short, fat and skinny. The common denominator of this awkward squad was a white ten-gallon hat, which each member of the group was wearing, just a bit sheepishly.

Fifteen minutes later, the cowpokes emerged cautiously from their bus at Appleby College, a boarding school for boys on the western outskirts of Oakville. A conservative and respected Toronto bookmaker was standing with a group of newspapermen when the white ten-gallon hats began to gather uncertainly around the door of their bus.

"If those bums are the members of the Calgary football team," the bookmaker said with a sigh, "I'll lay three-to-one that Ottawa will clean their clocks next Saturday afternoon."

I was making $130 a week minus income tax at the time. Before the bookmaker closed his mouth on his Corona-Corona cigar, I bet him a week's salary on Calgary at three-to-one.

For once, Les Lear, the tank-shaped playing coach of the Calgary team, smiled indulgently at the derisive chuckles that greeted the first appearance of his oddly assorted players at Appleby College. Lear normally had the disposition of an arthritic grizzly when his teams were criticized, but on this occasion, he could afford to be tolerant. Lear knew something.

"Take a look at my cowboys!" Lear cracked to the eastern press. "We have Jewish cowboys, Negro cowboys, Chinese cowboys, Greek cowboys. You name it—we got 'em."

Sure enough, the Calgary Stampeders had at least one Jewish cowboy: Rube Ludwig, a defector from the Winnipeg Blue Bombers. They had two of the pioneer Negro cowboys: Woodrow Wilson Strode, now a featured motion-picture performer, and Chuck Anderson. They had at least two Greek cowboys: Rod Pantages and Pete Thodos. And they had a Chinese cowboy in the bustling person of Normie Kwong.

There was an even more incongruous cowboy: Fritz Hanson, who had been the hero of Winnipeg's first Grey Cup victory thirteen years earlier. Hanson had been reactivated as a Calgary player though one of his legs had been almost torn off six or seven years previously when a grenade exploded prematurely on a military firing-range.

Lear could afford to smile that Sunday afternoon in Oakville because he was reasonably confident that Calgary could beat Ottawa. Lear had scouted Ottawa thoroughly the previous day. He and his American quarterback, Keith Spaith, had flown from Calgary to watch the Rough Riders beat Hamilton in the eastern final. Furthermore, Lear had the assistance of two full-time, unofficial, unpaid eastern scouts—Don Crowe and Don Durno—who provided him with vital information on the Ottawa team.

Now, in 1970, it seems utterly incomprehensible that there was little pre-game scouting in Canada twenty-two years ago. There was no exchange of game films. In fact, a year later, Calgary was accused of piracy when they managed to get their hands on a film of a Montreal Alouettes game before they played Montreal for the Grey Cup.

In 1948, the Calgary coach knew almost everything that was worth knowing about the Ottawa Rough Riders. On the other hand, Ottawa hadn't bothered to scout the Stampeders. Furthermore, the Rough Riders took the Stampeders just a bit lightly because no western team had won the Grey Cup since 1941.

Everyone knows that Calgary beat Ottawa 12–7 in that Grey Cup game. Everyone knows that Calgary scored its first touchdown on the hoariest of old-fashioned subterfuges—a sleeper-play pass from Spaith to Norman Hill, who now is an eminent Winnipeg neurosurgeon.

Everyone knows that Calgary scored the winning touchdown on an improbable Ottawa lapse. Ottawa's Bob Paffrath tossed a lateral pass wildly and his teammate, Pete Karpuk, was mesmerized by the sight of the bouncing ball. Woodrow Wilson Strode solemnly picked up the fumble and ran to the Ottawa 10-yard line. Pete Thodos plunged over the Ottawa goal line on first down.

Concerning that 1948 game, I remember best the remarkable reformation of Lovable Leslie Lear.

Coach Lear was a sturdy chap who could drink a quart of rye before breakfast without batting an eye. However, on the Sunday morning following the game, I sat with him in his Royal York Hotel suite while, carefully, he diagrammed the key plays for me on sheets of foolscap. He showed me the diagrams of the Ottawa formations that he had obtained on his scouting trip the previous week. We were there for a couple of hours while Lear sipped coffee and orange juice. An unopened bottle of rye sat prominently on the desk.

Lear's oldest and dearest pal, Ches McCance, was banging on the suite door and howling indignantly. "I know that you're in there, you blankety-blank," McCance was yelling. "You win the Grey Cup, and you act like a blankety-blankety. You can't kid me—I knew you when you were poor, you blankety-blank Winnipeg hillbilly."

Lear refused to unbolt the door as he listened to his dearest friend's noisy recriminations. You may not believe it, but there were tears in Lear's eyes.

"Geez, I'd like to go out with old Chester and bust a few windows," he said earnestly. "But this is the one day in my life when I have to act dignified."

Tarzan the Wonder Husky

Southam News
January 26, 1972

DOGSLED RACING isn't included in the official list of events that will be contested at next week's Olympic Games in Sapporo, Japan. From our viewpoint this is a very regrettable omission because Canada would be a sure-pop cinch to win the Olympic gold medal in dogsled racing.

Many years ago, the Olympic Games officials solemnly decided that, in the interests of international amity, dogsled racing shouldn't be included in the calendar of events. The Olympic Games officials were motivated by the widely acknowledged overwhelming superiority of Canadian sled dogs. A dogsled race at the Olympics would be strictly no contest! The Canadian team always would win by as far as a strong-armed farm boy can throw a big red apple.

The Olympic officials were correct, of course. Canada would have won the gold medal with such monotonous regularity that all those underprivileged little countries, such as Russia, China and the United States would have sulked. The first thing you knew, Russia, China and the United States might have withdrawn from the Olympic Games.

Modestly, we are prepared to acknowledge that Canada raises the world's largest, strongest and toughest sled dogs. We have some Canadian dogs that are so strong that they could tow the Empire State Building on a sled and beat those canine bums from Russia, China and the US of A.

If you're a student of sports history, you may recall the only occasion on which another country had the temerity to challenge Canada's supremacy in dogsled racing.

The US newspapers bellowed that Leonard Seppala had the world's swiftest team, simply because his dogs lugged a load of diphtheria serum from Fairbanks to the stricken community of Nome, Alaska. Hell, we have Canadian dogs who could have run *backwards* to beat Seppala's time from Fairbanks to Nome!

Seppala and his lead dog, a mutt named Balto, were very big stuff in the US newspapers in the ensuing months and it became necessary for Canada to defend its dog-racing honour. Eventually, Emile St. Goddard, a trapper from Les Pas, Manitoba, was selected to represent Canada in an international championship. The record book reveals that St. Goddard whipped Seppala four straight times. In the final race, he contrived the supreme canine insult by offering to give the weary Balto a ride on the Canadian sled.

Yet, St. Goddard's sled dogs really weren't outstanding by Canadian standards. His lead dog, Pierre, subsequently retired in disgrace when he permitted himself to be thrown, two out of three falls, by a seven-hundred-pound bear that St. Goddard was attempting to trap. For that reason, although Emile St. Goddard's name is listed in the Canada Sports Hall of Fame, Pierre's name isn't mentioned. Canadian dogdom doesn't honour losers.

Canada has produced countless sled dogs that, by comparison, would make Pierre look like a lily-livered runt. The greatest sled dog ever raised in Canada was Tarzan, lead dog for Jules Cornwall.

Tarzan was approximately the size of a Japanese station wagon. He was part husky, part Labrador and, after looking at him, you'd have to suspect that a muskox got into that act, too.

Jules and his lead dog Tarzan became one of the great silent legends of the North; a silent legend because officials of the Canadian Humane Society persuaded Canadian newspapers to refrain from printing details of the gruesome denouement.

Undoubtedly, Jules Cornwall's team was the swiftest and strongest ever to run an ice-bound trail. Wop May once offered to race Cornwall's team from Edmonton to Fort McMurray. Wop was flying his old single-engine Fokker. Admittedly, Wop was held up a bit by headwinds, but he was pretty damn surprised when he found Tarzan waiting to lick his hand on the Fort McMurray airstrip.

Well, Cornwall was out with his dog team one winter. They had been on the trapline for three months. One night, sitting in his tent, Jules decided that he'd like to see his old girlfriend, Olga Iktuk. Olga lived 1,200 miles away in Inuvik. But Jules hitched up his team and they set out.

Jules Cornwall's yearning for his inamorata resulted in a northland tragedy. Jules and his team fought their way through three weeks of continuous blizzards. Six of the dogs dropped dead of exhaustion. Finally, only Jules Cornwall and Tarzan were left alive and, two days earlier, they had shared their last tin of beans.

As they sat in their tent that fateful night, Jules said to his dog, "You are my faithful friend, but in the great tradition of the northland, I must kill you and eat you. A starving man always eats his dog."

Tarzan understood. He nodded his head as he looked at his master. Then, Jules Cornwall made a mistake. Jules Cornwall neglected to take the first bite. Instead, Tarzan ate his master! He ate him right down to his hobnailed shoes.

After he had slept off the effects of his supper, Tarzan arose and he made the incredible journey through the blizzard, all the way back to Edmonton.

Tarzan, in his remaining years, became a public figure in Edmonton, spending every day lying on the steps of the old city hall. The old dog had one peculiarity. When anyone called a greeting to him, Tarzan wouldn't bark a reply. Instead, he would smile a slow, wise smile—and he would emit a very loud burp.

The Coleman Awards

Southam News
April 5, 1972

A THIRTEEN-YEAR-OLD SON can be a pain in the ear for an ancient sportswriter who asks nothing from life but peace and quiet. All those silly questions! Did you ever play in the Rose Bowl game? Did you ever play hockey against Rocket Richard? Did you ever have a date with Lana Turner? Did you ever own a horse that ran in the Kentucky Derby?

It must be very distressing for a thirteen-year-old boy to be saddled with a father who never was able to beat Jesse Owens at the Olympic sprint distance of 100 metres or 200 metres. Worse still, imagine having a father who never dared to go fifteen rounds with Joe Frazier!

Even when a thirteen-year-old boy becomes resigned to the fact that his father is engaged in such a lamentably sedentary occupation as sportswriting, he may be miffed by obvious parental mediocrity. Well, for gawd's sakes, *every* kid can't have Errol Flynn for a father!

The situation worsens when a thirteen-year-old reaches the stage where he reads the daily papers. For instance, the thirteen-year-old in our household was perusing a journal the other morning as, sulkily, he spooned oatmeal mush into his big, wide kisser.

Without looking up from the paper, he said with a groan, "I see where you didn't even win a National Newspaper Award this year. Boy, you sure must be writing lousy stuff."

Resisting the impulse to give him a good stiff clout on the lug, I maintained a gentlemanly silence. As a matter of fact, I turned off the power unit in my hearing aid. Nevertheless, the silence rankled. It's about time that I put this upstart critic in his place by listing publicly some of the honours that have been bestowed upon me during my long and inglorious career in the communications industry.

I can hardly wait to see the look of awed admiration on the little rat's face this morning when he reads this paper and discovers that his father, in the past has won an Oscar, an Emmy, the Gridiron Club Award, a Peabody Award, the Neilson Award, the Foster Hewitt Trophy and the Southam National Journalism Award.

Too long, modesty has impelled me to hide my light under a bush. In the interests of maintaining peace in my own household, now I strip away the veil of secrecy and reveal the details of these prize-winning performances:

NEILSON AWARD, 1959: This is not the same Neilson Award that is made annually to the number-one television personality. This Neilson Award was made by the Neilson company and it was won by me for my complete set of hockey pictures, which used to be packed in every bar of Jersey Milk.

OSCAR, 1955: The Academy of Motion Picture Arts and Sciences snobbishly ignored my script for the unfilmed classic, *Pride of the Argos*. This award was made to me by Oscar Berceller, the former proprietor of the Winston Grill on Toronto's King Street, and it commemorates my incredible feat of consuming sixteen double martinis at one sitting without blowing my upper plate.

EMMY TELEVISION AWARD, 1963: This was a special award "for courage above and beyond the call of duty" after I interviewed Gene Kiniski on three separate occasions on national television. Gene wrecked the studio three times, but I emerged with nothing worse than a twisted larynx.

GRIDIRON CLUB AWARD, 1971: This isn't the same prize that is offered annually by the Gridiron Club of Washington, DC. This award was made by the Gridiron Club of Portage La Prairie, Manitoba. It commemorates the fact that, over a period of thirty years, I lost more money than any other newspaperman betting on losing western teams in the annual Grey Cup games.

PEABODY AWARD, 1949: The George Foster Peabody Awards for television and radio writing weren't inaugurated until 1952. This particular Peabody Award was made by Eddie Peabody, the famous banjo soloist who was, for many years, the star of the Fanchon and Marco and the Keith-Orpheum vaudeville circuits. It was given to me when I won a ten-thousand-dollar bet for Peabody by rolling a "hard six" on the crap table at the opening night of the Desert Inn in Las Vegas, Nevada.

FOSTER HEWITT TROPHY, 1950: This is a very special prize given occasionally to an outstanding radio performer. I won it for telling the same Howie Morenz anecdote *ten* times in one season on the national network in those old Hot Stove League hockey intermissions.

SOUTHAM NATIONAL JOURNALISM AWARD, 1972: This is the most coveted prize in the world of Canadian newspapering. It is awarded to the foreign correspondent who submits the most colourful, precisely detailed and significant expense account. The judges were unanimous in their decision this year: probably they were dazzled by the fact that my expense account was lavishly illustrated with colour photographs taken inside one of those Japanese bathhouses in Sapporo.

I trust that my thirteen-year-old son reads this list of splendid achievements this morning. I will be completely mollified only if he chokes on his oatmeal mush.

Literary prizes—hell, they're old stuff to me! I have won so many of them that, among my understandably jealous colleagues, I am known as "Destiny's Tot."

The McGill Man

Southam News
July 7, 1972

MAX BELL died less than two furlongs from the plot of green grass on which he scored one of his first sporting triumphs. From Max's room in the Montreal Neurological Hospital, you could look right down on the football field in Molson Stadium. Two furlongs? That's a pretty accurate guess; a man standing on the 55-yard line could hear you calling from Max's window.

On a misty October late afternoon, many years ago, I sat in an upper row in the concrete stands and watched Max Bell kicking for the McGill Juniors. Gawd, how he could kick that ball!

He was magnificently disciplined in athletics, as in every other phase of his life. He had a funny little habit. In each kicking situation, just before he called for the ball to be snapped to him, he'd make a complete turn of 360 degrees on the spot from which he had decided to punt. He'd make this funny little complete pivot and he'd clap his hands to call for the ball.

He never wore a helmet. He stood there, bare-headed and very serious. As he let the ball slide from his hands, his right leg swung in a perfect arc; his spiral punts rocketed 60 to 70 yards every time. Sitting high in the stands, you could see Max's foot strike the ball and then, slightly delayed, you could hear the echoing sound—PUNG!—while the ball was soaring in the autumn twilight. He kicked McGill's opponents right out of Molson Stadium!

It was the same thing in hockey. Max had cartilage removed from his left knee and the doctor told him that he'd never play hockey again. That doctor didn't know Max Bell.

Max spent eight hours each day sitting on the corner of his study desk and swinging his leg continuously to stretch his healing knee. He was back playing hockey in five weeks.

He won his "Big M" as a member of one of the greatest teams in the history of intercollegiate hockey. His teammates included Dr. Maurice Powers, Jack McGill, Nels Crutchfield, Gordon Crutchfield, George McTeer, Bert McGillivray, Ken Farmer, Hugh Farquharson and D'Arch Doherty.

Max Bell took me to McGill University. Our fathers were long-time friends, and when my time came to go to college, I was shipped east in the care of Max, who already had spent one year at McGill. It didn't turn out quite the way our parents anticipated: on the eastbound train, I introduced my "keeper" to the mysteries of handicapping racehorses. The incident turned into a lifetime running gag: Max always said untruthfully that the eastbound trip "cost me hundreds of thousands of dollars."

Actually, Max quickly became one of the two or three most successful handicappers whom I've known in my long career around racetracks. He approached horse racing as he approached every other enterprise: he appraised every facet of the sport before he became involved totally. He and Wilder Kipley started out with a couple of cheap horses that they raced under the name of Arby Stable. Before he had exhausted the possibilities of racing, Max's horses had won the Irish Derby and the Queen's Plate.

Bell became a legend in his lifetime, but peculiarly enough, most of the stories about him were true. He never took a drink of alcoholic beverage and he never had a smoke in his fifty-nine years. He never wore a hat—except once!

He flew to England to see one of his horses, Arctic Blue, run in the Epsom Derby. He felt that he should dress up for the occasion, so he went to Moss Bros. in London and rented the complete rig. He went out to Epsom wearing striped trousers, a swallow-tailed coat, a grey weskit and a grey top hat. A photographer took a picture of him at Epsom, simply to record the remarkable fact that Max once was seen in public wearing a hat.

He was pleasantly and harmlessly nutty on the subject of his physical condition. On a train or in a hotel, he'd often sit stripped to the waist, exercising with one of those spring-cable chest expanders. One night, I walked in on him at his suite at the Palliser Hotel in Calgary. He had just finished his exercises and, clad only in his underwear shorts, he was indulging in a cool orgy—he was eating three different-flavoured scoops of ice cream from the same dish.

Max Bell reluctantly accepted his public image as "the sporting millionaire oilman-publisher" but the secret of his strength as a human being was the fact that, even when he became extraordinary wealthy, he never lost the common touch. He sat in the boardrooms of Canada's greatest corporations but also he was welcome in the tack rooms on the backstretch at Calgary's Victoria Park.

Max never kept an unlisted telephone number and his phone was open to anyone who called. There were occasions when N.R. Crump, the chairman of the Canadian Pacific, couldn't reach Bell on the telephone because Max was speaking to Doc Burns, the racetrack tout of saintly memory. And you could bet that Doc had phoned collect; and you could bet further that he was attempting to "borrow" money; and you could bet even further that Max gave him the money.

Max Bell never turned down an old friend or a cause that he considered to be just. Just before he underwent his second-last brain operation, he calmly accepted the possibility that he might not survive the ordeal. So he instructed his office to make his personal donation of forty thousand dollars to Hockey Canada.

Have I Ever Been Wrong?

Southam News
September 2, 1972

MONTREAL—HERE'S A FLATLY POSITIVE PREDICTION that Canada will win at least seven of the eight games in this hockey series with the Soviet Union. The Russians might scratch out a tie in one of the four games that will be played on Moscow ice.

This prediction isn't influenced by flag-waving chauvinism. This is a cold-blooded prognostication based on a comparison of Team Canada 1972 and the national team that represented Canada in Stockholm in

April 1969. Our country hasn't entered one of those world tournaments in the last three years since 1969.

First, I am one observer who is convinced that the Soviet team of 1972 *isn't* as good as the Russian national team that played at Stockholm in 1969. The Russians didn't bring Anatoli Firsov and Vitali Davydov on their present invasion of Canada. Or Alexander Ragulin, who long has been the linchpin. The absence of two well-established stars, plus the fact that the number-one defenceman is suffering from an acute case of "the slows," adds up to a Russian team that is slightly substandard. Furthermore, I saw this same Russian team in Sapporo seven months ago, and they were tied by the relatively harmless Swedes. The Soviets lacked their customary poise in Sapporo.

No, no, Ivan Ivanovich! You've picked the wrong year to test yourself in a match with Canada's professionals!

Now let's turn back to the 1969 tournament in Stockholm when Canada's national team lost a total of six games. The young Canucks were beaten twice by the Soviets, twice by the Czechs and twice by the Swedes. It was a very immature Canadian team and it compiled one of our worst records in a world tournament.

Yet there was a peculiarity about the two Russia–Canada games. In both games Canada was outscored rather handily but—strangely enough—they had a pretty fair share of the territorial play.

There was one department in which the Canadians fell down badly—shooting. The Canadians had almost as many shots on the net as the Russians in the two games but the Canadians had only one or two men who could shoot hard enough to break a mirror. If there had been even one Canadian in Stockholm who could shoot in the manner of Dennis Hull or Frank Mahovlich, our young Canadian team might have fluked out a win over the well-drilled Russians.

Now you can see the point I'm making about this 1972 series. The Canadian professionals will overpower the Russians with vastly superior artillery. Canadian shooting will be the dominant factor in all eight games.

If you listen to all the reverse propaganda, you can give the Russians a big edge in physical conditioning; you can accept the suggestion that the Russians are individually stronger (I doubt it); you can accept the fact that the Russians are better skaters (quite possible); but, in the final analysis, the series will boil down to shooting and goaltending.

And in both of those departments, Canada will have a big edge. Every single man on Team Canada 1972 can shoot the puck harder than any member of Canada's 1969 national team. The carnage may be frightful.

Young Vladislav Tretiak, the Russian goalie who celebrated his twentieth birthday only ten days ago, shyly told a press conference Friday morning that he never has had a tooth knocked out since he became a goaltender at the age of eleven.

I doubt seriously that he'll be able to make the same boast when this series ends in Moscow on the night of September 28.

A few of the more bloodthirsty chauvinists in the media were mildly disappointed when Coach Harry Sinden didn't nominate Dennis Hull of the Chicago Black Hawks to play in tonight's first game. Those chauvinists had been cracking their knuckles in glee as they contemplated goalie Tretiak's probable reaction the first time that Dennis fires a rocket past his head. Nevertheless, Coach Sinden performed a highly polished job of "psyching out" the Russians when the Canadian squad held its final full dress rehearsal in the Montreal Forum Friday afternoon.

The Russians had completed their own practice two hours earlier but they remained in the Forum to have their first live view of their rivals. Meanwhile, some of the Canucks had been attending a huge open-air public rally at Place Ville Marie, and when they reached the rink, they were wound up like a two-dollar alarm clock.

The result was that the Canadian practice session yesterday afternoon was at least twice as robust and exciting as any of the practices that they staged in the past three weeks at Toronto's Maple Leaf Gardens.

Keenly aware that the Russians were sitting on the east side of the Forum watching them, the Canadians deliberately unlimbered all their big guns. Every shot that missed the net hit the backboards with a "bang" that could have been heard all the way to the Caughnawaga Indian Reservation.

The Canadians skated at absolute peak speed and, all the while, they laughed and joked noisily, giving the distinct impression that they had much more speed in reserve. As a matter of fact, it may have been the most startling workout in the history of North American professional hockey. Even veteran reporters who have been watching hockey since the era of Howie Morenz were mildly bewildered. One poor old newspaperman was rushed to hospital for observation: he got a nasty chill from the cold wind that was created when Yvan Cournoyer swished past the press seats in a blur of snow and mist. Hospital reports last night indicated that the newspaperman may have a very slight case of pneumonia.

Coach Sinden's "show" had been a four-star smash hit.

Later a couple of reporters had a sneak interview with Rick Noonan, the Canadian superagent who has infiltrated the Russian team's dressing room in the capacity of trainer.

"What did the comrades think of the practice?" Noonan was asked.

"They," replied Noonan, rolling his eyes significantly, "were highly impressed."

Whose National Game?

Southam News
September 4, 1972

MONTREAL—You could smell the dank imminence of disaster when Valery Kharlamov sped past centre ice at 2:39 of the second period.

Valery baby was really tramping! At 2:40, the score tied 2–2, Kharlamov made a move that completely undressed Canadian defenceman Don Awrey. Poor old Donald's athletic supporter fluttered right into the organ loft of the Montreal Forum. The speeding Kharlamov shot the puck between the long padded legs of Ken Dryden who, momentarily, was frozen in startled immobility. Dryden had anticipated the inevitable shot, but Kharlamov fired the puck too swiftly and too accurately for Dryden to block its flight into the Canadian net.

That goal was the absolute gasser, chaps! School was "out" at that point. The Soviets had overcome a 0–2 deficit and they had taken a 3–2 lead. Less than eight minutes later, Kharlamov scored another goal and the Russians' complete mastery of the situation was evident to even the most myopic chauvinist in the strangely silent territory that extends all the way from Corner Brook, Newfoundland to Port Alice, British Columbia.

You looked down on the ice where—with the game only half

finished—Canada's best professional hockey players were perspiring in impotent frustration. The Canadians were being beaten soundly at the game that they invented, and there was absolutely nothing that they could do to avert, or even to delay, the denouement.

But let's have no blubbering at the breakfast table this morning. Just eat up all your Wheaties. The Soviets beat the whey out of our hockey team, but there's a second game scheduled for tonight.

As often is the case when an outstanding upset occurs in the world of athletics, many Canadians were looking for someone to blame after the National Ego had been effectively deflated on Saturday night. One Canadian hockey player—who shall remain nameless, because he was angry and frustrated when he spoke—blamed Canadian newspapers for lulling the hockey players into a false sense of security.

"The newspapers printed too much guff about our superiority over the Russians," the Canadian player growled. "We read so much about it that we began to believe it."

I am one of the many Canadian reporters who saw this same Russian team play in the Olympic hockey tournament in Sapporo less than seven months ago. This same Russian team, in winning the Olympic championship in Sapporo, didn't appear to be strong enough to beat the Minnesota North Stars or the St. Louis Blues.

These Russians aren't supermen. Simply, they're superbly conditioned athletes who came here to *play as a team.* They're the very same hockey players who performed only moderately well in Sapporo.

On Saturday night, they beat Canada with teamwork, skating ability, superior physical conditioning and excellent positional play. But *teamwork* was the most important factor in their victory. The Russians played as a cohesive unit whereas the Canadian professionals recklessly concentrated on hunting for goals.

Even as I emerge slowly from trauma and reflect on the sobering lessons of Saturday evening, I can't remember more than one or two occasions when the Canadians were detected in the act of backchecking with true professional diligence. I felt sorry for the Canadian defencemen who constantly were facing three-on-two crises.

The Canadians who genuinely distinguished themselves on Saturday night were the 11,818 spectators within the Montreal Forum. They were a fine sportsmanlike crowd and they gave you a feeling of pride.

They gave the Russians a genuinely friendly greeting; they applauded the brilliant plays of the visitors; and, quite properly, they gave a few mild razzoos to the Canadians when several of our disgruntled athletes became unnecessarily physical in the final two minutes of the game.

In the past thirty-six hours, the airwaves have been choked by quotations from individual players offering explanations of the Canadian defeat. Brian Glennie, who played on Canada's last national team in 1969, didn't dress for Saturday's opening game, but he was apprehensive when he saw the Canucks skate onto the ice.

"Emotionally, our guys were *up* too high," Glennie said. "I saw this happen with our last national team in Stockholm, but it can happen to professionals, too. Some of our guys, who normally mind their own business, were trying to throw their weight around. They were just too keyed up emotionally. You beat yourself when you lose your cool."

Phil Esposito said later, "We should have had a couple of games against other teams before this series began. This first game will do us more good than twenty-five practices. I missed three goals tonight that I never would have missed in mid-season form."

Harry Sinden and John Ferguson emerged with honour from their initiation as international coaches. Sinden offered no alibis—in rationalizing the defeat, he paid high tribute to the Russians.

"There's no doubt about it; they were much the better team," Harry said flatly. "They outplayed us in almost every department. I really didn't expect the Russian team to skate as they did for the entire sixty minutes. Their goaltender [Tretiak] surprised me. We got beaten by one fine hockey team."

While promising some Canadian lineup changes for the second game, Sinden said, "To tell the truth, I wasn't too disappointed by the way we played."

To which, a reporter asked, "Were you surprised by the way the Russians played?"

"I was stunned!" Harry replied bluntly.

You said it, Harry. You said it for yourself, for me, and for twenty-one million other Canadians.

On Saturday, this columnist predicted that Canada would win seven games in this series, while one game would be tied. Saturday's ego-deflator forces me to revise that prediction very drastically. Now I believe that the eight-game series will result in seven wins for Canada and one for the Russians.

A Few Words from Captain Phil

Southam News
September 11, 1972

VANCOUVER—Forget about that little 5–3 defeat in Vancouver, When we get those unsuspecting Slavs back on their home ice in Moscow, we'll hammer 'em—four straight!

The Canadian spectators are proving to be of invaluable assistance in the perpetration of this masterfully conceived subterfuge. Some of the Canadian spectators are booing our hockey players—thus deluding the Russians into believing that Canada has lost confidence in our team. The Russians are gobbling up the bait like lagniappe. By the time they get back to Moscow, they'll be so overconfident that they will fall into our trap—KABOOM!

Even some of our hockey players are contributing to this sly scheme. Phil Esposito did a grand job Friday night, pretending publicly that the boos of the Canadian spectators were irritating him.

"I was very disappointed with the people here," said Phil, as reporters feverishly wrote down his remarks in three languages. "I was very disappointed in the people in Winnipeg on Wednesday night. We're playing in this series because we love Canada—and we're being ridiculed by our fellow Canadians."

All this dutifully was reported to the official Soviet hockey delegation by three KGB men who were posing as foreign correspondents. The KGB men had a bit of difficulty transcribing and translating the remarks of Mr. Bill Goldsworthy, another Canadian player who was asked to comment on the reactions of the fans in Vancouver's Pacific Coliseum.

Friday night's script called for Mr. Goldsworthy to take first-period penalties, both of which would open the door for goals by the Russians. The fans responded dutifully by giving Goldsworthy a razzoo of quite impressive proportions.

Later, when Goldsworthy was asked to comment on the behaviour of the spectators, the vehemence of his reply blew out all the transistorized recording equipment in the building. He used some words that left the KGB agents looking at one another in utter befuddlement.

All in all, the Canadian spectators and the Canadian hockey players, acting their roles to the verge of travesty, managed to convey to the obviously duped Russians a picture of degrading Canadian disunity. Oh man, I can hardly wait until we get to Moscow—and show them that we were only fooling! This Canadian team will win four straight in Moscow. We've just been setting up the Russians for the Big Surprise!

I confess, though, that there were occasions on Friday night when the Canadian acting almost fooled me, too. May the good Lord forgive me, but there were moments when I almost permitted myself into being deluded that the Russians were the better team.

However, as the game wore on, my keen eyes began to detect subtle evidence of Canadian improvement. Mind you, the improvement wasn't apparent in the results of *Friday* night's game, but these were secret little improvements that bode well for the future.

For instance, the Canadian power play was vastly improved Friday night. The Canadian power play didn't yield a single goal by the Russians. Previously, the Canadian power play had given up a total of three goals in the first three games of the series.

Seriously, though, it isn't surprising that some of the Canadian players are irritated by the undeserved heckling from the spectators.

These players, in being invited to play for Canada at the international level, received "an offer that they couldn't refuse." Any man who turned down the invitation was derided as something dangerously akin to a traitor. These players were told by news commentators such as myself that this Russian team didn't appear to be overly impressive in winning the Olympic gold medal in Sapporo in February.

These players were brought into camp in Toronto and—in a training period of three weeks—they were expected to get into a physical condition that would equal the physical condition of the Russians—who had been training for *eleven months.*

Then, when our players go out on the ice and get their clocks cleaned in two of the four games, many Canadians suddenly get uptight and act as if this were the end of the world.

It seems to me that this would be a very appropriate occasion for

Canadian hockey fans to grow up, overnight, and begin to act in the manner of mature adults.

Really, there isn't much to choose between these two hockey teams. Russian hockey has improved more quickly than anyone expected, but I'm convinced that this particular Russian team has been playing *over* its head in this series.

And, although the Canadians haven't been able to match the Russians in skating in the first four games, the Canadians are certain to improve in this department within the next two weeks.

Comrade Boris Kulagin, the co-coach of the marvelous Muscovites, is a very shrewd cookie. Interviewed through an interpreter last night, he was asked if he expected to wrap up the series as soon as it shifts to Russian ice. Kulagin peered at his inquisitors stonily and replied, "We think that the Canadian team will play better and better in each game."

You said it Boris—but you really don't know the half of it! This Canadian team is just warming up for the greatest hockey comeback since the Toronto Maple Leafs lost the first three Stanley Cup games to the Detroit Red Wings in 1942.

Four straight, Boris! The Volga boatman had better get busy and start bailing—because your ship is going to be sunk without a trace.

One for All the Marbles

Southam News
September 28, 1972

MOSCOW—IF CANADA WINS TOMORROW NIGHT, we'll refer to it as the "Hockey Game of the Century." However, if Russia wins, we'll refer to it as the night when Comrade Bobrov dumped the overalls into Grandma Sinden's chowder.

Paul Henderson and goalie Tony Esposito combined to set up tomorrow's epic sports confrontation when Canada defeated the Soviet Union 4–3 in last night's seventh game of this international series. Paul scored the winning goal at 17:54 of the final period. But, up until that point, Esposito had been busier than an entire troupe of Japanese jugglers.

If it hadn't been for Tony's heroics between 5:15 and the ten-minute mark of that third period, we wouldn't be looking forward to tomorrow's game with any great interest. If Esposito hadn't stolen at least half a dozen goals from the Soviet marksmen in that pressure-packed space of four minutes and forty-five seconds, the Russians would have wrapped up the ruddy old world championship last night. Tomorrow's eighth contest would have been robbed of all meaning.

As it is, the Canadians now have come from behind, with true professional élan, to deadlock the series at three victories for each team, with one game tied. Without the slightest blush for my chauvinism, I confidently expect the onrushing Canucks to cop the duke tomorrow night.

Let us hark back to those excruciatingly tense four minutes and forty-five seconds in the third period. Tony had been weak and jittery and he was complaining of a tummy ache before the game. It's a lucky thing for our side that Esposito wasn't healthy: he's always at his best when he looks as if he needs a blood transfusion.

Anyhow, it started to snow in Moscow about the beginning of the third period and Tony suddenly must have felt that he was back home, in dear old Sault Ste. Marie. No one could fault Esposito when Alex Yakushev tied the score at 3–3 at 5:15 of that period. It was Russia's second power-play goal of the night. It was another of those occasions when there simply were too many Russians on the ice for Tony to handle. And, as far as that goes, Yakushev was far and away the best forward in the rink last night.

Scenting victory after that tying goal, the Soviets really shifted into overdrive. They put on their single greatest burst of the entire series. Obviously, they felt that one more goal would be sufficient to win the world championship. They damn nearly chased the perspiring and hard-working Canadians out of the rink. But, stretching, tumbling, diving and kicking in an unbelievable display of calculated acrobatics, Esposito held them at bay.

He stopped their sustained attack just seconds before the bell sounded for the teams to change ends at the middle of the third period. The Russians never attained quite that same pace again. I think that Tony broke their spirit—possibly he gave them a light inferiority complex that will continue through tomorrow evening.

And let me tell you something about Henderson's winning goal!

The teams were playing five-a-side because Gary Bergman and Boris Mikhailov were serving five-minute penalties after they attempted to precipitate the outbreak of World War III.

Well, there was a faceoff in the Canadian end and, just before the puck was dropped, Henderson caused a delay by skating over to speak to Bobby Clarke. I don't know what Henderson said to Clarke, but Clarke turned around to look at his defencemen, Serge Savard and Guy Lapointe. Bobby motioned to Lapointe, indicating that he wanted him to move over, slightly to the left and behind the faceoff circle. Then, for approximately the five hundredth time in this international series, Bobby Clarke won a faceoff. The puck slid back swiftly into the corner to his left. Lapointe got the puck and cleared it behind the net to Savard.

Meanwhile, old Paul was heading for Dreamsville and he really was tramping. There was smoke coming from Henderson's skates as he headed across mid-ice. Savard gave him a hard leading pass just before Paul reached the red line. At that point, Henderson gave a long blast on his whistle, just like a runaway locomotive, and he bore down on two startled Soviet defencemen.

Henderson was moving so swiftly that the defencemen didn't even get his number. He shoved the puck through the feet of the defenceman to his left. The puck hit the heel of his skate as Henderson made an abrupt diversion around the poor chap. The puck was waiting for Henderson behind the bewildered defenceman and Paul promptly hung that puck in the net. His rising shot performed a neat depilatory job on goalie Tretiak's right armpit. That was the sixth goal that Paul Henderson has scored in this series. However, from the viewpoint of most Canadians, it was the most important goal of his entire lifetime.

A tie last night would have been disastrous for Canada. It would have meant that, even if Canada won tomorrow's final contest, the series would have ended in an inconclusive draw.

Fortunately, tomorrow's finale will be refereed by Uve Dahlberg of Sweden and Rudy Bata of Czechoslovakia. Dahlberg and Bata handled last night's game and they were a vast improvement over Josef Kompalla and Franz Bader, those two incompetent kooks from West Germany.

As usual, Canada received the larger share of the penalties last night but, judged by the rather strict standards of European hockey, Canada probably deserved them, too. Dahlberg and Bata performed a rather capable job of keeping things in hand, particularly when Bergman and Mikhailov staged their bench-emptying ruckus just before Henderson scored the winning goal.

Mikhailov took Bergman into the boards at top speed behind the Canadian net. Boris put his arms around Bergy's neck a bit too affectionately and Bergman lashed out with his arms. At that juncture, Mikhailov kicked Bergman in the legs five times with his skates while Bergman punched Boris's head, very hard, against the yielding meshed wire above the boards. For a few seconds, Boris's noggin was bouncing around like a ping-pong ball. Yvan Cournoyer and Rod Gilbert also essayed to take a shot at Mikhailov, who responded by kicking them, too. If Boris ever loses his job with the Soviet national hockey team, he's a cinch to get a job with the Bolshoi Ballet. He's the best high-kicker to be seen in the country since Nureyev defected.

Oh, it was a rather jolly evening for the Canadian visitors, though a few strident voices are beginning to croak after a week of steady roistering.

And I wish that those Canadian television flacks would cease this practice of asking the Canadian crowd to give a phoney display of enthusiasm for the cameras. This "crowd reaction" provided a great boost for the Canadian team last Friday but now, after three games, it is losing its spontaneity.

Never a Doubt

Southam News
September 29, 1972

MOSCOW— I DON'T KNOW what the heck you were worrying about. I kept telling you that Canada would make a clean sweep of this series on Moscow ice. I can hardly wait to get home to have a few words with those wisenheimers who have been sending me all that charming mail.

Mind you, there were a few occasions yesterday when the confidence of even the most loyal Canadian wavered. At the end of the second period, when the Soviets were leading 5–3, things looked so bleak that a couple of us went up to the press bar on the fourth floor of the Luzhniki Ice Palace and ordered some of those salami sandwiches that they import from Minsk. They only import the bread from Minsk—the salami runs wild around here.

We were washing down the salami with a stout drencher of chloride of lime when a courier dashed in with the news that Phil Esposito had reduced the margin to 5–4 on a pass from Pete Mahovlich.

"Order me a double vodka," said my Canadian companion. "This is the only place to get a really dispassionate view of the game."

He was just downing his double vodka when the courier rushed back with the further intelligence that Rodrique "Mad Dog" Gilbert, the comely right-winger, had scored a clean-cut fistic decision over Evgeny Mishakov at 3:41. The courier panted the news that both players were serving major penalties.

"Crimey," howled my Canadian companion as he coughed the raw vodka through the gaps in his front teeth. "This must be the end of the world. Gilbert has gone berserk. We'd better get back into the arena so that we'll have a good seat when the bomb goes off."

Well, we got back to our seats soon enough to see Alan Eagleson logging more ice time than Don Awrey and Marcel Dionne have logged in this series.

The Eagle flew down from his perch, screaming wildly, when the goal judge failed to turn on the red light as Yvan Cournoyer tied the score at 12:56. This was the same goal judge who flashed the red light only for a split second when Paul Henderson scored the winner in the sixth game on Tuesday night.

Anyhow, a full platoon of Soviet militia grabbed Eagleson as he left his seat. They were giving him the heave-ho right out of the ruddy building when the Canadian hockey players, brandishing their hickory staves, converged on the boards immediately adjacent to the spot where the Eagle was going down for the third time.

Peter Mahovlich vaulted the boards and plunged into the crowd of militia. The other Canadian players were ready to follow Pete when—suddenly and inexplicably—at least ten militiamen retreated, leaving Eagleson resembling a pile of garbage. The players picked up Eagleson as, pale-faced and badly shaken, he was almost entirely a passenger while they propelled him clear across mid-ice to the other side of the rink and the security of the Canadian team's bench.

Never in the history of organized hockey has there been such an extraordinary spectacle. The Russian players and the crowd stood in stunned silence as the Canadian hockey team took matters into their own rough hands.

Come to think of it, Eagleson, with his glasses dangling from one ear, was the centre of a scene that was absurdly reminiscent of Eliza and Little Eva fleeing across the ice in that famous hominy-and-grits melodrama, *Uncle Tom's Cabin.*

Eagleson's feet hadn't even dried out after his first trip across the ice when he bounded over the boards again. This time, Alan and almost every member of the Canadian hockey contingent—from coach through civvy-clad non-playing members of the squad to physiotherapist and stick boy—was slithering and sliding madly to converge on the doorstep of the Russian net, where Paul Henderson had just finished scoring the winning goal of the entire damn series at 19:26.

Once again, the same goal judge didn't flash the red light as Henderson picked up his own rebound and shoved the puck under shell-shocked Vladislav Tretiak. The two referees didn't need the glow of the red light to tell them that the puck was in the net. At least thirty Canadian lunatics were pointing at the puck. They were yelling deliciously and they were clouting Henderson until his skull was ringing like a Chinese gong.

These heroics are becoming old hat to Henderson. He scored the winning goal in each of the final three games as Canada rushed to a genuinely thrilling triumph in the unofficial world championship of hockey. As a matter of fact, Paul also scored the fourth Canadian goal—which should have been the winner—in last Friday's opening game on Moscow ice. That was the simply revolting occasion on which the Canadian team suffered a six-minute defensive lapse in the third period and blew a three-goal lead.

"Unbelievable, unbelievable," Henderson kept muttering later in the dressing room as he shook his ringing head. He told reporters that Ron Ellis gave him the puck for his first shot. "Then," he said, still wagging his noggin incredulously, "I shoved my own rebound under him [Tretiak]."

You and I have our own highly emotional opinion of the type of hockey entertainment that was provided in this eight-game series, but the assistant coach, John Ferguson, probably expressed it for everyone.

Bill Brennan of the Detroit *Free Press* asked Fergy, "Did you ever see such a good hockey series?"

"Never, never," Ferguson replied firmly. Then, giving the matter approximately one second of thought, he said in amendment, "Well, maybe that series two years ago, when we [Montreal Canadiens] beat Boston in the first round of the Stanley Cup playoffs."

In view of the fact that I haven't been backward in expressing my opinion over the past four weeks, I have a compulsion to add that, for me, never has there been another hockey show that has matched this one in sustained excitement.

Remember, for a moment, that this was a Canadian team that was beaten on its home ice. Then, after being booed by some of their own nutty countrymen in Vancouver, these hockey players came all the way to unfamiliar Moscow and they beat the Russians before a partisan Russian crowd.

As our old horse-racing friend, defenceman Serge Savard, shouted in the dressing room last night, "A good racehorse always comes from behind to win. We won like a good racehorse. We did it the hard way—we came from behind."

Phil Esposito, who shared with Henderson the role of Canada's outstanding individual players over the series, put it a bit more bluntly.

"I thought that we had the series under control Tuesday night when we got some pretty good officiating from Dahlberg and Bata," growled Espo, who wore himself to a shadow with his selfless display in the past month. "Then, tonight, we get that [obscenity] German as a referee and he damn nearly screws us out of the championship."

Mr. Esposito was referring to Mr. Josef Kompalla, a West German alleged hockey referee who must be the last word in cloth-headed guffins. Kompalla almost penalized the Canadians out of the rink in the first period and the lid blew off when he gave Jean-Paul Parise a very, very questionable interference penalty at 4:10.

Parise lost his head when Kompalla added a misconduct penalty. Kompalla almost lost his head, too, because Parise rushed at him with his stick raised high over his left shoulder and he acted as if he would decapitate the referee. Kompalla ordered Parise to the dressing room with a match penalty.

Around the Canadian bench, the occupants almost went insane. In fact, a few did take leave of their senses. A Canadian threw a chair onto the ice, where it disintegrated. Someone else near the Canadian bench threw another chair onto the ice. For a moment, it appeared possible that Coach Harry Sinden might take his team to the dressing room and refuse to finish the game.

Fortunately for the prestige of Canadian hockey, the game was continued to its successful conclusion. The Soviets were leading 1–0 at the time of Parise's expulsion. But it must be acknowledged that the display around the Canadian bench did little to enhance our reputation in world diplomatic circles.

I must confess that I shared a bit of the Canadian team's feelings of rancour. I felt that the Soviets took a dead set on us yesterday. The Russians, of course, controlled all of the seat sales and last night, for the first time, they inserted an organized cheering section of approximately three hundred persons, directly in the middle of the Canadian rooting section.

This Soviet "fifth column" did its level best to counteract the Canadian cheering. One stalwart girl had a Soviet flag that she waved violently every time the television cameras turned on the Canadian section.

I wish that you could have been in the rink with me. It was the damnedest feeling, to stand there at the end of the game, listening to three thousand Canadians, thousands of miles from home, singing "O Canada" as they glowed with pride. Then they began to chant, "We're number one! We're number one!"

I looked at the spot where the Russian infiltrators had been sitting among the Canadians. Every last one of them had disappeared within thirty seconds after the dramatic end of the game—flags and all.

One mild complaint: after lunch on Wednesday, Paul Henderson made a prediction that Ronnie Ellis would score the goal that would win the series for Canada. Paul Henderson is a fine hockey player, but as a prognosticator, he's a bum. Now, if ever you're looking for really valuable predictions, just read this column.

Fanging Mr. Jellyroll

Southam News
August 27, 1973

IT HAS COME TO MY ATTENTION that while I was covering the football beat in western Canada I was libelled in the sacred precincts of the House of Commons by Otto Jellyroll, a wet-eared political tyro who represents the Toronto constituency of High Park–Humber Valley.

Mr. Jellyroll referred to my distinguished newspaper confrere, Richard E. Bedclothes, and me as "bigoted opportunists." Furthermore, he recklessly accused us of being the authors of "anti-Canadian remarks."

Otto chose to open his big yap in the sanctuary of the House of Commons, a circumstance that protects him from legalistic reprisal. However, Otto needn't have worried on that score because Mr. Bedclothes and I are old-fashioned newspapermen who never would resort to lawsuits in dealing with our public detractors.

Okay Otto, you asked for it! Some older, wiser politician should have taken you aside and he should have warned you to avoid name-calling contests with a pair of newspaper columnists.

I am fully aware of Otto Jellyroll's sporting background. He is a former figure skater who brought honour to this country by sharing a world championship. However, he has gone a bit to fat since he became a politician and regrettably some of that fat appears to have lodged between his ears.

Where the hell do you get that stuff about "bigoted opportunists" and "anti-Canadianism," Otto? If you bothered to read the printed evidence carefully, you'd damn well know why Mr. Bedclothes and I consistently have questioned Montreal's financial capability for staging the summer Olympic Games in 1976. Stop twiddling your thumbs while you sit in your House of Commons seat, Otto—get off your butt and go on over to the parliamentary library to study the files of your country's daily newspapers. It's all there in the files, Otto, in black and white!

I can't speak for Mr. Bedclothes, but I can reiterate my own reasons for opposing the staging of the Olympic Games in a Canadian city. I emphasize that I'm opposed to the Olympic Games being staged in *any* Canadian city—not only Montreal but Toronto, Winnipeg, Vancouver, Edmonton, Calgary, Ottawa or Prince George.

I'm opposed to the *cost* of the Games! I have evidence of the costs of staging the Olympic Games in Tokyo and Munich. You know as well as I know that the 1976 Olympic Games will cost five hundred million dollars. Already we have some hint of those "hidden costs." The CBC is being forced to budget eighty million dollars for new television equipment for the Olympic Games. And they don't know how they're going to be able to make any further utilization of that particular equipment after the Games have been completed.

I argue that instead of spending five hundred million dollars on a two-week spectacle the same money could be spent much more wisely over a twenty-year period in providing new sports and recreational facilities for *all* the citizens of Canada.

You could build Canada into a genuinely athletic country with an expenditure of five hundred million dollars spread over twenty years. You could build arenas and stadia in Trois-Rivières, Sherbrooke, Halifax, Charlottetown, St. John, London, Hamilton, Windsor, Saskatoon, Regina, Moose Jaw, Edmonton and countless other smaller Canadian communities that need such facilities. You could open up thousands of acres for ski runs, public golf courses and public tennis courts. You could take three thousand of our best young Canadian athletes and expose them to intensive training programs.

So think very carefully about it, Mr. Jellyroll, before you commit the error again of referring to me—even in the sanctuary of the House of Commons—as a "bigoted opportunist." When you employ the word bigot you are implying that I am anti-French or anti-Quebec. If I am anti-anything, I may plead guilty to the charge of being strongly opposed to stupidity in the House of Commons.

As for your "anti-Canadian" slur, I suggest that you take another close look at all those newspaper files in the parliamentary library. I accept, with equanimity, the fact that I could have been described as many kinds of a son of a bitch in my time, but no one ever could describe me as an anti-Canadian son of a bitch.

I trust, Otto old chap, that you're not suffering from the delusion that all you Progressive Conservatives who were successful in the last election were sent to Ottawa because your policies enthused the electorate.

Forget it, Otto. You guys simply were washed into Ottawa on an anti-Liberal groundswell that was sweeping across the land. Now we discover that you PC guys are just as ineffectual as the Liberals. For gawd's sake, don't precipitate another expensive election. Don't rock the Ship of State!

In the unlikely event that the Progressive Conservatives are asked to form the government before 1976, I believe that there's an appropriate cabinet portfolio awaiting you. You should be appointed Federal Midwife to Mayor Jean Drapeau of Montreal.

"Midwife?" you ask.

Yes. You may recall that approximately one year ago Mayor Drapeau stated loftily, "The Montreal Olympics no more can have a deficit than a man can have a baby."

Well, Mayor Drapeau is *pregnant*, just as surely as the good Lord made little apples. And the federal government will be compelled to appoint a midwife to bring His Worship safely through his painful *accouchement.*

One Helluva Stubborn Cat

Southam News
August 15, 1973

THE WORLD'S BIGGEST DOG-SWIMMING RACE will be staged at the Canadian National Exhibition in Toronto on Sunday. The canine swimming marathon is staged annually as a memorial to Rex, the hero dog that once fought an epic battle with Doc Black's sabre-toothed cat named Maud.

In all the long history of the animal kingdom there never has been another who was as tough as Maud. Doc Black's cat terrorized the entire East End of Toronto—the whole waterfront area from the original Woodbine racetrack right down to the gas works.

Doc Black was a veterinary surgeon with a large racehorse practice. His veterinary hospital still is in operation on Queen Street East, just past the corner of Morse Street and, presently, the resident veterinarian is Doc Black's grandson. In the small garden behind the hospital there are a cairn and a plaque recording the fact that Maud won 104 consecutive fights against all comers.

Old Doc Black always was secretive about Maud's background. It is possible that he acquired her on one of his big-game hunting expeditions in Africa. Maud looked as if she might have been sired by a small panther. Her teeth were distinctly peculiar—two incisors, one each side of her mouth, protruded—and they were sabre-edged. It's a damn cinch that Maud hadn't been foaled in the hayloft on an Ontario farm. No sir, not *that* cat!

Maud loathed dogs. She abided human adults; she adored small children; but she hated dogs with an intensity that bordered on psychosis. She could put up with the horses that came to the veterinary hospital for treatment. Doc Black's dog practice fell away to zero while Maud was around the place.

Maud used to lie on the veranda in front of Doc Black's house, which adjoined the hospital. She used to lie there, waiting for dogs. Whenever a dog appeared on the street, Maud would jump him. She would leap right on his back and sink her claws into his hide. Really used to beat the heck out of them. When the dog was in full flight, ki-yi-ing in terror, Maud would leap from his back and, stiff-legged in triumph, she would strut back to Doc Black's veranda. Man, she simply whipped the tar out of every dog that made the mistake of venturing in the vicinity of the Queen–Morse intersection!

The canine population of Toronto's East End was panic-stricken. Dogs who wished to go from downtown Toronto to Balmy Beach used to sneak aboard the Queen Street electric trams so that Maud wouldn't see them when they passed Morse Street. Some dogs even walked all the way north to Danforth Avenue to avoid Maud's territory.

After Maud had scored 103 knockout victories over her canine foes, the dogs of the East End held an emergency meeting. They called in Rex, a dog that was the acknowledged heavyweight champion of the Bloor–Danforth strip. Rex was a cross between a Newfoundland and a Labrador retriever. Rex listened gravely while the East End dogs explained their state of peril and, a bit reluctantly, he agreed to take on the formidable Maud.

The big confrontation took place on a summer Sunday afternoon. Maud was lying in her accustomed spot on Doc Black's veranda when Rex casually sauntered across the intersection of Queen and Morse. Hundreds of dogs, curious but cautious, were cringing in doorways two blocks away, awaiting the battle.

Maud immediately sprang to the attack. She leaped on Rex's back and she sank her claws into his shoulders. Rex had anticipated the assault, but he was surprised by Maud's strength and ferocity. Screaming in pain, Rex ran due south along Morse Street with Maud clinging to his back. Rex ran madly until he reached the shore of Lake Ontario and he plunged into the cold water. Maud hated water but refused to relax her death grip.

Rex attempted to drown Maud. He submerged and he swam underwater, but Maud refused to quit. Rex kept swimming right across the lake in the direction of Toronto Island. It was one of the most amazing swimming feats in the history of the animal kingdom. Rex kept plodding along, weighed down by a savage sabre-toothed cat.

About every fifty yards, Rex would submerge and he would swim underwater until he felt that his lungs would burst. Maud didn't let go of her hold but, after they had gone a mile, Rex could sense that she was weakening.

Well, when Rex finally struggled ashore on Toronto Island, just beneath the lighthouse at the Eastern Gap, Maud still was clinging to his back but she was unconscious and half-drowned. When Rex fell down on the beach, exhausted, Maud simply tumbled from his back and she lay beside him.

After he had recovered his strength, Rex looked at Maud and he detected that the pulse in her throat was throbbing faintly. He began to give her mouth-to-mouth resuscitation. He worked on her desperately for fifteen minutes until Maud finally opened her eyes.

Maud stood up, but she didn't express any gratitude. She just wound up with her right forepaw; she slugged Rex on the kisser; and, with one punch, she knocked him absolutely cold!

Then, stiff-legged, Maud walked across Toronto Island to the docks and boarded the first available ferry boat for downtown Toronto. Maud was one hell of an unforgiving cat.

That, however, was Maud's last fight. Her unnatural submersion in the cold waters of Lake Ontario proved to be fatal. She contracted pneumonia and, a few days later while she lay gasping on Doc Black's veranda, she just keeled over and expired.

Rex went to the funeral. He felt that it was the least he could do. He stood in that little back garden with tears in his eyes as old Doc Black conducted the simple but dignified burial ceremonies.

Rex was much too decent a dog to object, even when old Doc Black erected the plaque, on which were engraved the words: "Maud, The World's Toughest Cat. 104 Victories; No Defeats." Rex didn't object though he knew in his heart that Maud's record actually was "103 Victories; One Draw."

Christmas Story

Southam News
December 24, 1973

DUSK WAS SETTLING SOMBRELY on Christmas Eve when Charlie heard the car turning off the roadway into the stable yard. He heard the tires of the big car crunching the frozen snow. Instinctively, Charlie glanced at the old-fashioned alarm clock that was clicking noisily atop the trunk in one corner of the tack room. The clock showed 4:46 p.m.

Charlie stood up and pulled on his coat and tweed cap. Then he picked his mitts from the two wall pegs on which they were hanging. He opened the tack-room door carefully and he went out to meet them.

He stared indifferently at the big car as it lumbered to a stop directly in front of his door. He knew that there was only one person who could be visiting him on Christmas Eve.

"Hi, old-timer," shouted the Boss as he opened his door and squeezed his bulk past the steering column. The Boss was a big man, the type of former athlete who packs on weight when he becomes wealthy in his middle years. His size was accentuated by his long winter coat with its full Persian lamb collar.

The girl got out of the far side of the car and she came around to stand beside the Boss. "You know Helen," he said briefly and Charlie touched the peak of his cap politely to acknowledge the introduction. The girl really was extraordinarily beautiful. She was at least twenty years younger than her companion; she smiled easily, her eyes lighting up her whole face with genuine warmth.

"Everything okay here, Charlie?" asked the Boss, nodding toward the row of stall doors that already had been closed against the cold of the winter night.

"Everything is fine," Charlie replied quietly. "The yearling was a bit colicky a couple of days ago. I gave him a shot of Bells and moved him into the stall next to the tack room so I can hear him at night." As he spoke he opened the upper half of the door on the first stall and the two men looked in. "He's cleaned up the oats from his afternoon feeding," said Charlie. "I moved the stud horse down to a stall at the other end of the row."

The two men went from stall to stall, opening the upper doors and looking in. The girl, after exchanging glances with Charlie, didn't join in the token examination of the horses. She went into the warm tack room and she stood appraising the meagre comforts of old Charlie's little home. She went out once to get a paper bag and a fairly large flat cardboard box from the car.

When the two men returned to the tack room Charlie poured three cups of coffee from a metal pot that had been simmering on the hot plate. The Boss opened the paper bag and he gave Charlie a bottle of very expensive whisky. In the same gesture he slipped two one-hundred-dollar bills into Charlie's hand, saying, "Merry Christmas, old-timer."

"Well, same to you," said Charlie uncomfortably, shoving the banknotes into his pocket without looking at them.

"I brought a present, too," the girl said, ripping open the cardboard box. She pulled out a warm, fleece-lined car coat with a big collar. Laughing with infectious pleasure, she insisted on Charlie modelling the new coat right there. Her laughter tinkled in the tiny room as she buttoned the coat on the old man.

"Helen worries about you," the Boss grunted.

"Yes," said the girl firmly. "I wish that you'd move out of this tack room and live in the farmhouse. It's silly to have that heated house sitting there empty most of the time. You could have someone come and visit you for Christmas."

"This is where I belong, miss," Charlie said civilly. "I've been around horses all my life. I like to sleep here, close, so I can hear them if they need me."

"Well, it's time to go," the Boss said brusquely. There were some things he hadn't bothered to tell the girl.

The girl began to follow him through the door and then, in one other warm, generous, natural impulse, she turned and hugged the old man and gave him a great big kiss.

Charlie, fingering the buttons of his new coat, followed her through the door and he watched her skip over the frozen snow to get into the car.

The car drove down to the far end of the shedrow and made a U-turn. As it was passing the tack-room door on its way out the girl made the driver stop. She rolled down the car window and, with her eyes glistening strangely, she called out, "Merry Christmas, Charlie—and take care of yourself!"

Oddly touched by the sincerity in her beautiful face, Charlie raised one hand in salute and he said, "You take good care of yourself too, miss."

It was perhaps three hours later that Charlie made his final round of the stalls. He opened each door and he spoke quietly to each horse. Then, he returned to his tack room; he hung up his new coat carefully and he turned down the volume of the radio. He opened the new bottle and he poured a stiff drink.

"One drink for remembering," he said softly and he went over and opened the trunk in one corner of the room. He pulled out a packet of letters and he sat down on the edge of his cot. He extracted a couple of faded photographs from an envelope and he looked at them thoughtfully as he sipped his drink.

When the glass was empty Charlie replaced the photographs and the letters in the trunk, which he locked. He sat down on the cot and he looked at the bottle. "One drink for remembering—and a second drink for sleeping," he said aloud. He poured the second drink and he tossed it off in a single gulp. He pulled off his shoes and he examined the alarm clock to be sure that it was set for four thirty in the morning. Then, still wearing most of his clothing, he pulled the blankets over him and, as he settled down, he reached up and switched off the overhead light.

In the stall directly next to old Charlie's cot the yearling colt nickered softly. On that Christmas Eve the colt instinctively was conscious of his own destiny: the coming victories, the defeats, the roar of the crowd. Old Charlie didn't hear him. Old Charlie was dead to the world, dreaming, dreaming, forever dreaming.

9

1974–83

Just a Tad Stubborn

Southam News
January 14, 1974

It's too bad Indian Jack Jacobs didn't live long enough to watch his old teammate, Bud Grant, coaching the Minnesota Vikings in yesterday's Super Bowl game against the Miami Dolphins. Watching the game on television in the privacy of his own home, Indian Jack undoubtedly would have made some sardonic remarks about quarterbacks "who are slaves to the coach's game plan."

Indian Jack had a lofty contempt for game plans designed by head coaches. Jacobs was a hard-headed quarterback who preferred to improvise his own plays in moments of crisis. The individualistic conduct did not endear Jacobs to his football coaches. There were some—notably the late George Trafton of the Winnipeg Blue Bombers—who endured Jacobs's intractability rather gracelessly.

Jack came into professional football at a time when quarterbacks were beginning to be pampered specialists: men who went on the field only when their team had possession of the ball; men who nestled next to the head coach on the sidelines, exchanging words of wisdom while the opposing team had possession.

This modern type of game, with offensive platoons and defensive platoons alternating on the field, wasn't Indian Jack's idea of football. Indian Jack wanted to be on the field for sixty minutes every game; he wanted to play defensive halfback as well as quarterback. He loved to tackle and, indeed, was one of the most savage tacklers in the game. He wanted to kick field goals and he even wanted to do all his team's punting.

Canadians who remember Jacobs in his five seasons with the Winnipeg Blue Bombers think of him primarily as a quarterback with a compulsion to throw a pass on sixty-five percent of his plays. The truth is he was one of the greatest all-rounders ever to perform in football. He was born in Holdenville, Oklahoma; played college football at the University of Oklahoma; and then, after a short shift in the armed services, played in the NFL for the Cleveland Rams, Washington Redskins and Green Bay Packers. Canadians probably have forgotten that in the 1947 season with the Packers, Jacobs was the leading punter in the NFL.

Man, but he was a vicious tackler! I remember a playoff game in Winnipeg's Osborne Stadium when Jacobs threw a pass that was intercepted by Rollie Prather, Edmonton's great two-way end. Prather hated Jacobs and Jacobs hated Prather. Well, Prather began to sprint toward the Winnipeg goal line and Jacobs sprinted toward Prather on a collision course.

As they converged, Prather swung his right elbow at Jacobs's head. If the blow had landed, Jacobs would have been decapitated. But Jacobs ducked, just as he dismantled Prather with a tackle that rocked the dome of the Manitoba parliament buildings three hundred yards away.

In all my years of watching football, I remember only one other open-field tackle that was as brutal as the Jacobs–Prather wipeout. I recall Nate Shore of Winnipeg hitting Royal Copeland of the Toronto Argonauts head-on in a Grey Cup final. They met with such a crash both were knocked unconscious.

The good Lord alone knows how many more records Jacobs would have inscribed in CFL statistics if he had been willing to accept the authority of his coaches. George Trafton reached the stage where he simply refused to use Jacobs. There was one crazy Winnipeg–Edmonton 1953 playoff game when Trafton had *two* quarterbacks on the field at the same time. Trafton had Joe Zaleski on the field to call the plays and Jacobs to then execute them.

It was in the third game of those western playoffs that Jack Jacobs gave the greatest performance of his Canadian career. Trafton kept Jacobs on the bench in the first half and Edmonton went into an 18–6 lead. (A touchdown counted for only five points in Canada in that era.)

The Winnipeg team's executives huddled in the cold Edmonton grandstand at halftime and Ralph Misener was delegated to serve an ultimatum on coach Trafton. Misener, a former president of the Blue Bombers, had hired Trafton after the 1950 season. So Misener went down to the dressing room and ordered Trafton to put Jacobs at quarterback for the remainder of the game—or else.

Jacobs's first pass of the second half was intercepted. But after that he completed fourteen passes for 243 yards and three touchdowns. Winnipeg won 30–24. That was Indian Jack Jacobs's finest hour.

Off the field, Jacobs was an extroverted athlete of the old school. There was a night in a room in the Royal York Hotel, before a Grey Cup final, when there was a great deal of drinking and a great deal of lie-swapping. The cast of characters in the room included Jacobs, Glenn Dobbs, Ches McCance, Les Lear, Don Durno, Dougie Pyzer and Bob Cunningham. About two o'clock in the morning, Old Jake, who was making heavy weather, said wearily, "If I pass out, be sure to put me to bed in room 613."

So an hour later, they picked him up and got an assistant manager to unlock the door of room 613. He emitted a shout of fright when he saw a very large, naked, tough-looking man lying on the bed.

It was only then that anyone realized Indian Jack Jacobs was not the registered guest for room 613 at the Royal York Hotel. Indian Jack happened to be the registered guest in room 613 at the *King Edward* Hotel, five blocks to the northeast!

The Ghosts of Road Trips Past

Southam News
February 13, 1974

Cherry Hill, New Jersey—There is at least one Canadian traveller, a young Toronto woman, who is prepared to go to the witness stand and testify the Holiday Inn in this winter paradise is haunted. The young lady vows she actually saw two ghosts in the corridor of the third floor of this hotel at three thirty Monday morning.

The management of the Holiday Inn sternly denies any possibility the hostelry is haunted. However, the local innkeeper conceded a few guests other than the young lady from Toronto also reported they had been awakened by weird noises in the corridors of the hotel in the ungodly hours of darkness prior to Monday dawn.

"It's very mysterious," said Jack Franzen, manager of the Cherry Hill Holiday Inn. "We checked the carpet in the corridor and found what appeared to be one set of soapy wet human footprints. They were exceptionally large feet but I can't guess why they left *wet* prints.

"The hotel's swimming pool was locked at midnight. We can't figure how anyone could get all the way from the pool to the third floor of the hotel without leaving some wet tracks on the stairs. Maybe the young lady in room 311 simply was having a nightmare. Anyhow, we've completely discounted the theory that our hotel is infested with spooks."

The young woman, whose identity is being guarded until the ghost case is solved, left Cherry Hill on an early morning plane Monday to return to her desk at the Global Television Network offices in Toronto. As concerned friends led her aboard the plane, she kept repeating, "I saw them. Honest to goodness, I saw two of them!"

The young Toronto woman's presence in the Cherry Hill Holiday Inn should be explained at this point. Global Television had sent a crew to Cherry Hill to televise a World Hockey Association game between the Toronto Toros and the Jersey Knights. It was only a coincidence the Toronto Toro hockey players happened to be staying in the same hotel as the television crew.

Sunday afternoon, prior to the game, an old Toronto sportswriter was sitting in front of his typewriter in a Cherry Hill hotel room, laboriously pecking out a column. He heard a rustling sound and saw a sheet of notepaper being shoved under his room door. Slowly, he went over to the piece of paper and picked it up. He opened the door and peered into the corridor—not a soul was in sight.

The note read: "You're always writing about the laughs you had years ago, on road trips with the NHL teams. You should take a few trips with WHA teams—you've been missing something!"

The old sportswriter thought nothing more about the note until three o'clock the following morning when the telephone rang furiously beside his bed. At the other end of the telephone line, a voice was intoning in a sepulchral voice, "This is the Ghost of Seasons Past. There's an old-style hockey party swinging in room 212. Come on down and regain your youth."

"I'll be right down," said the old sportswriter, rolling over in bed and falling asleep again instantly. Precisely ten minutes later, the telephone bell rang. As the old sportswriter put the receiver to his ear, he heard the same sepulchral voice intoning, "This is the Ghost of Seasons Past. If you won't come down to our party, we're going to bring our party up to you."

"Thank you very much," said the old sportswriter, getting out of bed to make sure the night lock on his hotel room was securely bolted.

I always thought ghosts moved on soundless feet. However, the Ghost of Seasons Past proved to be very, very noisy. Within a minute after the second phone call, fists thumped thunderously on the old sportswriter's bedroom door. There was more than one ghost, obviously, because at least two eerie voices could be heard keening in the hotel corridor. They sounded like exceptionally merry ghosts.

Well, the young woman from Global Television was occupying the bedroom directly next to the old sportswriter's bedroom. Being awakened by the loud thumping on the door, the young woman thought someone was hammering at *her* door. Alarmed, and thinking the hotel must be afire, the young woman leaped from her bed and she flung open the door of her room.

She screamed as she was confronted by two white ghostly figures. The two figures were covered from head to toe in shaving cream, which had been squirted from aerosol cans. (The ghosts must have used the contents of at least three or four aerosol cans.) The two ghosts appeared to be wearing nothing but their thick coating of shaving lather.

Before the young woman's scream had rebounded from the opposite wall, one ghost turned and fled down a nearby flight of stairs. The other ghost, momentarily transfixed in utter astonishment, stood long enough for some of the shaving cream to wet the carpet, outlining the prints of his large feet. Then he fled, too, without even bothering to bid the young woman a polite "good night."

Complete silence descended abruptly on the Cherry Hill Holiday

Inn. The night watchman, making his rounds, glanced rather incuriously at a set of wet footprints outside a door on the third floor. Inside that particular room, an old sportswriter chuckled himself back to sleep.

One Vote for the Deacon

Southam News
April 5, 1974

Vancouver—The selectors for the Canada Sports Hall of Fame are gathered here in solemn conclave, pondering the annual lists of nominees for enshrinement. Regrettably, until now, no one has bothered to nominate that saintly gentleman, Deacon Jack Allen, who was one of British Columbia's most colourful sporting figures in an earlier era.

Deacon Allen possibly would be disqualified from consideration because he was born in the Excited States. Indeed, he was born in Sacramento, right next door to the home of Ancil Hoffman, who managed Max Baer to the world heavyweight boxing championship. And, before coming to Vancouver, John Finlay Allen tarried briefly and profitably in Anchorage, Alaska, until the local constabulary asked him to leave.

Mr. Allen operated two taxicabs, but the constabulary complained that his taxis appeared to be devoted exclusively to the transportation of large cases of Canadian whisky, which were unloaded surreptitiously from ships in the harbour.

Never a man to bear a grudge, Mr. Allen cheerfully booked passage for Vancouver. And, before boarding his ship, the good Deacon donated his two taxicabs to the Anchorage Police Department and they became the first two cruisers in the history of Alaskan law enforcement.

Arriving in Vancouver in 1920, the Deacon lived in Canadian cities for forty-four years until his death in Toronto. In that period his boxing promotions took him for a couple of years to Madison Square Garden in New York where he served as assistant matchmaker to James Joy Johnston, known affectionately as "the Boy Bandit." It was fortunate that the Deacon was the most carefree and emotionally resilient of all men because many of his boxing promotions proved to be hilarious disasters.

He guaranteed two fighters ten thousand dollars each for a

championship bout in Vancouver and, three hours before the fight, the city suffered an unprecedented twelve-inch snowfall. Less than one thousand customers managed to make their way through the blizzard to the arena.

He decided to move to Toronto after he promoted a Vancouver bout between Max Baer and a forgettable opponent named James J. Walsh, billed as "the Alberta Assassin." The old twelve-thousand-seat Vancouver Arena burned to the ground two hours after the conclusion of the alleged fight.

"Someone is trying to tell me something," said Deacon Allen as he watched the building being consumed by flames. So, before the ashes cooled, he boarded a train for Toronto and moved into the Walsingham Hotel on Jarvis Street, a hostelry known far and wide as "the Dancing Pig."

Through the next two decades, Allen's cluttered little room in the Dancing Pig became a late-night stopping place for two generations of newspapermen, wrestlers, boxers, stock salesmen, plainclothes detectives and a Chinese taxi driver named Nine Dollar Charlie. The Deacon had some lean years but, always, he managed to scrape up enough money to provide drinks for his scores of uninvited guests.

The Deacon seldom went to sleep before daylight, so nocturnal visitors knew they'd be welcome at any hour. I don't know how many persons had keys to his room, but the list must have been lengthy.

One of the keys belonged to a heavy-drinking blonde named Miss Halifax. She was so-named because when the Deacon was absent she'd use her key to get into the room and use his private telephone to make lengthy and expensive long-distance calls to some mysterious friend in Halifax.

One night, the Deacon was magnificently foxed with the grape when he came home with $3,500 in cash, the receipts of a fight show at Massey Hall. The Deacon had great piles of newspapers against every wall of the room. When he was drunk, which was frequently, he had a habit of hiding his bankroll in the piles of newspapers. After all, a lot of people had keys to his room and he never was sure whether Miss Halifax might bring some of her nutty friends into the room after he'd passed out.

Late the next afternoon, Tommy McBeigh and I let ourselves into the room with *our* keys. The Deacon still was in his pyjamas and staggering around, pulling down the piles of newspapers. "I came home with $3,500 last night and can't remember where I stashed it," he said. "Help me pull these newspapers apart."

There must have been at least five months of newspapers in the room—three daily papers for five months come to approximately 450. We were down on our knees when Old MacKelvie, the night clerk, who wasn't yet due on duty, let himself into the room with *his* key.

"What are you kooks doing on the floor?" asked Old MacKelvie.

"We're looking for my $3,500," answered the Deacon.

"Well, you were very drunk when you came home after the fights last night," said Old MacKelvie. "You were carrying your entire bankroll in a paper sandwich bag. So, I took it away from you and I put it in the hotel safe."

When Deacon Jack Allen dropped dead of a heart attack one October evening in 1964, he was carrying what he described customarily as "the necessities of life." Clutched in his arm as he fell was a roasted chicken, two bottles of good French wine and a copy of the *Daily Racing Form.*

Scalper

Southam News
April 22, 1974

JOCKEY FLEMING, who was buried Sunday in Montreal, was the last of the old-fashioned ticket scalpers. It's true that countless younger ticket hustlers are thriving illegally on the streets of major Canadian cities today but none of these johnny-come-latelies can ever hope to attain the Jockey's exclusive plateau of international notoriety.

Jockey Fleming's story is a seventy-five-year testimonial to ingenious human connivance. He went to his death with an unblemished record: in his entire lifetime he never once soiled his hands by stooping to what is described customarily as "honest labour."

The Jockey began the adult phase of his business career as a racetrack tout but graduated quickly to the considerably less hazardous occupation of a ticket scalper to major sporting events.

A racetrack tout lives a precarious existence. A tout is harried relentlessly by insensitive racetrack detectives who, in the old days, had the nasty habit of giving the tout a crude kick on the buttocks when they ejected him from the grounds. A racetrack tout generally is despised by other gentlemen in the confidence games.

Fleming pioneered ticket scalping in Montreal. For more than fifty years his beat was a four-block strip of Peel Street, extending from Mount Royal Hotel on the north to the Windsor Hotel on the south. His illegal activities were always tolerated by the worldly Montreal constabulary who regarded him as a harmless pest.

In Montreal, the most lucrative commodity for scalpers always has been professional hockey tickets. For a man with Jockey Fleming's social connections, no great difficulty was ever associated with putting his hands on hockey tickets. For one thing, the players of visiting teams who came to Montreal to play games at the Forum always had tickets. In the era when NHL salaries were limited to seven thousand dollars per year, the management of the teams magnanimously provided their players with a couple of tickets to each game.

In those days, the visiting teams stayed at two Montreal hotels: most of them stayed at the Mount Royal and the others at the Windsor. On the morning prior to a game, Jockey Fleming would canvass the players in the lobbies of these hotels. They would trade him their pairs of tickets in return for a bottle of bootleg whisky or cash to the face value of the tickets. The Jockey had no difficulty scalping those tickets, at a profit of four hundred or five hundred percent, to his eager clients who habituated the Montreal tenderloin.

I remember one morning watching Jockey Fleming circling the lobby of the Windsor in agitated conversation with a ticket scalper named Dutchy. They kept circling the lobby, chattering excitedly, until they reached a chesterfield on which was sitting Dr. Horace McIntyre, the estimable physician who was medical officer for the Toronto Maple Leafs.

"Doc," said Jockey, as they stopped in front of the seated Dr. McIntyre, "what would you say is wrong with me?"

Dr. McIntyre looked at Jockey thoughtfully and said, "I'd say you're suffering from an anxiety neurosis."

"Did you hear that?" Fleming cried triumphantly, poking Dutchy in the chest with one bony forefinger. "That's exactly the same thing the head-shrinker said up at the nuthouse!"

It is possible Jockey Fleming's chronic state of insecurity resulted from an incident in the late 1920s when liquor hijackers, who were on the lam from US authorities, used to take up lengthy residence in the Mount Royal Hotel while their lawyers were attempting to settle the beef back home. This was the type of exile that was described colourfully by Damon Runyon in his fine short story "The Lily of St. Pierre."

Anyhow, Jockey Fleming ingratiated himself with a couple of these well-heeled gunzils who were in residence at the Mount Royal. In return for money, he provided them with liquor, betting facilities and female companions. One afternoon, he persuaded them to bet five hundred dollars on a horse that was running at the old Dorval track.

Fleming simply stuck the five hundred dollars in his own pocket because he had been assured by a conniving trainer the horse in question was a "stiff." Quite improbably, the horse won and the payoff price was ten-to-one. Fleming had no way of scraping up $2,500, so he disappeared from Peel Street and he went into hiding for two months—until the two very angry gentlemen received executive clemency and they returned to their bootlegging activities in the United States.

Throughout the next forty-five years, when the Jockey practised his peculiar habit of peering over his shoulder nervously in hotel lobbies, it's possible he was expecting to see those two US hijackers, coming back to collect their $2,500.

In his old age, Jockey Fleming became increasingly dishevelled and ill. He was barred from the lobby of the Mount Royal and in his final years his office was the drugstore in the basement of the hotel. He sat at the coffee counter in the drugstore, on the mournful lookout for those few veteran visiting hockey men who seldom failed to provide him with tickets that he could scalp at a handsome profit.

He died in his lonely little apartment last Thursday night. It was ironic Thursday was the very night when the Montreal Canadiens bowed out of the Stanley Cup playoffs, depriving the Jockey of any further opportunity to scalp hockey tickets this season.

Indians 1, Cavalry 0

Southam News
August 8, 1974

FORT CHADBOURNE isn't listed in the *American Racing Manual,* the invaluable publication that provides all pertinent information concerning racecourses on this continent.

And I can't find the names of Colonel R.J. Dodge or Chief Mulaquetop listed among the former leading trainers of thoroughbreds in North America. These omissions prove only that the computers that collect information for the annual editions of the *American Racing Manual* aren't infallible.

John I. Day, the scholarly director of information for the Thoroughbred Racing Association, has provided us with the details of a nineteenth-century match race that was contested on the Fort Chadbourne track and that could provide a sequel to that eminently successful motion picture entitled *The Sting.*

Fort Chadbourne was a US Cavalry establishment in Texas, officered by a group of sporty gentlemen who amused themselves by conducting intramural races with their thoroughbred horses. The officers raced their horses two or three times a week and these regular speed trials were observed with interest by some roving Comanche braves, who were "squatting" outside the fort.

Colonel Dodge was irked by the fact that the Comanches were openly derisive about the quality of thoroughbreds that raced at Fort Chadbourne. The Comanches, after watching the officers conduct their races, would chuckle among themselves; they would place their fingers tightly over their nostrils; and they would make other obviously rude gestures.

Somewhat nettled by these Indian knockers, Colonel Dodge summoned Chief Mulaquetop of the Comanches to his office in the fort.

"See here, my good man," said the colonel sternly. "We don't like you chaps sitting around, giving the razzoo to our racehorses. Our officers are riding some very good thoroughbreds."

"In your hat, Colonel," said Chief Mulaquetop with studied insolence. "Those horses of yours couldn't beat a fat man hobbled with the gout. I have an Indian pony back at my hogan that can spot your horses twenty pounds at any distance."

"Bring on your pony," roared Colonel Dodge. "We'll whip the tar out of him. We won't even bother to race one of our best horses against him. We'll bet you any amount of money on the race."

"We're a very poor tribe, Colonel," said Chief Mulaquetop sadly. "But, I imagine that we can scrape up five hundred dollars for a friendly little wager. One of our braves just received a remittance from his grandfather in England."

The match was made. On the morning of the race, Chief Mulaquetop trudged into Fort Chadbourne leading a scruffy horse covered with hair six inches in length. Behind the long-haired horse trudged the Indian "jockey," a 160-pound brave, carrying a stout club.

"Good Lord, what an ugly bag of bones," quoth Colonel Dodge when he appraised the Indian challenger. "I hope that the war department doesn't cashier me for stealing five hundred dollars from these Comanches. To give them a sporting chance, we'd better run our third-best horse against them."

The course was six furlongs. The cavalrymen of the fort and the grinning Comanches gathered near the finish line. It was a good race, but the Indian pony, ridden expertly by his oversized jockey, charged from behind to win by half a length.

"That's the way the cookie crumbles, Colonel," said Chief Mulaquetop quietly as he collected his winnings of five hundred dollars. "But we're good sports and we'll give you a chance to get even. My pony needs only thirty minutes to regain his wind, and then we'll race again, against one of your *better* horses. I'll leave the five hundred dollars in the kitty; the bet will be double-or-nothing!"

"You're on!" replied Colonel Dodge and he ordered his officers to bring out the second-best thoroughbred in Fort Chadbourne. He reckoned that Indian pony, after running one race, would be easy meat in a second heat. Silence descended on the cavalrymen of Fort Chadbourne as the second race was run. The Indian pony defeated the cavalry's thoroughbred by a full length.

"My pony's all tuckered out, Colonel," said Chief Mulaquetop as he sauntered up to Colonel Dodge. "But I'm willing to give you one more chance to get even. Let my pony have an hour's rest and we'll race again, but this time we want to race against the best horse in the fort."

"Agreed," replied Colonel Dodge. "But I warn you that I'm going to run my own thoroughbred mare, who was sired by the great Lexington."

"My pony will choke her to death," said Mulaquetop confidently. "The bet is two thousand dollars or nothing. And this time I'll have to ask you to add a case of whisky to the pot because some of my braves are getting powerful thirsty, sitting out here among the crazy white men in the midday sun."

To spare you any further harrowing details, the Indian horse, running his third race in less than two hours, beat Colonel Dodge's magnificent thoroughbred mare by twenty yards. As he crossed the finish line, the Indian jockey turned round in his saddle and he jeered at his defeated white rival. The two-thousand-dollar losing bet cleaned out the personnel of Fort Chadbourne until the next payday. As Colonel Dodge paid the two thousand dollars to Chief Mulaquetop, he said soberly, "That Indian pony is quite a runner! If you shaved off that six inches of hair all over his body, I wonder what we'd see?"

"Well, we're a roving band of Comanches," Mulaquetop replied solemnly. "We roved through Kentucky last year. Maybe one of those Kentucky horse breeders forgot to lock his gate at night."

"Well, you just rove your way the hell out west to Nevada or California," said Colonel Dodge. "You've worn out your welcome in Texas."

"Okay, Colonel, and thanks for your hospitality," said Chief Mulaquetop as he hefted the case of whisky on his shoulder and shuffled away toward the gate of Fort Chadbourne. He turned and he added, "Don't report us to the Better Business Bureau."

You may think that I'm kidding, but this infamous match race really took place. You can get confirmation by writing to John I. Day, Thoroughbred Racing Association, 5 Dakota Drive, Lake Success, New Hyde Park, NY 11040.

The Fourth Estate Follies

Southam News
December 11, 1974

Clyde Gilmour, the distinguished Canadian motion-picture critic, has been shouting hosannas for the latest remake of *The Front Page*, a film scheduled to appear in some of our major cities next week.

At heart, Mr. Gilmour is a nostalgic journalistic bum from Medicine Hat, Alberta, and although his critical faculties are impeccable, his enthusiasm for the new picture probably is heightened by the fact that *The Front Page* is evocative of a rowdy era of newspapering of which he personally has some salty memories.

As originally scripted in 1928, *The Front Page* was an exercise in genial lunacy, concocted by Ben Hecht and Charles MacArthur. Nevertheless, several of its most important roles were inspired by real newspapermen. The character of Walter Burns, the managing editor, was modelled on Walter Howey, managing editor of the old Chicago *Herald-Examiner*. And the living prototype of reporter Hildy Johnson was Gene Fowler, a wildly ingenious scribe who came to Chicago from Denver. In his tamer moments, Fowler wrote such memorable books as *Timberline, Good Night Sweet Prince, The Great Mouthpiece, Trumpet in the Dust* and *Salute to Yesterday.*

Although the antics of the characters in *The Front Page* undoubtedly defy present-day credulity, they were commonplace in their era. Not so many years ago, you could go into the newsroom of many Canadian dailies and flush a covey of very weird birds.

At the first Canadian newspaper for which I worked, there was a distinguished reporter who owned a St. Bernard dog that followed him faithfully on his appointed rounds. Attached to the dog's collar was a small keg of rum. And when the reporter occasionally collapsed from fatigue on the snow-packed sidewalks, the dog stood over him obediently until the reporter restored his strength with a refreshing swig from the small keg.

Sobriety, you will gather, was not a cardinal virtue among journalistic personnel in those days.

Even sports editors and sports columnists were not the dignified, well-clad and scholarly creatures they are today. One Canadian sports editor had a glass eye. In fact, he had a *collection* of glass eyes. He had a special bloodshot glass eye that he inserted carefully in his empty eye socket on those mornings when he was suffering from particularly debilitating hangovers.

One sports editor for whom I worked in my youth had a nervous habit of munching copy paper while he was sitting at his desk thinking. He was heedless of the fact reporters laboriously had written their stories on the copy paper on which he was munching. That particular sports editor, who eventually became Henry R. Luce's official biographer, ate some of the best stories I ever wrote.

There was a sports reporter friend of mine who, when temporarily bereft of employment, kept body and soul together by playing the mouth organ in beer parlours in return for free drinks. And there was a sports editor who "dreamed winners." In his alcoholic slumbers, he'd dream he was watching a horse race. Carefully, he'd remember the number of the winning horse. The next day, he'd go out to the track and bet on that particular number—with astounding success.

Peculiarly enough, this sports editor only "dreamed winners" when he had been drinking one particular brand of beer. If he made the mistake of drinking any other brand of beer before he went to bed, he dreamed losers.

You think that I'm kidding, eh? Well, Mr. Gilmour, or Mr. Himie Koshevoy, of the Vancouver *Daily Province*, and I could use up every inch of space in this estimable journal if we ever had time to detail the eccentricities of the many delightful kooks with whom we have worked in this sweaty newspaper business.

When I go to see *The Front Page*, I'm certain I'll find myself cracking my knuckles gleefully and thinking about Cy. If ever there was a Canadian reporter who should have been working around Chicago in the era of *The Front Page*, that reporter was Cy.

Cy was, to say the least, very unpredictable. He used to live with a female handwriting expert who really never understood him very well. One night, when he was slightly foxed with the grape, he clumsily wrecked their little apartment and the female handwriting expert complained to the editor of the paper. So Cy was banished to another paper in distant Regina.

About two weeks later, Cy lurched into the newsroom of the Regina newspaper, roaring drunk. He leaped atop a desk and, very noisily, pretended to be driving an unruly team of horses. Art Raymond, the managing editor, stormed out of his office and shouted, "Cy—one more screwball act like this and you're fired!"

Cy jumped down from the desk; he threw his arms around Art's neck and burst into tears of gratitude. Hugging the embarrassed editor, Cy howled, "Mr. Raymond, I love you! You're the first son of a bitch who's paid the slightest bit of attention to me since I arrived in Regina."

Once, in a very confidential mood, Cy told me about his one little secret eccentricity: he always wore a hat on his head when he went to bed. He wore his hat to bed because he suffered from a recurrent nightmare. In this nightmare—which visited him two or three times a week—a flock of woodpeckers burst through the glass of his bedroom window and they attempted to drill holes in his skull.

Amos and Tansey

Southam News
March 18, 1975

WHEN VERY OLD HORSE PLAYERS go into winter hibernation and lie down to sleep away the snowy months, they murmur respectfully a little prayer: "Dear God, Please let me see just one more spring."

Another spring . . . another thoroughbred horse-racing season opening Wednesday in Toronto . . . and I'm sitting here, wondering if I should go up to the site of the old Thorncliffe track and place a few flowers on Amos's grave. Because, in the long ago, every spring when the time came for the opening of the thoroughbred racing season, Amos used to be standing just inside the Thorncliffe gate, waiting for Tansey.

Waiting for Tansey?

Amos was a dog, a big black Newfoundland owned by Frank Stocker, the assistant superintendent of the Thorncliffe track. Amos wasn't merely big; he was about the largest dog in history; he stood shoulder-high to a tall Indian.

Tansey was a tout. Tansey was a tout who came into Canada every spring from Florida. Tansey was big—about six feet three and he must have weighed 250 pounds. Tansey was one hell of a performer with the knife and fork. When Tansey sat down at the table, he went through food like a swarm of boll weevils going through a field of cotton. Man, could he eat!

The chef who presided over the hot-food counters in the Thorncliffe grandstand was a bespectacled gentleman named Andy. In those days, you gave Andy fifty cents and he carved you huge chunks of ham or beef that were placed between two slices of bread. Andy gave you what amounted to a full meal for fifty cents.

Amos adored hambones. Each day after the last racing patron had shuffled home, Andy would select the biggest, juiciest hambones from his counters and give the hambones to Amos—until Tansey came into the picture!

Tansey persuaded chef Andy that his need was greater than Amos's. "I gotta keep up my strength," Tansey said. "I gotta be strong if I hope to make a living touting all them suckers. Now, if I have them hambones to gnaw on back in my rented room I can keep myself physically fit and mentally alert."

So Andy started giving the hambones to Tansey at the end of each racing day.

Well, you should have heard the uproar the first time Amos saw Tansey leaving the grandstand with the hambones tucked under one arm. Amos was chained outside Stocker's little office building and Amos was so damn mad he almost pulled the structure off its foundations. When Tansey had a head start of approximately fifty yards, Stocker, just for the heck of it, unhooked the chain from Amos's collar.

Amos took to running and Tansey took to running, too! They sprinted down the roadway to Thorncliffe's big iron gate with Amos gaining at every jump. Tansey just made it through the gateway into Millwood Drive and Amos, barking furiously, stopped when he reached the gate. Amos had been trained never to go beyond that big iron gate.

Tansey pulled to a stop out on Millwood Drive, sweating, panting and laughing. He shouted at the furious Amos, "Tough luck, old dog, but I need these here hambones."

Every evening after that, Tansey and Amos staged their own footrace. The regulars from the backstretch used to gather to watch the fun. One night, the official Thorncliffe clocker pulled out his stopwatch and timed Tansey going two furlongs in 49 2/5 seconds, which in those years, was damn close to a world record. And don't forget Tansey was carrying a couple of heavy hambones.

On more than one occasion there were some rather noisy automobile collisions when startled motorists swerved to avoid Tansey as he sped through the gate out into the traffic on Millwood Drive. The collisions were noisy but no one was ever hurt.

Personally, I believe Amos could have caught Tansey any time he felt like it. But the old dog simply got his kicks chasing Tansey. It was one of those love-hate relationships that the psychiatrists ponder so thoughtfully these days.

Each spring, Amos waited inside the Thorncliffe gate for Tansey to make his appearance, fresh from Florida. Year after year, the two of them staged their evening footrace, with the hambones as prize.

Then, one night, a letter from the US arrived at Tansey's Toronto boarding house. The US had got into World War II and Tansey, who was a reservist, got his call. He was ordered to report within twenty-four hours.

Although the hour was late, Tansey got a taxi and drove to the Thorncliffe gate. He knew Amos would be on guard just inside the locked gate. Tansey got out of the cab and peered through the bars at Amos. He said softly, "I gotta go, old dog. Mr. Roosevelt wants me to straighten out some Krauts, over in Europe. But when I get through in Europe, I'll be back. You wait here for me, eh, old dog."

Tansey didn't make it back from World War II. But the next spring, Amos went down to the Thorncliffe gate to wait for him. Three nights in a row, after the opening of the racing season, Amos waited. Then, on the third night, Amos lay down in the grass just inside the gate. The evening breeze was whirling the dust in the Thorncliffe driveway. Amos looked into the distance through his clouding old eyes and gave one little affectionate growl and died—just like that.

Waiting for Tansey.

Chatahoochee Smith

Southam News
April 25, 1975

FORTY YEARS AGO, a good Samaritan motorist braked his car to a stop when he saw a small truck stuck hopelessly in the deep mud on the shoulder of the old Number One Highway between Regina and Winnipeg.

The motorist got out of his car, walked across the highway and peered inside the truck. There were no apparent casualties, but the truck contained a peculiar cargo. There was one grizzled man sitting in the front seat, singing to himself as he awaited rescue. In the back were two thoroughbred racehorses and a barber chair. The horses, one of which was sprawled over the barber chair, had an expression of resignation on their careworn faces.

The driver of the mired truck was Chatahoochee Smith, the gypsy horseman who, when spring came each year, closed his little barbershop on Eighth Avenue in Calgary and went away to the races. One of the horses in the back of the truck was Chatahoochee, the old chestnut mare from whom Smith acquired his racetrack nickname. The other horse was a nondescript plater that Smith had acquired for three hundred dollars.

That was the way Chatahoochee Smith travelled in the Depression years: two horses and a barber chair in the back of the truck as he drove from track to track. When the horses were bedded down in their stalls at each track, Chatahoochee put his barber chair in a sunny spot at the end of the shedrow and, with fellow horsemen as his customers, he practised his tonsorial profession to acquire cash to provide sustenance for himself and his noble beasts.

Chatahoochee finally died, just two days ago, in a Calgary nursing home at the age of eighty-two. He was one of the last of the truly colourful western horsemen. Chatahoochee has gone to his final reward, but his name is certain to live on in the picturesque legends of the West.

He was born in Dundas, Ontario, and was christened Walter Edward Smith. But for some obscure reason of his own he always signed his documents as Jack Smith.

One of his sisters, who was living in suburban Toronto until a couple of years ago, was a teacher of elocution, which probably explains Chatahoochee's histrionic ability. He became a national celebrity in 1964 when he appeared in a beautiful film, *Woody's Wish,* which Michael Magee produced for the CBC. Chatahoochee co-starred with a horse named Woody's Wish and, in the final scene, the old horseman was sitting in a tack room reciting a racetrack poem entitled "The Ballad of Chatahoochee."

Actually, the poem was written by Bill Galvin of the Ontario Jockey Club, but with the harmless imaginings of old age, Chatahoochee ultimately managed to convince himself that he personally was the author of the ballad.

Western horsemen seldom were given stabling accommodation at Toronto's old Woodbine in the 1930s. But, on the urging of Jim Speers of Winnipeg, Major Palmer Wright—the punctilious secretary of the Ontario Jockey Club—once agreed to provide stalls at Woodbine for four horses trained by Chatahoochee Smith.

Little knowing what was in store for him, Major retired to sleep in his private bedroom in the directors' building at Woodbine on the night when Chatahoochee arrived from the West.

After his horses had been unloaded and placed in Woodbine stalls, Chatahoochee examined his surroundings. It was a moonlit night and, as he stared across the track, he could see all that lush green grass.

Many months had passed since Chatahoochee's horses had seen green grass. He decided they needed an immediate change of diet. One by one, he led his four horses across the track and turned them loose to gambol on the greensward of the infield. Little did he know he was trespassing on holy ground—he was permitting his shaggy cayuses to romp on Woodbine's carefully manicured steeplechase course, which was Major Wright's particular pride and joy.

The major was awakened at the crack of dawn by a distraught watchman banging on his bedroom door. While the watchman babbled and pointed to the infield, the major peered through his bedroom window. Major Wright almost burst a blood vessel when he saw Chatahoochee's scruffy animals desecrating his beloved steeplechase course. Never again was Chatahoochee Smith granted stabling accommodation at Woodbine.

The little barbershop on Calgary's Eighth Avenue has long since disappeared. The hair clippers, the scissors and the old straight-edged razors had been retired permanently before they persuaded him to enter that Calgary nursing home. No man ever was destined to stay among us forever and now Chatahoochee Smith has gone to a faster track.

Inheriting Lochinvar

Southam News
December 5, 1975

As Yuletide approaches and this troubled world desperately requires some stabilizing reassurances, it's a pleasure to be able to report Michael Lochinvar Levinsky is still alive and well and residing at Sully's Gym in west central Toronto.

Michael Lochinvar Levinsky, cheerfully shabby and uncombed, has been shuffling around Toronto gymnasia for more than thirty-five years. Much busier and stronger men have worried themselves into graves but Michael, who never has troubled his mind with anything more important than the source of his next meal, simply goes rolling along like Ol' Man River.

If ever you've attended a boxing show, professional or amateur, in Toronto in the past thirty-five years, you're certain to have seen Mike. He's that little guy in the suit two sizes too large for him, cupping a cigarette carefully in one hand and wearing a wistfully tentative little smile as he nods back at all the regulars who greet him. Those regulars who attend fight shows and hang around gymnasia are Mike's People, though to be truthful he can't identify many of them by name, even those he sees four or five times a week.

Mike's almost non-existent memory span might have proved a handicap to a more complicated man. But Mike has gone through life in an almost constant state of euphoria. People always have liked little Mike and they have looked after him, protecting him from the slings and arrows of fortune. The Care for Mike program has placed no great strain on any of his benefactors because his wants are simple: a couch on which to rest his tousled head, a couple of meals a day and the occasional package of cigarettes.

When Mike first arrived in Toronto from his native St. Catharines, he cherished the harmless delusion he had been a pugilist of great renown. Quite unexpectedly, he would grab a guy by the arm and launch into the story of how he had fought Jack Dempsey or Joe Louis or Jimmy McLarnin or any other champion whose name happened to have been mentioned in the ringside conversation.

His stories were preposterous, of course, because Michael Lochinvar Levinsky was an uncoordinated little fellow, weighing about 115 pounds soaking wet. However, even in the very beginning, no one ever mocked Mike when he aired his fantasies. And when Dempsey or McLarnin or Jack Sharkey or any of his other imaginary opponents came to town, they'd agree gently with Michael's version of their gory combats.

The story of Mike's life over the past thirty-six years boils down to the fact that people are always inheriting him. The late Deacon Jack Allen, a whimsical, ill-starred fight promoter, inherited Mike when Levinsky arrived in Toronto from St. Catharines. When the Deacon died in 1964, Mike was automatically inherited by Earl Sullivan, the proprietor of the athletic club that is known as Sully's Gym.

Peculiar how it all began. The Deacon had this training gym on the second floor of a building on Bond Street. One afternoon, a couple of fighters were sparring in the ring and the Deacon noticed this very shabby little guy watching them closely.

"Scat," cried the Deacon and he chased the little guy down the long flight of stairs into Bond Street. Four more times during that afternoon and the ensuing evening, Allen chased the little guy out of the gymnasium. Then, about midnight, the Deacon locked up the joint and he went home to his bedroom in the Walsingham Hotel, to which he always referred as "the Dancing Pig."

The next day about noon, the Deacon unlocked the front door of the joint on Bond Street and climbed the long flight of stairs to the gymnasium. There standing beside the ring with a tremulous smile on his face was the little guy who had been chased out of the gymnasium five times the previous day. Michael Lochinvar Levinsky had sneaked into the gym the previous night when Allen's back was turned and he spent the night sleeping under the ring.

"I just inherited him," the Deacon used to cackle as Mike, smiling uncertainly because he knew the conversation was about him, would go about his chore of sweeping the gymnasium floor. For twenty-five years, the Deacon kept Mike in meals and cigarettes and provided him with a bed in the successive gymnasia that Allen rented.

Mind you, Mike didn't *always* sleep in the gym. Joe Fink, who died just a few months ago, was another of the Good Guys who kept an eye on Mike. Joe was the perpetual night clerk of the old Variety Hotel and Mike often used to drop into the hotel to get out of the cold. When there was a midnight checkout by one of the casual guests, Joe Fink ceremoniously would escort Michael Lochinvar Levinsky to the newly vacated room and permit him to bed down comfortably until morning.

When we buried the Deacon in October 1964 Mike rode home from the graveyard with my wife and me in the funeral director's seven-passenger Cadillac. When we reached our house, Mike said thoughtfully that maybe the funeral director could give him a lift down to Queen Street. We saw him drive away, a tiny rumpled man alone in the back seat of a huge limousine.

Well, within twenty-four hours, Sully had inherited Mike. Sully told me Mike just walked into Sully's Gym and made himself at home. He fixed up a cot for himself, and he has been there for the past eleven years plus.

Probably because the usual emotional stresses of day-to-day survival make no impression on him, Michael Lochinvar Levinsky will outlast all of us.

Young Boswell and His Grizzlies

Southam News
May 20, 1978

HISTORIANS, in their scholarly preoccupation with the Grand Design, often ignore colourful and trivial truths.

For instance, local football historians are making much of the fact that this is the twenty-fifth season in which Vancouver has operated a team in the Western Conference.

WRONG!

Vancouver had a team in the Western Conference in 1941. The Grizzlies played an eight-game schedule with the Winnipeg Blue Bombers and the Regina Roughriders. They won only one of those games and they lost the other seven.

Local historians also would have you believe that no Vancouver football player was named to an All-Canadian team until 1963 when, overtaken by a sudden attack of brilliant acuity, the All-Canadian selectors decided that seven Lions—Joe Kapp, Willie Fleming, Tom Hinton, Lonnie Dennis, Tom Brown, Dick Fouts and Norm Fieldgate—were worthy of national recognition, all in the same season.

Wrong again!

Bill Garvin of the Vancouver Meralomas was named as middle-wing (right tackle) on the All-Canadian team selected by a panel of sports commentators for *Maclean's* magazine in 1934. Your eastern Canada correspondent doesn't profess to be a historian but he remembered something about primeval Canadian football in Vancouver during the years when there was a league known as the Big Four. The participating teams—with occasional substitutions resulting from financial anemia—usually were the Meralomas, UBC Thunderbirds, Vancouver Athletic Club and North Shore Lions. Vancouver newspapers applied the derisive nickname "the Wolves" to the VAC team after a hilarious incident in which they refused to complete the final five minutes of a game with their bitter rivals, the Meralomas.

Rugger was the socially elite sport in British Columbia in the 1930s and Canadian football existed precariously. Nevertheless, BC annually met the Alberta champions in the four-province playoffs that produced a western representative for the Grey Cup game. In 1934, the Meralomas made history when they eliminated the Calgary Tigers. However, the Regina Roughriders, with six US imports in their lineup, came to Vancouver for the western finals and they subdued the Meralomas in a two-game total-points series.

Thereafter, the three other western provinces snootily excluded BC from their playoffs. Beginning in 1935, they formed their own three-team league comprised of Winnipeg, Regina and Calgary. For the 1939 and 1940 seasons, they grudgingly accepted the membership of the Edmonton Eskimos.

Snubbed by their short-sighted prairie neighbours, Vancouverites struggled along with a four-team BC league. However, the dream of getting into a Western Conference wasn't completely dead. In November 1940, I.A. "Tiny" Rader, in concert with an impecunious but starry-eyed local newspaperman, concocted the hare-brained scheme of assembling a Vancouver all-star team and bringing the Calgary Bronks to town for an exhibition game.

Enlisting the moral support of sports editor Hal Straight, the addled pair persuaded the late George Norgan to loan them one thousand dollars to pay for the Calgary team's rail transportation and a single night of accommodation at the Georgia Hotel.

Despite heavy rain, the game attracted 3,800 spectators. George Norgan got his one thousand dollars. Bob Brown, proprietor of Athletic Park, collected the largest rental he ever had received from a Canadian football contest, and the cash surplus was used to pay the dental bills of Vancouver players who had lost their teeth during the 1940 season.

Recklessly emboldened by the meagre success of their all-star experiment, Rader and his Boswell decided to make a bid for Vancouver's inclusion in the Western Conference for the 1941 season. The formation meeting of the Vancouver Grizzlies was held on a wet winter evening in the tiny kitchen auditorium of the old Vancouver *Daily Province* building, a room in which dietician Marian Cassellman conducted daily cooking classes for bored housewives.

By mere chance, a visiting Winnipeg spellbinder named Mark Long dropped into the meeting and the chairman invited him to speak. Long was so persuasive that, when ten-dollar memberships were offered to his listeners, they sold like—well, er, they sold like manhole covers.

Coincidentally, Calgary and Edmonton were deciding to suspend football operations. Winnipeg and Regina were looking for another city to round out a three-team league. The Vancouver Grizzlies, long in enthusiasm but short in capital, were the obvious patsies.

The Grizzlies sold enough ten-dollar memberships to hire Greg Kabat of the Blue Bombers to come to Vancouver as playing coach. Kabat brought along Bill Hiendl, a Winnipeg high school fullback who had been coached by Kabat at St. Paul's College. Larry Haynes, All-Canadian end, and halfback Jimmy Gilkes came from the Calgary Bronks. Gordon Gelhaye, a bulky American lineman, reported from Edmonton. Joe Budnick commuted from Seattle for games. These "imports" received minimal financial remuneration while the local players performed only for the sheer glory of competing.

The truth was that the Grizzlies were overmatched. In that 1941 season, the Winnipeg Blue Bombers were on their way to their third

Grey Cup victory in a span of seven seasons. In December 1941, Winnipeg defeated the Ottawa Rough Riders 18–6 in one of the most thrilling Canadian finals of that era.

Anyhow, the Grizzlies 1941 season began with Regina coming to town for two games within three days. Regina won the opener 4–1 before a rain-soaked crowd of three thousand on the afternoon of Saturday, September 13. Two nights later, Vancouver scored its only victory of the entire season, beating Regina 7–6 on a touchdown by Jack Horne.

With only three days of rest, the Grizzlies then embarked upon a horrendous road trip that boggles the imagination. They took the train to the Prairies and they played *four* games in seven days! So help me, gawd! They played in Regina on Friday, September 19; they played in Winnipeg the next afternoon; they returned to Regina for a game on Monday night; and, on the Thursday night, they concluded their road trip with another game in Winnipeg.

Crazy, eh? The Grizzlies were beaten four times on that ludicrous road trip but, in their fourth game in seven days, they held the Canadian champion Blue Bombers to a 12–5 score.

Let's never hear any disparaging remarks about those old Grizzlies. After all, when the BC Lions were admitted to the Western Conference in 1954, they won only one game and lost fifteen games in their first season.

Big Atch: The Cast Never Changed

Southam News
November 1, 1978

TWO OF THE MOST PLEASANT ASSASSINS in the history of the sport—Kaye Vaughan and Ron Atchison—will be admitted to the Canadian Football Hall of Fame in official ceremonies in Hamilton on Sunday night.

Kaye and Atch had a great deal in common though they laboured in different conferences, Vaughan with the Ottawa Rough Riders and Atchison with those burly weedbenders, the Saskatchewan Roughriders. On the field both men were alleged to be hyperaggressive with a tendency toward mayhem. Off the field both men were warm, friendly, humorous and highly articulate.

Both men were—and still are—characters. They played in the CFL through the same years, roughly 1952 until the late 1960s, but they were throwbacks to an earlier era when football players in Canada received insignificant financial compensation and the rewards for their weekly exercises in cheerful violence were confined largely to the pre-game and post-game parties. Vaughan came to the Ottawa Rough Riders from Tulsa University in 1953. He played twelve seasons in the CFL and twice was selected as the outstanding lineman in Canada. He was a two-way performer who won all-star honours offensively as well as defensively. He was selected as an all-star offensive guard and an all-star defensive tackle.

He took up skiing and married Lucille Wheeler, the Canadian girl who won a world championship in the alpine sport. One night Vaughan was being interviewed on a national television network and the interviewer asked him, "Why would you, a man who grew up in the flatlands of the southwestern states, decide to take up skiing as a sport?"

"Well," drawled Kaye, smiling into the camera, "if you're going to spend a winter in Ottawa, you have only two choices—either you take up skiing or you become an alcoholic."

Unlike Vaughan, Ron Atchison didn't go to university. He grew up in Saskatoon and he dropped out of school to become a carpenter. He joined the Saskatchewan Roughriders and became a professional football player when he was only eighteen, in 1952. He played for Saskatchewan through seventeen seasons.

Atchison is a Bunyan-like legend in western football. Throughout most of his career he wore a plaster cast on his right wrist and opposing linemen and ball carriers always kept a wary eye on Atch's right arm. Referring to the wrist cast, Toronto offensive centre Norm Stoneburgh used to mutter aggrievedly, "I realize that Atch is a carpenter by trade, but I wish to gawd that he wouldn't bring his hammer onto the football field."

There are some good stories about Atchison. As a kid, he didn't own any football equipment, and when he turned out for his first practice with the Saskatoon Hilltop juniors, he was wearing a pair of knee-high rubber boots. He told the coach he was a carpenter, so the coach kept him around to assist in constructing the small clubhouse that the Hilltops were building on the edge of their practice field.

When he wasn't banging nails into the new clubhouse, Atch also was demonstrating that he was a hell of a football prospect. Glenn Dobbs, who was coaching the Roughriders, heard about Atchison, and he invited the young carpenter to the pro team's camp. Atch arrived in Regina on his motorcycle, carrying only a few extra pairs of socks and underwear. Because of his refreshing naïveté, Atch immediately was adopted by the pros of the club, and although he was only eighteen, Dobbs gave him a contract.

He became a perennial All-Western selection at middle guard and defensive tackle. And looking back on it I don't recall that injuries caused him to miss more than a half a dozen league games between 1952 and 1968.

The amiable Atchison once precipitated a player riot when the Roughriders were playing a pre-season exhibition game against the Toronto Argonauts at Varsity Stadium. Dick Fouts, Toronto's huge defensive end, maltreated a Saskatchewan offensive lineman.

In this emergency, Saskatchewan coach Frank Filchock sent Atchison onto the field to play offensive tackle against Fouts. On the first play thereafter, Atch is alleged to have kicked Fouts in an area that is described euphemistically as the vital zone. In the ensuing melee, which involved all the coaches and players on both teams, Bobby Kuntz of the Argos, employing his helmet as an equalizer, slugged Bill Glass of the Roughriders over the bare head.

Atch had a thing about footwear. As I told you, he wore a pair of knee-high rubber boots to his first practice. In the second game of the 1967 western finals Calgary was playing Saskatchewan on an ice-covered Regina field. In the fourth quarter, the only player who wasn't slipping and sliding on every play was Ron Atchison. Sitting on the bench, he doffed his football shoes and he donned a pair of brown suede slip-on Hush Puppies.

It's a matter of history that with Atch wearing those street shoes the Roughriders won the game and subsequently they went on to score their only Grey Cup victory in the long history of their football club.

If Pocket Knives Could Speak

Southam News
February 28, 1979

There's a famous old hockey story connected with the inscribed gold pocket knife that was discovered recently in a Toronto pawnshop.

Dr. Ernest Lewis, a Toronto dentist with strong hockey affiliations, brought the gold pocket knife to the press box at Maple Leaf Gardens Saturday night, seeking an explanation of the engraved inscription. The penknife was inscribed to "Odie Cleghorn, who guided us to victory." Also inscribed were a date—April 7, 1928—and the name of the donor, John S. Hammond.

Professional hockey is a sport that has produced many colourful legends but also it's a sport that was built on many colourful truths. And April 7, 1928, is a historic date in the saga of the Stanley Cup. It was the occasion on which the veteran coach Lester Patrick donned the goaltending pads and went into the New York Rangers net to thwart the Montreal Maroons in the Montreal Forum.

The story of the Rangers first Stanley Cup triumph in 1928 has been written and rewritten, but because Odie Cleghorn's gold pocket knife has been found in a Toronto hock shop it can survive another telling.

Because Ringling Brothers' Barnum & Bailey Circus had been booked into Madison Square Garden for April 1928, the Rangers were compelled to play the entire three-out-of-five-game Stanley Cup final series in the Montreal Forum. The Montreal Maroons, generally regarded as a shoo-in, won the opening game 2–0. The second game was scoreless in the second period when a shot by Nels Stewart hit Ranger goalie Lorne Chabot on the left eyeball. The Rangers didn't carry a spare goaltender. The Maroons refused to permit the Rangers to use Ottawa's Alex Connell, who was sitting in the Forum as a spectator alongside King Clancy.

Pittsburgh coach Odie Cleghorn and Toronto's Conn Smythe were among the well-wishers who charged into the Ranger dressing room to offer advice in this crisis. The room was bedlam.

Always a man for dramatic gestures, grey-haired Lester Patrick donned Chabot's pads and went into the Ranger net. Before leaving the dressing room, Lester asked Odie Cleghorn to take over the coaching duties behind the New York bench.

History records show that Lester allowed only one goal and the Rangers defeated Montreal 2–1 when Frank Boucher scored after seven minutes and five seconds of overtime. Then, with Joe Miller of the New York Americans guarding their net, the Rangers went on to win two of the remaining three games and the Stanley Cup.

A few years before he died, Frank Boucher provided a hilarious sidelight on this incident in a book that he wrote with the assistance of Trent Frayne. Boucher recounted that Lester, who gloried in his somewhat theatrical performance, was shouting defiance at the Maroons, adjuring his Rangers to "Let them shoot! Let them shoot!"

But, according to Boucher, the Rangers on the ice also could hear the voice of emergency coach Odie Cleghorn howling passionately, "DON'T let them shoot! For God's sake, don't let them shoot!"

Anyhow, the above explains the existence of the gold pocket knife that was presented to Odie Cleghorn by John S. Hammond, the president of the New York Rangers. Still unexplained is how Odie's memento finally made its way to the Toronto pawnshop where it was found last week.

I know one sad fact. The Cleghorn brothers, Sprague and Odie, had long and colourful careers in the NHL but they amassed no fortunes. And when the two brothers died, only two days apart in 1956—Sprague on July 11 and Odie on July 13—both were stone broke.

Little Blackie's Great Big Score

Southam News
April 4, 1979

THIS IS THE TRUE BUT HEART-RENDING STORY of Little Blackie, who bet 1,700 smackers on a sterling steed named Occult in the second race at Hialeah a week ago yesterday.

Now, it is well-known to one and all that Little Blackie is no better than the good Lord intended him to be. In fact, Little Blackie got the big heave-ho from Canadian racetracks more than twenty-five years ago for unsportsmanlike activities. The track dicks are rather narrow-minded about these shenanigans. The track dicks gave Little Blackie the boot and told him to never darken the door of a racetrack again, even if he lives to be 180. Blackie disappears from all his old Toronto haunts for many years. There is a rumour that he is living on a little farm, growing potatoes and cabbages and other knick-knacks for the dinner table. No one in Toronto really believes this rumour because Little Blackie is sadly underequipped for the agricultural life. In fact, Little Blackie is underskilled in almost everything except, maybe, petty larceny.

Well, it is a matter of surprise to all parties when Little Blackie surfaces again in Toronto, just a few months ago, and he expresses a desire to make a modest wager on racehorses from time to time. No one wishes to handle Little Blackie's action because even twenty-five years in absentia have not improved his credit rating with the flinty-hearted bookies, who have memories like old elephants.

Little Blackie finally makes contact with Honest Sam, a cautious small-time book who reluctantly agrees to handle Blackie's action on a very limited basis. "You are not my favourite pin-up boy, Blackie," says Honest Sam. "You're limited to fifty dollars per diem and the money always must be up front. You put fifty smackers into my mitt and then you can have fifty dollars of action."

They go along in this fashion for several weeks. Little Blackie wins a few wagers and he loses more than a few. Honest Sam is content because he doesn't let Blackie bet until he has Blackie's fifty dollars in his basket. Then, last Monday, Blackie walks into Honest Sam's joint. "I wish to wager $1,700 to win on Occult in tomorrow's second race at Hialeah. I have the cash with me," he says, flashing a big roll of bills. "It is not all my own dough. My mother wishes to bet and my brother-in-law wishes to bet, along with a few cousins."

"You are out of your bleeping mind," screams Honest Sam. "I will not take a $1,700 wager from you even if the race took place yesterday and I know that your steed finished in the can. I am a very small book and I do not handle that kind of action. And I do not lay off to other bookies; I put all my action in my own basket."

"These are very harsh words, Sam," says Little Blackie, "but I forgive you. This is an emergency. My mother, my brother-in-law and all those cousins will kill me if I don't get them down on Occult. As an old pal, get me in touch with a book who can handle $1,700 in action."

"I am not your old pal but let it pass, let it pass," says Honest Sam. "There is only one man in Toronto who will let you on for that kind of dough. This one man is Mister Big. But I warn you—Mister Big remembers you and your brother-in-law from the old days when the racetrack dicks gave you the booteroo. He will not give you the Big Hello when you show your kisser in his joint."

So Little Blackie toddles over to Mister Big's office, which is situated in a building from which Mister Big operates several very legitimate businesses. Blackie lays the story on him and Mister Big doesn't blink. He just points to the basket on his desk and Blackie deposits the $1,700 therein. Mister Big *never* lays off to anyone. Mister Big keeps everything for himself, even if you wish to bet him ten thousand dollars that it won't rain tomorrow.

To cut a long story short, Occult wins the second race at Hialeah the next afternoon. Occult pays $8.20 for every two-buck wager. Little Blackie gets the winning price out of the *Daily Racing Form* that evening. He does a little simple arithmetic; he has $6,970 coming to him from Mister Big.

The next morning, Little Blackie hotfoots it to Mister Big's establishment. A man in a black hat and a black overcoat is blocking the office door. In sepulchral tones, the man in black tells Little Blackie, "Mister Big just croaked. I am the undertaker. My hearse is waiting outside and we're just preparing to take Mister Big on the first stage of his final journey to the big racetrack in the sky."

This is all true, so help me. There is no way that Little Blackie and his mother, brother-in-law and cousins will ever collect their $6,970.

There is a time-honoured gambler's maxim: dead men aren't required to pay off.

The Brass-Pounders

Southam News
April 11, 1979

THIS IS A FINAL SALUTE to the brass-pounders. This is a column for "insiders" and you can skip it unless you happen to be a newspaper sentimentalist or an old telegraph operator.

The brass-pounders will reach the end of the line at midnight Saturday. The amalgamation of the Canadian Pacific and the Canadian

National Telecommunications systems will become a *fait accompli.* At midnight Saturday, Jock Wilson and the five other surviving Morse operators at CPT in Toronto will pick up their "bugs" for the last time and they will walk out of the building into retirement. The six of them have given a combined total of 248 years of loyal service to the railway and newspaper businesses.

Telegraphy long has been an honourable and highly colourful profession. Someday a lively historian will get around to writing the saga of the "boomer" operators who roamed from job to job, their luggage consisting only of their precious telegraph key, an extra pair of socks and a bottle of rye whisky.

The "boomers" were a breed unto themselves. Usually they wore green eyeshades while they worked. They wore black dust-sleeves to protect their white shirts. When they had their fill of a trick in some town, they'd simply collect their pay and leave—without bothering to say goodbye.

When, finally, they ran out of money, many miles farther down the line, they'd walk into the chief dispatcher's office at a railway divisional point and they'd ask to be assigned to another job until they had collected another stake. The "boomers" seldom settled down until they became bored with constant travelling or until some pretty girl lured them to the altar.

The elite among the telegraph operators usually were assigned to handle stockbrokers' messages and newspaper communications. The telegraph operators often were better writers and better editors than the men whose copy they transmitted. I'd like to have ten dollars for every time that a telegraph operator composed a story for a reporter who, stupefied with the grape, had fallen asleep over his hot typewriter.

The telegraph operator was the newspaperman's good right arm. Not long before Ralph Allen died, he and I were recalling how we wrote out stories, coming home on the train after out-of-town hockey games. We'd persuade the conductor to stop the train at a wayside station in the middle of the night, then we'd get the station telegraph operator out of bed and sweet-talk him into transmitting our deathless prose. All that the operator received for his self-sacrifice were our grateful memories.

I could mention a hundred operators—including Jimmy Nickleson and Ira Kennedy and Sam Weisbrod and Al Rubin and Vern House—

who saved my reportorial career over the years. But I remember particularly the night that I walked into the Brandon CPT office after a boisterous evening and, for some reason, my fingers kept getting stuck between the typewriter keys.

The Brandon operator on duty was a tall, skinny man named Bill Scotland. He wore one of those green eyeshades and black dust-sleeves over his white shirt. After watching me attempt to extricate my fingers from the typewriter keys for ten minutes, he said quietly, "You just sit back there and dictate whatever comes into your head. I'll send it as you say it." It turned out rather well in the next day's editions of the Winnipeg *Tribune*.

Every young sportswriter's greatest moment came when he attended his first world championship fight—and he was assigned his personal telegraph operator. "Are you from the Vancouver *Province*?" asked the amused older man. "Well, I'm your postal telegraph operator." Man, that was living!

You sat there and you dictated to him, punch by punch, round by round. As quickly as you spoke, he transmitted your words to the newspaper office, countless miles away.

There was one telegraph operator who saved Jack Dempsey from losing his world heavyweight championship. For two days, I have been attempting to get the operator's name but no one remembers it. Anyhow, Dempsey was fighting Luis Angel Firpo in New York. In the very first round of that brief, wild brawl, Firpo knocked Dempsey right through the ropes and into the front row of newspaper seats.

Referee Jack Gallagher peered down at Dempsey uncertainly; it appeared unlikely that Dempsey could return to the ring before the count of ten had been completed. Suddenly, someone in the press row gave Dempsey a mighty heave and shoved him back into the ring. Dempsey went on to retain his championship, kayoing Firpo in the second round.

Many years later, it was revealed that the man who saved Dempsey's title was the postal telegraph operator who was sending the fight story for Hype Igor, an old-time reporter. The telegraph operator refused to accept a hero's role when eventually his identity was revealed. He scoffed at suggestions that any noble motive had impelled him to shove Dempsey into the ring.

"I didn't even know it was Dempsey," the old telegraph operator grunted. "All I knew was that some naked son of a bee was lying on my bug, and I wanted to get on with my job."

And so, we bid a fond farewell to the brass-pounders—the last of a remarkable breed.

Little Man, Big Heart

Southam News
June 23, 1980

AVELINO GOMEZ, who died after a horrifying racing accident at Woodbine Saturday, was an ageless elf, an intensely warm and colourful man whose attitude toward life and his own perilous profession always was joyous.

Let there be no tears of sadness for Avelino. Remember only the joy he brought to those who were his friends and the thrilling excitement and laughter he brought to those who watched him from the grandstands or the clubhouse lawns.

Remember particularly the laughter, because Avelino was a happy man who rejoiced when his antics bought grins to the faces of his public. And, indeed, it *was* his public, from the very moment when he made his first appearance on a Canadian racetrack in the autumn of 1955, until the moment of his death Saturday night. Never in the history of Canadian racing has there been another jockey who, through the sheer overpowering magic of his personality, dominated our thoroughbred sport for twenty-five years.

Avelino wasn't merely one of the greatest riders ever to throw his right leg over a horse's back. He was what we used to describe on the sports pages as a character. He was, in a sense, an anachronism, because he was a throwback to the Golden Age of Sports when such towering figures as Babe Ruth, Jack Dempsey, Earle Sande and Howie Morenz bestrode the sporting scene.

Gomez was the Gordie Howe of Canadian horse racing. Gordie still was playing in the NHL at fifty-two. Avelino listed his own age as fifty-two but I believe that he was fifty-four. When he won his first race in Mexico City in 1944, he took an affidavit that he had been born in Havana in 1926. As he grew older, he became a bit coy about his age and he changed his birthdate to 1928. The matter is unimportant. As I wrote at the beginning of this piece, he was ageless.

However, some facts are pertinent. He was only a fourteen-year-old pageboy in the Havana gambling casino when an uncle took him out to Oriental Park and put him on a horse for the first time. He got his first American headlines on June 22, 1949 when he rode six winners in a single afternoon at Ascot Park in Ohio. He had his first big payday in 1951 when he rode Curandero to win a purse of $113,000 in the Washington Park Handicap in Chicago.

In his younger years, Avelino was a reckless firebrand and, like Eddie Arcaro, frequently was in trouble with the stewards. He was sent home to Cuba from Vancouver after he "stiffed" a mount but Judge W.J. McKeon declined to register a suspension in the records of the Jockey Club.

On another occasion, he went home to Cuba, declining to report for US military service. A Buffalo congressman, years later, successfully introduced an Act of Congress that restored Gomez to good standing in the US.

But those hare-brained youthful indiscretions were all behind him when trainer Pete Prieto brought Gomez to Canada in the autumn of 1955 to ride Jack Stafford's horses. Earlier that year, Avelino had been a sensation in Mexico City, twice winning six of seven races in a single afternoon.

His performances in 1956, his first full season in Canada, were amazing. He won races in clusters: five on June 26 at Woodbine; five on August 22 at Fort Erie; five on October 15 at Woodbine. He rode 210 winners from only 898 mounts and his winning percentage of 28 was the highest in North America, surpassing even the impeccable Bill Shoemaker, whose winning percentage was 27.

But it was Avelino's charisma that excited Canadian racing enthusiasts. Ah, but he was a captivating little man! The crowds adored him and, perversely, some spectators hated him because he won too many races. Gomez, always an imp at heart, merrily provoked his hecklers by sticking out his tongue and performing gaudy little victory dances in the winner's enclosure and, occasionally, responded to the booing by giving his detractors a surreptitious one-finger salute.

The truth of the matter is that Avelino genuinely loved the racing crowds, even those who booed him. He looked upon himself as an entertainer—"Like Muhammad Ali," he said. He played on their love-hate relationship. When they booed him as he took his patented victory leap from the saddle after winning a race, he grimaced derisively at them and, when he disappeared from their view into the tunnel under the grandstand, he chuckled happily all the way back to the jocks' room.

Avelino Gomez was the consummate showman. He positively crackled with good humour and electric animation. On top of everything else, he was a superb athlete, a superb horseman and a warm, lovable human being whose personality was one of Canadian racing's greatest assets.

We mourn him but there will be no tears here. His greatest bequest to us is the memory of his contagious laughter. The rub is the certain knowledge that we shall never see his like again.

The Irish Cameo

Southam News
December 23, 1981

THE TINY OLD LADY was sitting in front of her television set when the younger man entered. She was propped up in a heavy upholstered chair, but only a few feet away was the wheelchair in which they take her downstairs to the dining room for lunch and dinner. Although she will be ninety-eight on Christmas Eve, she likes to be taken downstairs for her noon and evening meals.

As usual, she was looking for a sporting event on television. She insists on watching every game played by the Montreal Canadiens. This is a continuing habit from the years when her husband was a vice-president of the hockey club and she attended all home games, sitting in the front row of a box that the Montreal players passed as they clumped from and to their dressing room.

In addition to watching Les Canadiens, she likes baseball in summer, though now her attention span is very limited and she nods off to sleep occasionally. She still loves horse racing, a sport to which she was devoted when her husband was alive and they spent so many afternoons at the track—any track, anywhere.

"She watches all the sports," the nurse, with wonder in her voice, whispered to the man. "It's amazing. One night, I slipped down the hall to make a cup of coffee and when I came back she was watching a high school basketball game from a station in upstate New York. She was so interested in the game that she shushed me when I tried to ask her a question."

The man looked down at the tiny old lady in front of the television set and he found himself remembering the first time he ever saw her. She had arrived in the Canadian prairie city, fresh out of New York where she had married his widowed father in the vestry of St. Patrick's Cathedral on Fifth Avenue. He remembered being overwhelmed by her petite beauty, blue eyes, finely chiselled features and lustrous black hair—an Irish cameo.

He remembered her standing on the sidelines while he played football, her Fifth Avenue chic impervious to the wind and mud. When she visited his boarding school, his dormitory mates vied for her invitations to lunch at a downtown hotel. He remembered that her charm was pervasive and he recalled wryly his own slight pang of possessive jealousy when she greeted his dormitory mates as "my other sons."

Now when she spoke, her eyes brightened in recognition. A warm smile illuminated her face and she held up her arms to be embraced. She talked with animation for a few minutes, but the light in her eyes soon dimmed and, almost in mid-sentence, her gaze wandered back to the television set.

The man pulled up a spare chair beside her and put his large hand over her small delicate one. He was surprised to feel that her hand was quite cold.

Suddenly, the little old lady turned to him and said, "We had such fun, didn't we? We had such wonderful times at the racetrack. I always picked the winners. One afternoon, when we were at Belmont, a man in the next box turned to me and said, 'I don't know how you do it. I'm a horse trainer, but I can't pick as many winners as you do.'"

The man nodded. He had heard the story a thousand times. Her voice trailed away. She was watching the television set again. There were no sporting events on, so she settled for a soap opera. She grimaced at the banal dialogue. On one of the man's previous visits she had told him, referring to the soap opera's cast, "They're terrible people. All of them should be in prison."

She twisted her head. The lights in her eyes turned on again as she looked at the man in the chair beside her. But her mind was out there, on the western Prairies in the distant past.

"I remember the surprise birthday party you and your brother arranged for me one Christmas Eve in Winnipeg," she said. "You were only little boys, but you invited all the guests and you made all the arrangements at the Royal Alexandra Hotel."

She patted the man's hand. "Your brother always has been a very good boy," she said fondly. "You always were a bad boy, but you always could make me laugh, too. And it was your father and you who taught me to love sports."

It was, for her, a very long speech. She sank back into her chair, shading her eyes with a frail hand.

When she seemed to be asleep, the man rose and donned his topcoat. He leaned over her, gave her a soft kiss on the forehead and said, "In case I don't get back before Friday, Happy Christmas."

But she wasn't asleep. "Come back tomorrow," she said eagerly. "We'll go downstairs and have dinner together. Now don't just go away and forget me."

The man, unwilling to look back, headed for the door of the little room and said, over his shoulder, "I'll never forget you."

And I meant it from the depths of my heart.

Piffles Will Be Spinning

Southam News
February 21, 1983

Your correspondent, who deplores the erosion of nationalistic traditions in this country, cannot join in the general enthusiasm over Regina's proposal to build a steam-heated dome over the football stadium at Taylor Field. If Reginans persist in this mad scheme, they will have committed the final desecration of a unique Canadian sporting shrine.

Furthermore, they will have destroyed one of Canada's most cherished legends—the legend that the citizens of Saskatchewan are completely impervious to the cold of sub-Arctic winters and have the highest pain threshold of any large group of human beings in North America.

Up until now, Regina has been one of the few remaining Canadian cities where Real Men (no quiche-eaters) and brave womenfolk wear thermal underpants from October until April. Let us hope that this idiotic proposal to have a domed stadium in Regina is only a passing aberration and the scheme will be voted down scornfully by the stout-hearted civic ratepayers.

Until recently, Taylor Field was a stadium of such marvelous compactness that the spectators could lean out of their seats and pat the knobby skulls of the football players sweating on the sidelines. Then some genius decided to rebuild the west side grandstand completely, raising the seating capacity to 27,606. At the luncheon where the reconstruction program was announced, Don Harron was impelled to orate wonderingly, "Twenty-seven thousand seats for football in Regina? They must be planning to make this city the hemorrhoid capital of the world!"

Thereupon, they began to destroy the great Regina football tradition. They built a new dressing room in which the players' bare feet were protected by lush carpeting. They threw out the old pot-bellied stove around which two generations of Regina players had huddled to restore their circulation after coming off the frozen field. The veterans of the team were permitted to stand closest to the pot-bellied stove; rookies, forced into the background, warmed their frozen hands with cigarette lighters or wooden matches.

Regina football fans and the team management have earned a reputation for being magnificently ingenious. When the final two games of the 1951 Western championship were played in Regina, a record snowfall was predicted before the last game. Taylor Field didn't own a tarpaulin. In the emergency, volunteer truckers hauled tons and tons of straw from the nearby civic exhibition livestock coliseum. The field was covered with straw to protect it from the coming snow.

Soon after the final game began on the Saturday afternoon, nauseated players from both teams— Regina and Edmonton—were retching and gasping as their feet churned up the field that had been melting beneath the heat of the straw.

Quickly, it became apparent that the most recent event to be staged in the nearby livestock building was a pig show. And any player to survive that afternoon's activities will attest that pig manure is considerably more odoriferous than horse manure.

Neither dry cleaning nor repeated washing could eradicate the stench of that afternoon. The Regina players had to be equipped with brand new uniforms before they went east to play Ottawa in the 1951 Grey Cup final.

Incidentally, Taylor Field was named after Norman J. "Piffles" Taylor, who epitomized the traditional toughness of Regina athletes. Piffles was so pain-resistant that after having an eye knocked out of its socket in a lacrosse game, he refused to leave field. Actually, it was his glass eye that he lost. His real eye had been removed by a German machine gunner in World War I.

Piffles Taylor must be revolving in his grave if he has heard that his fellow Reginans have become such softies that they're contemplating putting a domed roof on the fabled stadium that bears his honoured name.